EDUCATION IN RETROSPECT

Policy and Implementation Since 1990

edited by

Andre Kraak and Michael Young

Human Sciences Research Council, Pretoria
in association with the
Institute of Education, University of London

Human Sciences Research Council
Private Bag X41
Pretoria 0001
South Africa

Institute of Education
University of London
20 Bedford Way
London WC1 HOAQL

ISBN 0 7969 1988 7

Technical editing and production supervision by Karin Pampallis
PO Box 85396, Emmarentia, Johannesburg 2029

Cover design and layout by Hilton Boyce
Vico Graphics, 8 Victory Road, Greenside, Johannesburg 2193

Printed by Ultra Litho (Pty) Limited
PO Box 40896, Cleveland, Johannesburg 2022

Cover photograph by Omar Badsha
(082) 459-1067

Acknowledgements

This book is a product of the collective wisdom of all those colleagues who participated in the HSRC Round Table on Tuesday 24 and Wednesday 25 October 2000, entitled An Education Policy Retrospective, 1990-2000: Analysing The Process of Policy Implementation and Reform. The Round Table was initiated as a forum for dialogue between government, policy analysts and critics from within the HSRC and beyond. We are indebted to the contributions of the following participants who made the Round Table such a success:

- Dr Ihron Rensburg, Deputy Director General, General Education and Training, National Department of Education
- Mr Khetsi Lehoko, Deputy Director General, Further Education and Training, National Department of Education
- Mr Ian Macun, Director, Skills Development Planning Unit, Department of Labour
- Mr Haroon Mahomed, Director, Gauteng Institute for Curriculum Development (GICD)
- Professor Linda Chisholm, Faculty of Education, University of Natal, seconded to the National Department of Education
- Professor Michael Young, Institute of Education, University of London
- Professor Joe Muller, School of Education, University of Cape Town
- Professor Jonathan Jansen, Dean, Faculty of Education, University of Pretoria
- Ms Rahmat Omar, Senior Researcher, Sociology of Work Programme (SWOP), University of the Witwatersrand
- Dr Nico Cloete, Director, Centre for Higher Education Transformation (CHET)
- Mr Botshabelo Maja, Chief Research Specialist, Human Sciences Research Council
- Dr Andre Kraak, Executive Director, Research on Human Resources Development, Human Sciences Research Council
- Dr Mokubung Nkomo, Executive Director, Group Education and Training, Human Sciences Research Council
- Dr Andrew Paterson, Chief Research Specialist, Education and Training Information Systems, Human Sciences Research Council
- Ms Shireen Motala, Director, Education Policy Unit, University of the Witwatersrand
- Dr Michael Cross, School of Education, University of the Witwatersrand
- Dr Nic Taylor, Chief Executive Officer, Joint Education Trust
- Dr Mark Orkin, Chief Executive Officer, Human Sciences Research Council
- Mrs Hersheela Narsee, Policy Analyst, Centre for Education Policy Development, Evaluation and Management (CEPD)

- Mr Michael Cosser, Chief Research Specialist, Human Sciences Research Council
- Mr Trevor Sehule, Lecturer, Faculty of Education, University of Pretoria
- Ms Sarah Howie, Senior Lecturer, Faculty of Education, University of Pretoria

The Editors would also like to thank Karin Pampallis for her excellent editorial work in bringing the book to print. The Human Sciences Research Council and the Institute of Education, University of London, are both thanked for their support of this joint venture.

Contents

Abbreviations

ADEA	Association for the Development of Education in Africa
ANC	African National Congress
ASAHDI	Association of South African Vice-Chancellors of the Historically Disadvantaged Institutions
BSETA	Banking Sector Education and Training Authority
C2005	Curriculum 2005
CEPD	Centre for Education Policy Development, Evaluation and Management
CETA	Construction Education and Training Authority
CHE	Committee on Higher Education
CHEPS	Centre for Higher Education Policy Studies
CHET	Centre for Higher Education Transformation
COSATU	Congress of South African Trade Unions
CTP	Committee of Technikon Principals
CUMSA	Curriculum Model for South Africa
CUP	Committee of University Principals [now SAUVCA]
DS	Development State model [Green and Sakamoto]
DoE	Department of Education
DoF	Department of Finance
DoL	Department of Labour
DQAD	Directorate of Quality Assurance and development
DSS	Division of Standards Setting
DSSD	Directorate of Standards Setting and Development
ERS	Education Renewal Strategy
ET	Education and Training
ETQA	Education and Training Quality Assurance body
EU	European Union
FEFC	Further Education Funding Council [UK]
FET	Further Education and Training
FETC	Further Education and Training Certificate
GEAR	Growth, Employment and Redistribution strategy
GET	General Education and Training
GICD	Gauteng Institute for Curriculum Development
GNVQ	General National Vocational Qualification [UK]
GNU	Government of National Unity
HAI	Historically Advantaged Institution
HBI	Historically Black Institution
HDI	Historically Disadvantaged Institution
HE	Higher Education
HRD	Human Resources Development
HSD	High Skills Diffusion model [Green and Sakamoto]

HSE	High Skills Elite model [Green and Sakamoto]
HSRC	Human Sciences Research Council
HSS	High Skills Society model [Green and Sakamoto]
HWI	Historically White Institution
IPPR	Institute for Public Policy Research [UK]
ISETT	Information Systems, Electronics and Telecommunication Technologies Sector Education and Training Authority
IT	Information Technology
ITB	Industry Training Board
JIP	Joint Implementation Plan
MAPPSETA	Media, Advertising, Printing, Packaging and Publishing Sector Education and Training Authority
MEC	Member of the Executive Committee
MTEF	Medium Term Expenditure Framework
NCHE	National Commission on Higher Education
NCVQ	National Council for Vocational Qualifications
NECC	National Education Crisis [later Co-ordinating] Committee
NEDLAC	National Economic Development and Labour Council
NEF	New Education Fellowship
NEPI	National Education Policy Investigation
NETF	National Education and Training Forum
NLRD	National Learners' Records Database
NQF	National Qualifications Framework
NSA	National Skills Authority
NSB	National Standards Body
NSDS	National Skills Development Strategy
NTB	National Training Board
NTO	National Training Organisation [UK]
NTSI	National Training Strategy Initiative
NVQ	National Vocational Qualification [UK]
OBE	Outcomes-Based Education
OBET	Outcomes-Based Education and Training
OECD	Organisation for Economic Co-operation and Development
PRISEC	Private Sector Education Council
PTSA	Parent-Teacher-Student Association
QCA	Qualifications and Curriculum Authority [UK]
R&D	Research and Development
RDP	Reconstruction and Development Programme
S&T	Science and Technology
SADTU	South African Democratic Teachers Union
SAQA	South African Qualifications Authority

SARS	South African Revenue Service
SAUVCA	South African Vice-Chancellors Association [formerly CUP]
SCQF	Scottish Credit and Qualifications Framework
SETA	Sector Education and Training Authority
SGB	School Governing Body
SGB	Standards Generating Body
SPDU	Skills Development Planning Unit
SRHE	Society for Research in Higher Education
SSETA	Services Sector Education and Training Authority
SSP	Sector Skills Plan
SWOP	Sociology of Work Programme
TEC	Training and Enterprise Council [UK]
TEC	Transitional Executive Council
TIMSS	Third International Mathematics and Science Study
THETA	Tourism and Hospitality Education and Training Authority
TEXTILES SETA	Clothing, Textiles, Footwear and Leather Sector Education and Training Authority
UK	United Kingdom
VET	Vocational Education and Planning
WSP	Workplace Skills Plan

Contributors

Michael Cosser is Chief Research Specialist in the Human Resources Development component of the Human Sciences Research Council. He was previously Head of the Division of Standards Setting at the South African Qualifications Authority.
mcosser@beauty.hsrc.ac.za

Anthony Gewer is Divisional Manager for Evaluation and Research at the Joint Education Trust. His expertise lies primarily in Further Education and Training, where his research work involves organisational transformation, FET policy implementation and curriculum design. He is currently managing the Monitoring and Evaluation of the Colleges Collaboration Fund, a large-scale project aimed at restructuring the technical college sector. He is also JET project manager for the Technical Colleges Responsiveness Project that, in collaboration with the HSRC, attempts to measure employability of college graduates. He is managing the research and evaluation of JET's Learnership Pilot in Small Business Development, focusing on out-of-school youth in the rural Eastern Free State.
agewer@jet.org.za

Jonathan D. Jansen is Dean of the Faculty of Education at the University of Pretoria. His current research concerns the study of mergers in higher education, comparative studies of policy transitions in Southern African education (Namibia, Zimbabwe, South Africa), and policy implementation in South African schools. Professor Jansen is a member of several associations, including the International Association for the Advancement of Curriculum Studies. His recent articles appear in Pedagogy, Culture and Society, Prospects: A Quarterly Journal of Comparative Education, and Higher Education.
JDJansen@postino.up.ac.za

Andre Kraak is Executive Director of the Human Resources Development Strategy research programme at the Human Sciences Research Council. Prior to joining the HSRC, Dr Kraak was a Senior Lecturer in Comparative Education and subsequently Academic Planner at the University of the Western Cape.
AHKraak@beauty.hsrc.ac.za

Ian Macun is currently the Director of the Skills Development Planning Unit in the Department of Labour. He has previously worked as a researcher and lecturer in Industrial Sociology at the University of the Witwatersrand and the University of Cape Town.
Ian.Macun@labour.gov.za

Johan Muller is Professor of Education and Head of the Department of Education at the University of Cape Town. He has written extensively in the sociology of knowledge and curriculum. Recent publications include a monograph entitled Reclaiming Knowledge (Routledge Falmer) and a co-edited volume entitled Challenges of Globalisaiton: South African Debates with Manuel Castells (Maskew Miller Longman).
jpm@education.uct.ac.za

Dr Ihron L. Rensburg played a pivotal role in the development and transformation of the South African education system. He was a cofounder and leader of the anti-apartheid National Education Crisis Committee, an arm of the United Democratic Front. At the time of writing his contribution to this book, Dr Rensburg had been a senior manager in the Department of Education since 1995. He was instrumental in developing, implementing and evaluating critical post-apartheid education policies and programmes. Under his leadership the development of outcomes-based education, Curriculum 2005 and new directions in the FET band took place. Dr Rensburg holds a PhD and MA (Sociology) from Stanford University, California.
sizeka@mweb.co.za

Michael Young is Professor of Education at the Institute of Education, University of London. He contributed to the NEPI Working Group on Human Resources and to subsequent developments that led to the establishment of the South African Qualifications Authority, and was recently appointed to the Panel to undertake a focused study of the development of the National Qualifications Framework. He has published widely on curriculum issues and the sociology of education more generally. His most recent book, *The Curriculum of the Future*, was published by Falmer Press in 1998 and is being translated into Portuguese, Japanese and Chinese.
m_young@ioe.ac.uk and tedpmmy@mentor.ioe.ac.uk

Chapter 1

Introduction

Michael Young and Andre Kraak

The broad aim of this book is to present and extend the dialogue between education policy makers and researchers that was initiated at the HSRC-sponsored Round Table that took place in Pretoria in September 2000. It brings together revised versions of the key presentations at the Round Table as well as two additional papers, and draws on the discussions that took place in response to the papers. The book is a dialogue in two senses. First, it is an ongoing critical reflection on education policy design and implementation throughout the last decade. Second, the book not only includes a number of chapters (by Muller, Jansen, Young and Kraak) that are critiques by researchers of policy and its implementation; it also includes several contributions (by Rensburg, Macun, Cosser and Gewer) that offer insider views of policy that to some degree reflect on the theories that underpin the critiques.

The focus of the book is on education policy in South Africa and the unique set of circumstances faced by both government and researchers. However, we want to stress not only the common global context that has shaped South African education policy, but also the wider relevance of the issues raised in South African policy debates. This global context is not just reflected in the demands of international corporations and organisations and the increasingly transnational character of labour markets, but in the policy options themselves and in the kind of critiques developed by researchers. The pressures for improved performance and for making public services more accountable, and therefore the search for measurable educational outcomes, are found to varying degrees in most countries, both developed and developing. No less widespread has been the increasing emphasis by governments on the economic role of education and its expression in the increased emphasis on human resource development. There have also been parallel efforts by researchers (Ashton, 1999) to find alternatives to discredited economic theories – whether those associated with the Left such as the economistic interpretations of Marxism, or the human capital approaches that have been endorsed by the Centre and Right. The tensions between a commitment to equality and social transformation and the associated intention to replace old institutions and practices with new ones, and the awareness that some old institutions and practices may need to be built on rather than abolished, is also not unique to South Africa. Likewise, the embeddedness of educational institutions and practices in the wider society and the enormous constraints that such embeddedness places on educational reforms fulfilling their more ambitious goals is part of the reality facing all reforming governments.

However, the lessons from the South African efforts to overcome the unique circumstances that have been inherited from apartheid dramatise the problems of achieving radical educational change in two important and distinct ways. The first is the urgency of the problems faced by the incoming government in 1994 and the extent of exclusion of the majority of the population from anything beyond elementary education. The second distinctive feature of the South African situation is the far closer link between those involved in policy research and theory and policy makers, practitioners and others involved in implementation than is found in most developed countries.

Background to the Round Table

It is widely recognised that the major priority of the second ANC-led government, elected in April 1999, has been the implementation of policies. To this end a National Strategy for Higher Education and two major reviews – one of Curriculum 2005 and one of the National Qualifications Framework – have been initiated. Furthermore, in the last two years a National Skills Development Strategy and a Human Resources Development Strategy have been launched, as has a new programme for work-based training (known as learnerships). These initiatives, together with the wider public debate and criticism of the new policies and their implementation, provided the intellectual context for the Round Table and for this book.

Briefing notes sent to contributors to the Round Table suggested that by the year 2000 education policies in South Africa appeared to have undergone a profound shift away from the original premises that had been established by the democratic movement in the early 1990s. Despite continuing official commitment to a unified and integrated system of education and training at all levels, policies appeared to retain the traditional divisions between education and training, and between colleges, technikons and universities. Furthermore, in contrast to the earlier endorsement of a progressive view of pedagogy and an outcomes-based approach to curriculum and qualifications, the emphasis of current policy and practice has tended towards more traditional notions of schooling, a 'back-to basics' view of curriculum and pedagogy, and a more 'managerialist' approach to education policy generally. Contributors to the Round Table were asked to consider a number of questions that follow from these claims. These were:

- To what extent do you agree that this shift in policy has taken place?
- What do you think has been achieved over the past decade in relation to the original policy goals?
- What constraints and opportunities for reform have been generated by:
  - (a) the form of the emerging post-apartheid state;
  - (b) the wider political and economic conditions within which the government is operating;
  - (c) the impact of international trends on developments in South Africa

(especially in relation to such policies as outcomes-based education, the integration of education and training, creating unified systems of further and higher education and training (FET and HET), and establishing a National Qualifications Framework?

- What do you think should be the role of educational researchers in the policy process and what alternative ways are there of conceiving of the relationship between policy, theory and practice?
- What ways forward are there for government and to what extent should the original policy goals be sustained or modified?

From the perspectives of the different areas of provision on which they were focusing, contributors were asked to consider the emerging character of education and training policy as a whole, how it might have been viewed in the early 1990s, how it might be described today, and what might have been the causal factors involved in any policy shifts. In particular, it was hoped that contributors would focus on two historical moments. The first was the period after 1990 when policies for a new system of education and training were launched, including the establishment of:

- integrated education and training;
- a single national Department of Education;
- a single FET band incorporating both senior secondary schooling and technical colleges;
- a single nationally co-ordinated system of HET; and
- a single qualifications framework (NQF) regulated by a single qualifications authority (SAQA).

The second moment that contributors were asked to focus on was the present period (2000/2001), when policy appears to be characterised by:

- major debates and uncertainties about the feasibility of earlier policy goals; and
- an awareness that the implementation of agreed policies for education and training has proved to be far more complex and difficult than was ever imagined by those involved in developing the policy.

Finally, contributors were asked to consider the extent to which they saw the difficulties associated with implementation as the 'teething problems' that any major reforms face or whether they called into question the basic assumptions of the original policy goals.

Issues in the implementation of education policy

Education policy debates within the democratic movement in South Africa in the early 1990s were visionary and, with hindsight, somewhat utopian. This phase of policy making reflected not only a commitment to social transformation and a break with policies associated with the apartheid era, but also the social location within the democratic movement of those individuals who were involved in policy making. The policy development process was led by a relatively small group of left intellectuals, none of whom had any direct experience of government. After 1994 many of those who had been involved in the democratic movement joined the new government that had the task of converting visions into practical policies. Some remained outside government and became critics, highlighting either the slow pace of implementation and the government's loss of radical nerve or the lack of realism of the original policies. All had to face the reality of the enormous practical difficulties of implementing radical change. Some of these difficulties were clearly linked to the gross inequalities inherited from the past – for example, the dramatic discrepancies in the educational provision available to the white, Indian, coloured and black communities – which a change of government alone could not overcome, at least not in the short term.

Others difficulties reflected less obvious social realities. In particular, there were the problems associated with building new institutional capacity and forms of trust and expertise in areas where they were previously absent. Regardless of government commitment or availability of funds, these new capacities could not be created quickly or easily. Policies can establish a new 'macro' framework or system of education and training as the goal and a vision to inform and shape future practice and policy. However, such a framework is not – as many (including us) hoped – something that can be put in place in the short term. It is these less 'political' realities that underlie some of the difficulties faced by those trying to implement policies and that can be brought to light by appropriate critical analysis. The problems of implementation are not necessarily an indication of the failures of South Africa's first democratic government or even that the original vision was wrong. Implementation of changes in a system with deep historical divisions and low levels of capacity is inevitably a slow process when compared to the relatively easy task of designing new policies. It is a process in which the experience of practice has to be drawn on to continuously interrogate the original vision, not to reject it.

We view the Round Table and this book as two small contributions to the education policy process. The original unified vision of a genuinely democratic system providing opportunities for all remains fundamental, and the theories on which this vision is based can inform the process of implementation and help make it more likely to be progressive as well as pragmatic. If this process of dialogue between research and implementation works and if the lessons from past mistakes in South Africa (and elsewhere) are not forgotten, some of the issues covered in this book will not need to be covered again. International experience, not the least from the UK, suggests that learning lessons from the failure of past policies is not easy. Because such lessons are often uncomfortable (for radical reformers as well as for governments), they are easily forgotten. Policies that appear to 'deliver' in measurable ways will always be attractive to politicians and policy makers under pressure. Similarly, utopian visions and critiques of policy based on them will always have their attractions for those such as researchers who are some distance from the context of implementation.

The recent shift away from the simplistic ideas implicit in the Curriculum 2005 (C2005) proposals is a good example of a constructive dialogue between researchers and policy makers at work. The recommendations of the committee reviewing C2005 (DoE, 2000f), that are reflected in the new Curriculum Statement, show a realism about how far improved levels of attainment can be achieved by the specification of outcomes alone. While retaining the vision associated with Curriculum 2005 and continuing to stress the importance of freeing teachers and their students from the rigidities of a curriculum laid down by central government, the New Curriculum Statement does not abandon the strengths of a curriculum based on identifiable bodies of knowledge and an understanding of how learning actually takes place. The importance of a critical role for theory and research is that it can help ensure that such realities do not become a retreat into conservatism or pragmatism, and to recognise that it is not possible to 'go back to basics', whatever they were.

This book presents a view of the general relationship between theory, policy and its implementation that applies to curriculum reform. However, the specific focus of this book is on:

- the role of qualifications (and in particular the role of the South African Qualifications Authority and the National Qualifications Framework);
- work-based learning (in particular the new learnership programme and the Department of Labour's National Skills strategy); and
- the broader issue of unifying the systems of further and higher education.

It does not seek to call into question the long-term vision of a unified system of education and training that could overcome existing patterns of stratification, division and inequality. However, it is unrealistic to envisage such a transformation as an immediate goal, with one kind of system being wholly replaced by another. It is not conservative or reactionary to recognise that overcoming divisions and inequalities is a slow process that cannot be guaranteed even by a progressive reforming government. Rather one must remember that the new forms of institutional arrangement that will be necessary to achieve such a transformation will take time, trust and considerable expertise to establish.

Theory, research and educational policy

Although the debate between different approaches to relating theory, policy and practice that this book seeks to promote arises from an analysis of the current situation in South Africa, our view is that it has implications wherever progressive reforming governments are in power. Two issues are stressed throughout the book. The first is the importance of a continuing dialogue between vision and theory on the one hand and policy and practice on the other. The visions developed by the democratic movement in the early 1990s and turned into policy after 1994 will themselves need revising in terms of the goals and aspirations that they articulate, both as new experiences and knowledge are gained and as the world of which South Africa is a part changes. However, visions and theories will always retain their critical role in challenging existing reforms and clarifying their purposes in terms of the continuing need to expand opportunities and reduce inequalities.

The second issue crucial to the link between research and policy implementation is the importance of developing and disseminating knowledge of pedagogic practice, in particular the links between teaching and learning. This is not just a question of improving techniques, but of rethinking assumptions about teaching and learning and the practical implications that follow. Examples include the importance of:

- the essentially *social* character of the learning process while at the same time not neglecting the centrality of individual learners;
- the need for a clear, progressive and unified system of qualifications in promoting learning, at the same time being aware that a qualification system is only one part of a system designed to promote learning as a process; and
- identifying the knowledge that is important for people to acquire, how it is best acquired, when the process of knowledge acquisition needs a school or college environment and when it does not, what knowledge can be learned as it is applied (as in the case of practical tasks), and when knowledge has to be acquired prior to application (as in any form of numeracy that takes the learner beyond specific contexts).

These aspects of implementing any educational process are among the 'micro' processes that determine the outcomes of any attempt to reform an education and training system. The more that government priorities are geared to implementation and delivery and not just to policy design, the more important these processes become. They underlie the importance given to curriculum inputs as well as outputs, and content as well as outcomes of learning in the new Curriculum Statement, and underpin more cautious approaches to unifying the systems of further and higher education and reducing the institutional differentiation that has emerged in recent policy.

However, recognising the extent to which these micro-processes impose constraints on the pace and even the direction of reform is only one aspect of a progressive approach to education and training policy. A policy for transforming a national system of education and training also needs to recognise that pedagogies, curricula and qualifications are not givens; they are the result of decisions and priorities and therefore need debating. Without this recognition of the extent to which intentionality is involved in implementation, the move away from the utopianism of the early 1990s could easily degenerate into a new form of conservatism and a licence for accepting the inevitability of existing inequalities.

The papers presented at the Round Table and the discussions that followed ranged widely, not only in the aspects of education and training policy that they covered, but in the kind of political, epistemological and pedagogic issues that they considered. The overriding concern of the contributors was to look back in order to look forward. In looking back there are clearly many different ways of periodising the changes in the policy process in South Africa between 1990 and 2001. However, several clear shifts of perspective and circumstance that have followed the apartheid era stand out. These are usefully described in the chapter by Jansen as

- *positioning*, which refers to the 1990-1994 period of democratic struggle and debate,
- *frameworks*, which refers to the early work of the first ANC-led government from 1994 when the proposals formed in opposition were converted into legislation, and
- the more recent *implementation* period that began in 1995-1996 and continues to this day.

The discussion that followed the presentations at the Round Table seemed to reflect a consensus on the part of all the participants that the end of the year 2000 was a time to stand back from the process of implementation, to reflect on the policies developed in the pre-1994 period, and to ask whether the reforms were moving in the right direction. There was also a suggestion that, six years after a democratic government was elected with a mandate to dismantle apartheid, there might be a case for reassessing the possible strengths as well as the well-known weaknesses of educational provision associated with that earlier era.

The timing of the Round Table and, we feel, this book, was appropriate for two reasons. Firstly, the book aims to be a contribution to the current range of policy reviews. Secondly, as was widely agreed by all contributors to the Round Table, there are many aspects of educational provision that are, at a fundamental level, not working and are proving remarkably resistant to reform. Examples are the large numbers of failing schools and colleges, the high levels of student dropout from universities, the number of universities in various forms of recruitment and financial crisis, and the continuing lack of administrative capacity in departments of education at both national and provincial levels. In relation to the specific reforms themselves, there was little disagreement on the problems. For example:

- The process of restructuring (and expanding) higher education appears to have stalled.

- The South African Qualifications Authority has created a large number of Boards, Bodies and Committees, and registered a growing number of standards and qualifications. However, there is very little evidence that these developments improve or expand opportunities for learning and qualifying 'on the ground'.
- The direction of the Curriculum 2005 reforms remains a highly contested issue and for some is seen as seriously mistaken.

These issues are addressed by contributors in terms of three possibilities. The first is that some (or all) of the reforms initiated since 1994 are fundamentally flawed. (This possibility is raised by Muller in his chapter on pedagogy, Chapter 4). From this perspective, some of the problems of policy implementation reflect the fact that progressive pedagogies are based on mistaken assumptions about teaching, learning, and the curriculum. Somewhat similar arguments are made by Young about qualifications frameworks (Chapter 2) and by Jansen about outcomes (Chapter 3). The idea of an outcomes-driven system was undoubtedly attractive to those involved in the democratic struggle. It appeared to offer a way of guaranteeing opportunities for all in sharp contrast to existing institutions and curricula, that had systematically excluded the majority. However, an outcomes-based approach to educational provision can also be seen as reflecting political pressures to find a short cut in the long road of building new forms of institutional capacity. It may also reflect a misplaced and somewhat uncritical enthusiasm for models developed in western democratic countries and a failure to critically examine their actual consequences.

The second possibility is that the problems with the first wave of reforms in post-apartheid South Africa are not fundamental or intrinsic to the reforms themselves which embody well-tested ideas that, though controversial, are also widely accepted within the international community. From this perspective, the problems are essentially about implementation, and the major issue is identified as a lack of capacity and more specifically a lack of leadership at national, provincial and institutional levels. (The chapters by 'insiders' – Rensburg, Cosser and Macun – tend to adopt this position.) These contributors do recognise that this lack of capacity has been exaggerated by the extraordinarily ambitious nature of the curriculum and qualification reforms themselves, and in the case of higher education, the political constraints on the options available for dealing with 'failing institutions'.

The third possibility recognises that although there are important lessons to be learned from the first two diagnoses, in terms of both the current analysis and the future direction of policy, they need not be seen as mutually exclusive. This is not a question of finding a compromise or a 'third way'. It is a recognition that in charting a future direction for educational policy, a number of quite distinct types of issues need to be distinguished. They are:

- *political* issues concerned with redress, overcoming inequalities, and extending participation to previously excluded groups; these are essentially, though not solely, issues about the expansion and redistribution of resources;
- *pedagogic* and *curricular* issues that underpin the achievement of particular educational goals; these issues roughly parallel the 'micro-processes' involved in learning and teaching that were referred to earlier; and
- *administrative* issues involved in expanding institutional and governmental capacity and co-ordinating different levels of government.

These three types of issues are clearly only separable analytically. Forms of school organisation and pedagogic and curriculum models are all at some level political and administrative. However, for policy analysis it is important to recognise that the types of issues have at least some autonomy from each other. For example, more participative forms of assessment and pedagogy may be more democratic and reflect a shift in power relations between teacher and learner and are consistent with certain political goals; however, they will not necessarily lead to the educational goals of raising levels of learning and attainment. Similarly, new curricula and forms of institutional capacity do not only reflect educational goals. They can also be a means for achieving broader and more overtly political goals, and it is partly by their contribution to these broader political goals that they must be judged.

Related to the third possibility is an issue that ran through many of the discussions at the Round Table. This is the relationship between the political culture forged in struggle and opposition in South Africa prior to 1994 and the very different political culture that is needed to underpin a high-performance system of education and training in a democracy that can 'deliver' the skills and knowledge needed by the majority of the population. A more specialised capability is likely to be at the heart of the new political culture that is needed. It follows, therefore, that priority may need to be given to developing the professional expertise of those working in education rather than the ideals of representativeness and stakeholder involvement that have been inherited from the years of struggle. The activities and newly-established traditions of a high-performance system will undoubtedly be based on specialist knowledge. However, in order for this specialist knowledge to be widely disseminated and not to become a source of new divisions, a major emphasis will be needed on the training and continuous professional development of the 'new' experts and specialists, and on innovative strategies for extending access and participation to the learners and potential learners from the sections of society that were disenfranchised and excluded by the old system.

1990-2001: policy slippage or policy maturation?

In Chapter 6 Kraak takes the specific case of higher education and argues that a form of policy slippage has taken place in South African education policy since the early

1990s. However, Muller [1] has questioned this view and pointed out that the other policy positions in existence at the time make the picture far more complex. There are undoubtedly problems in setting up the 'highly idealised' policy moment of the early 1990s as the benchmark for the evaluation of all later policy developments. There was a strong ideological intent in many of the early policy documents, which were written with an eye to policy advocacy rather than to implementation. It is unrealistic, therefore, to expect delivery in those ideal terms and to code every later policy permutation on a downward scale of lost idealism. If the factors that Kraak identifies as the causes of the policy slippage are kept in mind, it is difficult to see how the development of policy could have been different. An additional point made by Muller – and it is one of the themes recognised by Young (Chapter 2) – is that it is often the very same people that had the original policy vision who later express reservations about the policy. This raises some questions about the links between policy analysts, critics, policy makers and those involved in implementation, and how the latter are expected both to hold on to the original policy goals and at the same time deal with their internal contradictions and the incoherences involved in trying to implement them.

Muller suggests that the recent policy changes might be better viewed as an example of *policy maturation* when people come to be more realistic about what new policies can achieve rather than as *policy slippage* that emphasises the inevitable shift from idealism to pragmatism. Let us take two examples from among those discussed in this book to illustrate this point – the problems associated with implementing the National Qualifications Framework and the issues surrounding the restructuring of higher education. If we take account of the less polarised ideological climate of 2001, a somewhat different approach to both of these issues is suggested. First, in such a climate it is possible for policies giving priority to both equity and development to be explored as well as options that recognise the necessity of some differentiation in higher education, and that this does not preclude pursuing emancipatory goals. In the case of the NQF, it becomes possible to acknowledge the limitations of a qualifications-driven approach to policy while at the same time being aware that in a country like South Africa – where many sectors of the population have no possibility of gaining qualifications – no reforming government can afford not to give priority to qualifications reform.

While aware of the problems associated with approaches to qualifications that emphasise the specification of outcomes, many institutions and professional bodies (in the UK as well as in South Africa) have moved rapidly to give their own 'specialist' flavour to outcomes-based qualifications. Furthermore, the alliances that are needed between providers and users of qualifications can lead to new forms of trust that lie at the heart of more highly-valued qualifications.

1 This section draws on a summary by Jeanne Gamble of a symposium at the Higher Education conference held in Cape Town in March2001, in which Muller responded to papers by Kraak (on higher education policy) and Young (on the role of national qualifications frameworks).

Elsewhere, one of us (Young, 2001) has noted that in the last decade (at least in the UK) qualifications have been given an inappropriately large role in government proposals for reforming education. This illustrates another aspect of the lack of communication between policy visionaries and critics on the one hand and those involved in policy implementation on the other. In South Africa, this schism has been reinforced by a flawed process of 'stakeholder-driven' policy development, with teachers and practitioners on the ground often lacking the resources to cope in an entirely new curriculum and policy environment. Young (2001) argues that it is useful to distinguish between the intrinsic logic of a policy like the NQF and its *institutional logic*. The former refers to what a policy stands for and the wider goals it represents, and the latter to the power relations and social interests involved in the implementation of any policy. In the UK, and it seems likely in South Africa, a focus on the intrinsic logic of qualifications has led to the fundamental undervaluing of the institutionality of education. An examination of the extent to which specialist educational institutions –schools, colleges and universities – are likely to continue to be the major source of learning opportunities for adults as well as for young people is neglected. At the same time, and again especially in South Africa, the association of schools and colleges with their exclusive role in the apartheid era has meant that the idea of a national qualifications framework continues to represent hope for those who see no opportunities in the more conventional institutional learning or career pathways. This suggests that instead of setting up a polarity between developing a qualifications framework and strengthening institutions – that are dependent on each other – it is better to see them as alternative and in many cases complementary strategies for promoting learning and progression.

Our argument in this section has been that there has inescapably been policy slippage from the idealism of the early 1990s to the realism of a decade later. Furthermore, identifying the slippage is important not only for discussions about the next stage of policy development but also because it emphasises the continuing importance of articulating the goals and purposes of policy as a basis for evaluating actual reforms. On the other hand, the more pragmatic view of change as a process of policy maturation is also useful. It reminds us of the inherent fallibility of even the best of policy intentions. Perhaps it is not just a question of lost idealism, of policy makers giving way to practical exigencies or governments not willing to grasp the nettle. It may be more a matter of grappling with the complexities of educational reform, and of continuing to examine assumptions about knowledge and learning in different policies, as well as the multiple uses that can be made of qualifications by governments and individual learners. 'Getting it wrong' and admitting mistakes in a thoughtful and responsible way – whether as a policy theorist and researcher or as someone involved in policy implementation – has its advantages; it is likely to offer more hope for the future than the superficial advocacy of 'either/or' solutions.

The idea of policy maturation implies that both researchers and policy makers need to have the capacity to see that it is the simultaneous consideration of both the intrinsic and institutional logics of a policy – not a foregrounding of the one at the expense of the latter. The idea that all successful education is based on some form of institutionality and therefore depends on shared trust – especially between those who obtain, deliver and use qualifications – is not easy in our world today where competition rather than trust is its *leitmotif*. It is the continuing articulation of this fundamentally social basis of any educational policy that is one of the roles of debates in social theory and the continuing dialogue between those debates with educational policy and practice. Like policy slippage, policy maturation has its limitations as a perspective on changes in education policy. The idea of maturation implies that some kind of steady state or ideology-free period has been reached. In contrast, the idea of policy slippage is a reminder that the contradictions do not go away and the debate between ideals or theory on the one hand and policy on the other continues, although it may take different forms.

Three strategic issues for the future of educational policy and research

Rather than summarise the contents of the individual chapters in this book, this last section will explore briefly three issues that recurred in the Round Table discussions and that are the specific focus of several of the chapters. These issues are:

- the emergence of a so-called 'new realist orthodoxy' and its wider implications for future educational policy debates;
- the marginalisation of non-school (and non-university) aspects of educational policy; and
- the issue of institutional and sectoral differentiation.

These issues, we suggest, are important in themselves but also for the possibility that they could be pointers to new cleavages in the policy and research communities.

Orthodoxies old and new

Muller's chapter draws together a range of theoretical and empirical literature to challenge the ideas that became known as progressivism in the USA and child-centredness in the UK and that were a powerful strand of thinking in the Curriculum 2005 proposals in South Africa. Muller's main point is that whatever its other strengths, progressivism has tended to play down *the* crucial issue for any serious educational reform – what knowledge will future citizens need to acquire? Muller argues that by neglecting the question of knowledge – something that dominant groups have always taken seriously for their own children – progressivism inevitably sustains the inequalities that it claims to overcome. However, there is a broader policy issue that concerns the implications of the main alternative to progressivism – what some have seen as a return to traditionalism. Will it be the basis of a new cleavage within the Left in South Africa between an old progressive orthodoxy endorsed by the teacher unions and the new defence of content and traditional pedagogies by a small but influential group of intellectuals? This cleavage is expressed in the UK by Conservatives and the hardly less conservative New Labour Party.

On the other hand, a closer look at Muller's analysis suggests that he is not endorsing a traditionalist position and proposing that the curriculum is a given. He quotes Gramsci who argued that despite the strengths of the traditional Italian curriculum based on Latin and Greek, it needed to be replaced by a curriculum based on sciences and modern languages. Nor is he against the Vygotskian idea that learning is an active process of concept development. The danger that Muller points to is when a social constructionist view of knowledge is used to undermine the very idea that there is knowledge that young people need to acquire. What that knowledge is and how it is best acquired needs to be at the centre of the next stage of debates between theorists and policy makers, in relation to the school curriculum but also in relation to further and higher education and training, and adult and work-based learning.

Education beyond school

The three final chapters of the book document the lack of movement in a number of areas of policy concerned with post-school education in South Africa. Post-school education and training was given considerable emphasis in the 1990s, largely on account of the powerful role of COSATU within the Congress Alliance formed with the ANC and the Communist Party of South Africa prior to the first democratic election. However, since the formation of an ANC-led government the role of COSATU and the Congress Alliance itself has had far less impact on policy.

A key aspect of any education policy that aims to promote post-school and specifically work-based education is to establish a qualifications framework for accrediting learning that is not the outcome of attendance at school. The problems faced by the South African Qualifications Authority in accrediting any prior learning towards qualifications or to facilitate progression between work-based and formal learning and between vocational and general education is discussed by Cosser in Chapter 9. This is likely to be for a number of reasons, that need to be at the centre of future policy and research and that there is only space here to mention briefly. Examples are:

- ❑ mistaken priorities on the part of SAQA, that has devoted much of its energies to accrediting university-based qualifications;
- ❑ the relatively low national priorities given to work-based learning relative to schools and universities;
- ❑ the lack of pedagogic and assessment expertise outside the school system (in adult and community education and in work-based training) that is even more acute than in the schools themselves. Without a significant focus on developing pedagogic, curriculum and assessment expertise in adult, workplace

and community education the NQF, despite its potential, will remain an empty shell like much of the NVQ framework in the UK.

The second neglected area of post-school reform is the technical colleges (see Gewer, Chapter 8). This is an inherently contested area of policy. Should the major priority be the integration of senior secondary and technical college education in the new FET band of provision? The UK's experience of bringing the Departments of Labour and Education together is not a happy one. Since its incorporation into a single department, vocational education and education and training have been increasingly marginalised by the high political profile given to policies for schools. It is worth noting that some of the most successful systems of post-school education in Europe and Asia are not integrated. It may be that a more systematic focus on improving the quality of VET programmes and strengthening the distinct identity of technical colleges is more important than trying to create a seamless FET band of institutions that ranges from work-based learning to matric.

The final neglected aspect of post-school education is the poor nature of the links between education and the world of work discussed in Chapters 5 and 10 by Young and Macun. If we compare those countries in Europe, Asia and America that have succeeded in establishing such links – sometimes through employer-employee partnerships and albeit in very different ways – with countries like the UK and South Africa in which such links are far less developed, the issue appears to be not just educational but a much broader question of the place of education in national culture. The broad issue that the policies developed in the early 1990s by the reformed National Training Board hinted at, but that are in danger of being forgotten, is that whereas South Africa has a relatively powerful and effective (but unevenly distributed) group of universities and at least the basis of an effective school system, there is no tradition of partnership between trade unions, employers and providers of vocational education. There are strong parallels in the UK in how a similar situation is perpetuated – those in government departments and university Schools of Education invariably have had experience only of schools or universities (whether as students or teachers) and have little knowledge of technical colleges, let alone work-based training. In Chapter 5 on HRD strategies Young suggests that South Africa needs to look beyond the Anglophone countries for appropriate models if the schools bias in education policy is to be overcome.

The future of higher education

Despite the publication of a National Plan for Higher Education in 2001 and the continuing debate about structure that began with the National Commission on Higher Education in 1996, South Africa's system of higher education remains powerful (its research-led universities are unique on the continent) but unbalanced (in the proportion of students in universities rather than technikons and in the historical legacy of divisions between what were historically white and black universities).

Comparisons with other national systems suggest very different potential futures for higher education in South Africa – a single unified system that is highly stratified in the UK and the divided but less stratified systems that are found in other European countries are but two examples.

The two dominant positions on institutional and system differentiation in South Africa have been, first, a strong opposition within the ANC-aligned education policy community to all forms of apartheid-derived institutional stratification, and second, the concern of ANC and COSATU policy makers that institutional differentiation between education and training at all levels would accentuate already existent social inequalities in South African society. However, neither of these principles is easy to translate into policies that can be implemented, hence the sense of policy drift. It is possible that a more nuanced policy position could accept that certain forms of institutional differentiation in both further and higher education may in fact promote social and economic development and need not accentuate social divisions. Such an approach would derive from existing institutional forms and build on their existing institutional strengths. It would be important that this more incremental approach did not lose sight of international developments that indicate a weakening of boundaries and greater articulation between sectors such as further and higher education that have traditionally been quite separate.

Conclusion

Before concluding with the main arguments of this chapter, an important reservation needs to be stated. There are aspects of policy with which this book does not deal but that undoubtedly shape the policies with which this book is concerned. Four in particular are worth listing – funding, the language of instruction, the organisation of teacher training, and the relationship between national and provincial departments of education. This book has concentrated on issues relating more explicitly to questions of educational purpose such as curriculum and qualifications.

This introductory chapter has attempted to make a number of arguments. First it has made a case for the value of a retrospective analysis of policy both for policy makers and for researchers. Secondly, we have argued in ways that are exemplified in different chapters of the book that such a retrospective analysis needs to be based on (a) a recognition of the very different locations of researchers and policy makers, (b) an articulated theoretical framework, and (c) empirically-based international comparisons. Third, we have suggested that although globalisation is leading to common pressures on all countries, there is no one fruitful approach to policy analysis or the relationship between analysis and policy making. This relationship has changed in South Africa in the different periods between 1990 and 2001; it will change again and will be different in the situations of other countries. What is unlikely to change is the continuing need for theoretically informed critiques of policy that point to alternatives to what is often experienced as the given nature of the status quo as well as an awareness on the part of those who develop such critiques of the social and political constraints on any attempt at radical change.

Chapter 2

Educational Reform in South Africa (1990-2000): An International Perspective

Michael Young

Introduction

My own involvement in the educational reform process in South Africa began in the period between 1990 and 1994, first through the National Education Policy Investigation (NEPI) Human Resources Working Group and later with the National Training Board (NTB), the Congress of South African Trade Unions (COSATU) and the Centre for Education Policy Development (CEPD). My contributions to the debate in South Africa were related to my work at that time on the post-compulsory curriculum and the role of qualifications in the United Kingdom (UK), and was informed by similar theoretical and political concerns (Young, 1998, 2000). As well as being a UK perspective on education policy developments in South Africa, therefore, this chapter is also a reflection on certain theoretical ideas that have been central both to my analysis of the UK system of post-compulsory education and training, and to a number of proposals for reform in South Africa.

The broader theoretical ideas that I shall be concerned with arose from dissatisfaction with the educational implications of Marxist analyses of western capitalism and in particular the one-dimensional focus on de-skilling that followed from Harry Braverman's (1974) highly influential book, *Labour and Monopoly Capital.* Ideas such as flexible specialisation (Piore & Sabel, 1986) were used to argue that a more democratic alternative could emerge from the tensions in late industrial capitalism that would have profound implications for the kind of education system that would be possible, as well as its curriculum, qualifications and pedagogy. The story this chapter tells is of the confrontation between the democratic hopes that were embodied in the struggle against apartheid in South Africa and the reality of the kind of society and economy to which the abolition of apartheid led.

The urgency and speed of the political transformation in South Africa after decades of apartheid provides a European social scientist with the unique privilege of seeing idealism confronted with reality in ways that are rarely as clear and explicit in more stable and settled societies. The South African experience of reform dramatises the limitations as well as the potential of social scientists as both shapers and predictors of change. In doing so, it reminds us that social scientists are not so different from political activists and politicians; they tend to believe what they want to believe and choose the theories that seem most congruent with their beliefs. This tendency of the social sciences to embody a world view that may be at odds with reality is only a weakness if it is unrecognised. Without a vision shared with others and going beyond analyses, it is doubtful if social scientists would have had such a key role in the democratic movement.

In the early 1990s a number of concepts and theories were developed that resonated with the experience, the critique and the aspirations of activists in South Africa.[1] These ideas, particularly those for an integrated system of education and training and a single national qualifications framework, helped to shape the reform proposals that became incorporated in the first Election Manifesto of the African National Congress (ANC) and later in various education and training Acts. It is these ideas and the policies to which they led that I examine in this chapter. I want to try to separate two aspects of the ideas – the conceptual and the visionary (or, as some would call it, the utopian). I will argue that they were stronger in the latter – in pointing to a long-term future for a democratic education system for South Africa – and weaker in the former – they did not always provide the theoretical basis for the development and implementation of specific policies in the political and institutional contexts that were the legacy of apartheid.

Before embarking on a discussion of the theoretical ideas themselves, the following section begins by considering two methodological issues – the role of comparative studies and the relationship between theory, research and educational policy. However, these issues are not methodological in the narrow sense. In the early 1990s a major way for the leaders of the democratic struggle to distance themselves from the apartheid regime was to search for alternatives from overseas, especially those found in English-speaking western democracies. It follows that any retrospective review of the policy process in South Africa since 1990 cannot avoid asking to what extent assumptions can be made that South Africa is sufficiently similar to other countries for meaningful 'policy borrowing' to take place.[2] The relationship between research and policy is equally important, given the central role played by university-based researchers in helping to formulate the ideas that were developed by the democratic movement (Muller, 2000). Both issues – policy borrowing and the impact of research on policy – relate directly to my experience of trying to influence policy as a university-based researcher in the UK as well as to my links with the policy process in South Africa.[3] The third section of the chapter will consider, though not in detail, a number of specific theoretical ideas that shaped the early 1990s period of reform in South Africa as well as similar debates in the UK. This is followed in the fourth section by a discussion of a number of the key South African reforms that have parallels in the UK, how they

1 There is some similarity with the much less dramatic circumstances in the UK and the role of the IPPR publication *A British Baccalaureate* (Finegold *et al.*, 1990).
2 The point applies, of course, not only to policies but to analyses like that in this chapter.
3 For example ideas for a baccalaureate-type curriculum in England drew heavily on Scottish and French examples.

developed differently in the two countries, and the assumptions underlying them. The final section will offer some conclusions and an attempt to reconstruct a link between vision and analysis that might inform future theory and policy.

International comparisons and 'policy borrowing'

Background

Comparative studies have a long history in educational research and the social sciences generally. However, it is only recently that in education they have moved from being a specialist field (comparative education) to becoming a mainstream tool of both research and policy. This growing recognition of the value of comparative studies reflects the new global economic realities, the political responses to those realities, the similarities in reform goals in different countries, and the growth of policy borrowing itself. I shall discuss each of these factors in turn and then raise some cautionary questions about how particular comparisons, such as those between South Africa and the UK, can be misleading.

Global economic realities

It is increasingly recognised (e.g. Castells, 1996, 1997, 1998) that all countries regardless of their history or stage of development have to confront similar forces of globalisation and their impact on national economies. These global forces are leading to new kinds of social divisions and increasing doubts about the capacity of national states to overcome them, to uncertainties about the relation between growth and equity policies, and about the feasibility of balancing public and private provision. In relation to education, we have seen increasing expectations being placed on public education systems to deliver levels of attainment unthinkable even twenty years ago.

Political similarities

Different countries are reacting differently to these global forces. However, in the case of the UK and South Africa there are similarities in the political approach of the recently-elected ANC and Labour governments, especially as they impact on educational policy. A number of examples illustrate this point. First, in 1994 and 1997 both countries had very high expectations of their newly-elected governments after years of right-wing regimes. It also seems likely that they shared considerable over-optimism about how much a government with reformist commitments could actually achieve. Second, both governments were left-leaning, with official commitments to reducing inequality but without any major redistribution through the tax system. [4] Furthermore, they shared a largely non-interventionist approach to the economy which has had powerful, albeit unintended, consequences for education. In the UK, education is seen by the present Labour government as a major instrument for realising social

4 In the UK poverty has actually increased since 1997.

and economic goals. (Prime Minister Tony Blair is quoted as saying that education is the best economic policy that we have!) The education policies themselves have focused on supply-side measures and have left the all-important issue of demand to the market. Not surprisingly, it is possible to identify educational reform goals that are shared by the two countries. Examples include widening participation in higher education (HE), reducing social exclusion, promoting lifelong learning, emphasising employability as an educational goal, and promoting critical outcomes (or key skills as they are known as in the UK).

In relation to the specific educational strategies discussed later in this chapter, there has been a focus in both countries on:

- reforming qualifications and using them as a major lever of change (see Cosser, Chapter 9);
- developing a more co-ordinated and integrated system of further education and training (FET) [5] (see Gewer, Chapter 8);
- plans for restructuring higher education into a single co-ordinated, diversified system (see Kraak, Chapter 6); [6] and
- a shift in approach to the curriculum (see Muller, Chapter 4). [7]

South Africa and the UK: the limitations of comparisons

Notwithstanding the similarities to which I have referred, there are two reasons for being cautious about interpreting them too literally, over and above the obvious differences of history and geography between the two countries. First, they under-emphasise the major historical differences between the two countries. In the case of

5 In South Africa this takes the form of the FET band of provision linked though the National Qualifications Framework (NQF) and including senior secondary education, technical colleges and work-based training (the new learnerships). In the UK, it involves the merging of the Further Education Funding Council (FEFC) for Colleges and the Training and Enterprise Councils (TECs) that fund work-based training, and linking themwith the funding of upper secondary education through one national and forty-eight regional Learning and Skills Councils.

6 In the UK, an almost unified but highly stratified higher education system governed by a single quality assurance system and (at least potentially) a single qualifications framework is being created with similarities to the proposals from the Council for Higher Education in South Africa. The dilemma in the UK is whether the strengths of the old elitist system (high quality research and graduates) can be retained in a mass system for a projected one in two of each cohort.

7 In South Africa the shift is from a divided, fragmented and content-heavy subject-based system inherited from the apartheid years to the learner-centred outcomes-based education (OBE) model of Curriculum 2005. In the UK, the shift has been different and less dramatic - subjects remain but specifications replace syllabuses. Basic skills are being given priority, content is reduced and schools are allowed more flexibility to respond to the diversity of learner needs. Integration has been far less central to the English approach to curriculum reform and is expressed in cross-curriculum themes (and key skills for post-16 students). However, these reforms remain largely 'on paper' as the themes are not assessed and key skills are voluntary. For post-16 students in colleges or the upper forms of secondary schools, subjects and broad vocational fields have been unitised across a common framework with a common system of grading and similar names - A-levels and Vocational A-levels, and GCSEs and Vocational GCSEs. What is very different from South Africa is the enormous pressure on institutions competing for students through targets, and the League Tables ranking schools and colleges according to their examination results.

South Africa, the legacy of apartheid and the Afrikaner corporate state, the experience of resistance and repression, the greater legitimacy of 'stakeholders' such as trade unions and community groups, the extremely high levels of unemployment, the large informal and rural sectors, and the extent of inequalities are among the most obvious examples that have no direct parallels in the UK. In the case of the UK, the level of institutional capacity, the increasing integration into the European Union (EU), and the greater emphasis on markets as drivers of quality and accountability are examples of developments that have no direct parallels in South Africa.

Furthermore, there are two less visible differences which may be of even greater significance. The first is the powerful role in the UK of mediating groups and institutions such as schools and parents, a significant though weakened tier of local government, a qualified and unionised teaching force, and a relatively strong civil service with a tradition of political neutrality. All these groups and institutions act as barriers, limiting the extent to which innovative educational ideas – good and bad! – can become part of actual policy and practice. The other factor is the growing impact of 'electoral' politics in the UK and the increasing use of focus groups to 'test' the popularity of policies.

Another reason for caution in drawing conclusions from UK/South Africa comparisons is the danger of assuming that the UK represents the only alternative model and thus neglecting the importance of other European countries as well as Asian countries such as Japan and Singapore. These countries offer very different models for educational reform, that place a much greater emphasis on the role of the state in nation-building. The key elements of the alternative reform model suggested by these countries can be summarised as follows:

- They treat frameworks linking *institutions* rather than *qualifications* as the main drivers of reform.
- The approach to overcoming academic/vocational divisions is more concerned with enhancing vocational pathways than integrating vocational with general education.
- Increased participation in higher education is achieved by improving access and quality within a divided system (of polytechnics and universities) rather than by creating a single co-ordinated system.
- Less emphasis is placed on the role of individual choice, flexibility and the self-empowerment of learners.
- There is a stronger tradition of social partnerships between employers and the state in training and vocational education.

There are some signs of convergence between policies in the UK and other European countries (Green *et al.*, 1998) although the distinct traditions remain. In relation to the speed of the reform and the extension of opportunities, a number of Asian countries provide a powerful alternative model that is as relevant to the UK as to South Africa.

Research, theory and policy

The experience of being involved in attempts to influence reforms in the UK and in South Africa, coupled with the findings of a series of research projects concerned with the unification of academic and vocational learning (Lasonen & Young, 1998), have influenced how I have come to think about the relationship between research and policy as well as the possibilities of democratic educational change. I want to distinguish between four issues. The first is the importance of being clear about purposes and seeing educational reforms as means rather than ends. This links to the tendency, especially in the post-apartheid era in South Africa but found also in the UK, to polarise alternatives. A specific case, that I will discuss in more detail later in this chapter, is the polarisation of divided and integrated (or unified) systems of education and training.

The second issue refers to the need to be more cautious about the short-term possibility of democratic educational change and more aware that implementing any kind of egalitarian change is more difficult than radical social theory (or the democratic struggle) prepared us for. Real democratic educational change certainly does not follow in any straightforward way from a change of government. This links to the need to be aware that barriers to democratic reform are not always the result of right-wing governments or conservative vested interests; some forms of resistance to what are presented as progressive changes may have an educational rationale. The latter point is easily neglected by over-idealistic educational theories as well as by over-optimistic policy makers when they uncritically support democratic-sounding educational strategies such as participatory pedagogies and experiential learning and dismiss resistance to them as reactionary.

A third and related issue is the danger of over-politicising educational issues [8] – in other words, seeing all educational issues as extensions of an earlier 'struggle' (some may be, but not all).

It is important to distinguish between a 'political' discourse about democracy, participation and integration and an 'educational' discourse in which it cannot be assumed that more 'participatory' pedagogies, more representative committees or more integrated systems will necessarily achieve long-term educational goals such as increasing access and participation. Something highlighted for me by my experience of the reform process in South Africa and the highly charged political debates that occurred prior to the first democratic elections is the importance of separating *theoretical debates* about policy that tend to take place in research communities and *strategic debates* about implementation that lie at the heart of policy making.

8 Prior to 1997, like many on the left in the UK, I tended to see educational change as a struggle between a 'conservative' bureaucratic state apparatus and reformist politicians. When we finally elected a reforming government, some of us found a very different picture of bureaucrats eager to introduce reforms but being blocked by electorally-cautious Ministers.

Theories and critiques are bodies of ideas shared by research communities; policies, however, involve a much deeper and wider range of practices and interests of politicians, government officials, teachers, parents, and of course students. In a sense, then, policies are far more 'material' than theories, as far more is at stake. It follows that critiques of policies are very different from critiques of other theories. Not only may policies originate from sources other than the theories shown by researchers to underpin them, but alternatives to them are not just better policies (like better theories) – they involve changes in people's lives, identities and careers. These differences are important in every country, but are dramatised in South Africa where the 'policy making' and 'research' communities are so intertwined.

The final issue I want to raise that takes different forms in South Africa and the UK is the question of the relevance of educational research. In the UK there is enormous pressure on educational researchers to consult 'users' of every kind. The result is that the 'intellectual space' for research to go beyond the immediate and the pragmatic is reduced and the potential of research is weakened. This is primarily a pressure from government on researchers. However, it is also found in the tendency of researchers to accept that their role is to help make reforms work, when it may be that the reforms themselves and not their implementation are the problem. In the UK this can lead to a denial of the need for a distinctive theoretical space for university-based research and the need for research to operate at a distance from policy.

In this section I have argued that it is important to distinguish between theoretical and political analyses and to recognise that not all educational issues are first and foremost political in the sense of being about struggles for power. It follows that although education issues are always 'political' they also have a specificity that separates them from wider political conflicts. Educational research needs a distinct space separate from policy if it is to fulfil its distinctive role in the achievement of a country's educational goals.

Theoretical perspectives

Critical analysis of educational policy both in South Africa and the UK, though in different ways and to a different extent, has been shaped by a number of the same key ideas and debates since the early 1990s. These include those around social constructivism and post-modernism (Muller, 2000a), around progressive education (see Chapter 4), and no doubt others of which I am unaware. In this section of the chapter I shall consider a set of theoretical ideas that have had a particular impact on debates about curriculum, qualifications and pedagogy. My list is inevitably selective; it is chosen for a number of reasons. First, the theories discussed have shaped a number of the critiques of education policy. Second, they played a significant role in the South African debates and proposals since the early 1990s and underpin a number of the current reforms, in particular those concerning the National Qualifications Framework and the school curriculum. As was pointed out at the Round Table, this focus on curriculum and qualifications misses out major contextual issues concerning governance and funding. My justification for a more limited focus on debates about the curriculum and the qualifications system is that together they express different long-term visions of an education system as well as influencing specific reforms; it is these different visions that should have priority. Debates about the forms of governance and funding are important; however, they are concerned with the best way of achieving a particular vision in a democratic and affordable way.

The question of specialisation

Underlying the more optimistic scenarios for western capitalism since the late 1980s were arguments about changes in the industrial division of labour. The idea of flexible specialisation proposed by Piore and Sabel (1986) in their book *The Second Industrial Divide* was built on and developed by Robin Murray (1988) in the UK and John Mathews (1988) and others in Australia, who introduced the concept of post-Fordism. This analysis suggested that as competition became increasingly global the tensions in capitalism were forcing employers to take more seriously the potential productivity of their employees. This meant greater integration of managers and workers, more democratic workplaces, and a greater emphasis on skills development. The need for new links between workplaces and providers of education and training followed naturally from this analysis. With others I applied these ideas somewhat optimistically to education and developed the distinction between insular and connective specialisation (Young, 1998) that could be applied to changes in the curriculum, in the role of teachers, and in the relationships between school and work and the qualifications system. The implication of the analysis was that 'insular specialisation' (and, more emotively, divisions) – whether between subjects within the curriculum or between school and non-school knowledge – invariably created barriers to learning and underpinned educational and wider social inequalities. Insulation and its concomitants, division and separation, symbolised what I described as exemplifying a 'curriculum of the Past' (Young, 1998).

There were two problems with this analysis – one economic and one educational. The economic problem was of course that post-Fordism was a highly exceptional outcome of the collapse of Fordism, that only made its appearance in regions with a particular democratic political history (Emilia Romagna in Italy, Jutland in Denmark, and Bad Godesburg in Germany were the most frequently cited regions). Far more common, certainly in the UK, was the re-emergence of Fordism (in the service sector) and the neo- or hi-tech Fordism of Call Centres where the new technologies are used with new forms of managerialism to maintain hierarchical relations of production. The post-Fordist analysis was, therefore, at best over-simplistic in its claim that changes in the economy would provide the basis for a democratic curriculum of the future (Payne, 2000). It is clear now that, though there is no doubt that the form of capitalist production is changing under the impact of globalisation and new technologies from the old Fordist division of labour, the outcome is complex and uneven across the world. The educational issue that resulted from applying a post-Fordist analysis was the extent to which some of the divisions, boundaries and separations in the curriculum might have democratic and not just conservative and elitist educational possibilities (Young, 2000; Moore & Young, forthcoming).

This is an example of a tendency in both theory and policy that I referred to earlier. It polarises opposites, replacing one principle – insularity and division – by another – connectivity – rather than exploring conditions under which insularity or connectivity might have educational purposes and when arguments for keeping subjects separate might be no more than the preservation of vested interests. As with the economic analysis on which it is based, the insular/connective specialisation distinction does grasp some aspects of educational change and in slightly different forms has informed a number of analyses and proposals (Reich, 1991; Gibbons et al., 1994; Handy, 1994; Griffiths & Guile, 1999). However, it is in the development of new relationships between subjects and their connections rather than a polarisation between a subject-based and an integrated curriculum that we are likely to find models for the curriculum of the future (Moore & Young, forthcoming).

Overcoming academic/vocational divisions

A second and closely related theme in theorising about the curriculum in the early 1990s was the claim that the changes in the organisation of work pointed out by Piore and Sabel and others were undermining the traditional division between mental and manual labour. This view shaped the very influential publication in the UK of *A British Baccalaureate* (Finegold *et al.,* 1990) and many of the publications of the Post-16 Education Centre at the Institute of Education at the time. It also influenced my contribution to the NEPI Working Group on Human Resources (Young, 1998) and the later debates and proposals from the reconstituted National Training Board in the 1992-1994 period. The argument was that if divisions between mental and manual labour were being undermined by economic change, then academic/vocational divisions within the educational and training system must be sustaining them. There was, therefore, a powerful case for an integrated (or what in the UK was referred to as a unified) system that brought together education and training and general and vocational education. The idea of integration was an especially powerful one in South Africa in the early 1990s as it offered a clear alternative to the divisions that were such a dominant feature of the old apartheid system.

In the South African context, it is also relevant to note that the argument for a shift from a divided to an integrated system had a particular significance for trade unionists. It was linked by COSATU to the possibility of career and training opportunities through a single qualifications framework that would offer two possibilities systematically excluded by apartheid. These were:

- a structure for recognising (through the recognition of prior learning) the skills and knowledge of the many black workers who were skilled and doing skilled jobs but were neither qualified nor paid as skilled workers; and

- a ladder of opportunity for progression and promotion – 'from sweeper to engineer' was the most evocative expression at the time.

However, this focus on qualifications instead of institutions as the major lever of reform research in the UK and in South Africa was not as straightforward as it appeared. In the UK it unconsciously and uncritically mirrored the key driving role being given to qualifications by the Conservative government of the time. In other words it was clear, though not explicitly at the time, that a qualifications framework could have a number of quite contradictory goals. In the UK at least, the continuing role of qualifications as the main driver of educational policy has had centralising rather than democratising consequences for the education system. Furthermore, it has not led to a single NQF. Although both Tory and Labour governments have resisted the integration of general and vocational qualifications, government departments (the Department for Education and the Department of Employment), the regulatory authorities (the School Curriculum and Assessment Authority and the National Council for Vocational Qualifications, NCVQ), and the examining bodies were all integrated or merged. Only the qualifications themselves (academic and vocational) were kept separate. [9] It was a process of co-ordination rather than unification and its most obvious consequences have been a variety of forms of academic drift. Curriculum 2000, the most recent proposal for the post-16 curriculum in England and Wales, creates new possibilities for mixing between and bridging across academic and vocational qualifications within a common unitised framework. However, initial evidence is that this is leading to the expansion and greater separation of the general education route and a weakening of the vocational pathways; it is not leading to integration or equivalence.

It appears that the original analyses were too narrow and that divisions, at least in the UK, are not primarily a product of the educational system but of the society as a whole, despite the economic changes that are weakening traditional divisions between mental and manual labour. My conclusion is that we need to look again at (a) the origins of educational divisions in different countries, (b) the unintended consequences of making qualifications the driver of educational reform, (c) the purpose of integration and the extent to which it is the major or only strategy for reducing inequalities, (d) the lessons that may be learned from other countries where integration has not been a major issue or strategy (Lasonen & Young, 1998), and (e) the different forms that integration has taken in the UK and South Africa and the different roles that it may be playing. There is some evidence that whereas in the UK the co-ordination of general and vocational education within a common organisational structure has led to academic drift and little enhancement of opportunities for vocational education, the continuation in South Africa of separate Departments of Education and Labour

9 The most public reason for this was the political decision to preserve A-levels as the main access route from schools, both public and private, to university. By way of comparison, it will be interesting to see what the fate of the South African matric examination will be.

working within a single integrated National Qualifications Framework may have more positive outcomes.

In theory at least, an integrationist approach to education and training guarantees two possibilities. The first is that general, professional and vocational qualifications are part of a single system with progression being possible either through the school-university route or the vocational-work route. The second possibility arising from an integrated national qualifications framework is that work-based vocational qualifications will have to include a component of general education, thus breaking with the National Vocational Qualifications (NVQ) model of competence. As of June 2001, however, these are still no more than possibilities.

Pedagogic models

The third theoretical theme I want to consider concerns the kind of approach to pedagogy that should be characteristic of a modern democratic education and training system. Pedagogy was not a central theme in the debates of the early 1990s when the focus was, understandably, on more systemic issues. However, it is beginning to appear more explicitly in the debate about Curriculum 2005 (C2005) and its emphases on learner-centredness and 'freeing the teacher'. My contention is that the more reforms in South Africa get involved in the process of implementation, the more important the issue of pedagogy becomes.

In the UK the debate about pedagogy has its origins in a wave of new theories of learning that stress the extent to which learning is a socially constructed process involving what the American anthropologists Lave and Wenger (1991) refer to as 'legitimate peripheral participation' in communities of practice (see also Wenger, 1998). The ideas have been applied in the UK by Bloomer (1997) among others. It is not surprising that the idea of 'learning as participation' appears attractive in societies with histories of social exclusion such as the UK and South Africa. In the UK it has been taken up by adult educators as well as by those involved with young people who have become disaffected from school. However, again we have an example of misplaced theoretical polarisation. In this case it is the opposition between what Svar (1998) describes as two metaphors of learning. These are:

- ❑ 'learning as participation' that underpins the idea of learner-centredness and 'teacher as facilitator' that is associated in South Africa with OBE; and
- ❑ 'learning as acquisition' with its links with pedagogy as the transmission of a given body of knowledge.

Two problems have emerged in the UK with the 'participation' model of pedagogy. One I have already referred to – it tends to be applied to slow or disaffected learners who are least equipped to benefit from it. The second problem is that treating participation as the central feature of learning can deflect attention away from the development of new pedagogic strategies – in other words, the activities in which the learners might be encouraged to participate (Young, 2000). This is a particular problem with efforts to promote work-based learning in workplaces, that have no tradition of pedagogy or even instruction (Guile & Young, forthcoming).

Theories of knowledge and the curriculum

My final theoretical issue refers to the question of knowledge, which was somewhat tangential to the debates about qualifications and the curriculum in South Africa in the early 1990s but which has come to the fore recently in the C2005 debates. In the early 1990s, there was an assumption – at least in the discussions about qualifications – that shifting from the narrow concept of *competence* to the broader concept of *outcomes* as a basis for defining qualifications would allow space for debates about knowledge content. The question of knowledge tended to be avoided by focusing on notions of competence, partly because it was restricted to vocational qualifications and partly because it assumed that knowledge was always implied in competent performance in the workplace. This turned out not to be the case. As Muller (2000a) argues, either outcomes are too narrowly prescribed to take account of knowledge or too diffuse and difficult to assess. In each case knowledge content gets lost.

More generally, we need an alternative to another polarisation – one that refers to opposing epistemologies (Young, 2000). The traditional view that is defended and attacked in the UK is that the curriculum is a given body of knowledge to which learners, teachers and the community have to adapt. The paradigm case is the English academic curriculum associated with the nineteenth and early twentieth century public schools and copied by many grammar schools. It was based initially on the classics – Livy, Homer and other similar authors were prescribed texts. In the UK a modern version of this view of the curriculum is still widely held by, among others, the former Chief Inspector for Schools, Chris Woodhead. The opposite view – that comes from the sociology of knowledge and was first applied to the curriculum in my book *Knowledge and Control* (Young, 1971) – is that knowledge is not a given but is socially constructed. It follows that the curriculum is not a body of content but the outcome of political struggles over what counts as knowledge (to be transmitted). From this kind of social constructionist perspective, the task of the reformers becomes to replace a racist, sexist or out of date curriculum that differentiates learners by social class (and other divisions) with one that treats all learners as equal. This appears to be the aspiration of Curriculum 2005. Its most articulate expression in the UK is rather different and is based on arguments for a skills-based curriculum (Royal Society of the Arts, 1998), although it is also found in books influenced by post-modernist theory (Griffith, 2000).

The problem with this polarity is not the argument that knowledge and therefore the curriculum are not socially constructed, but with equating social construction either with political struggles as it has been by some in South Africa or an opposition between 'knowledge for the past' and 'skills for the future' as in the proposals from the Royal Society of Arts in the UK. Both polarities neglect the extent to which the conditions under which knowledge is actually acquired and produced are not arbitrary but have evolved over time. It seems likely that we need to look at some aspects of what have been dismissed as socially exclusive, elitist and even racist 'curricula of the past'. We need to distinguish between those elements of such curricula that are associated with preserving vested interests and maintaining social divisions and patterns of discrimination and those that may be the basis for transcending those interests and divisions and be necessary for certain types of learning – especially conceptual learning. Examples might be the continuing role for school subjects, and the need for curricula to take students away from their non-school everyday experiences and provide them with opportunities to explore ideas in new contexts. Elsewhere I have referred to this latter approach as a *social realist* [10] view of knowledge and the curriculum. It differs from most social constructivist approaches to the curriculum in that it recognises that there may be cognitive and not just political interests involved in claiming that some forms of curriculum organisation are 'better' than others (Moore & Young, forthcoming).

Conclusion

To conclude this section, I have argued that much theorising about education in the early 1990s, both in the UK and in South Africa, was too one-dimensional. As such, it ended in polarities that led to oversimplified policies that appeared attractive to activists but that sometimes turned out to be educationally misguided. The four strategies I have referred to are best seen as means instead of ends; they refer to one side of a complex and changing picture. To keep the ends or purposes of educational policy in mind we need a dual focus on:

- the roles of insular *and* connective forms of specialisation;
- the integration of general and vocational education as a long-term goal that in the short term is only one possible strategy for promoting greater parity of esteem of vocational education and hence enhancing the quality of learning;
- the view that pedagogies must encourage the acquisition of knowledge and skills as much as the active participation of learners; and
- the view that social constructionist and social realist approaches to knowledge can be complementary and not opposites.

This is not a proposal for compromise but for asking difficult questions about 'what works for what purposes'.

10 The term *social realist* as used here draws on Collins (1998) who argues that, contrary to traditional sociologies of knowledge, the social character of knowledge is not the grounds for relativism but for the objectivity of knowledge.

Key reforms in South Africa and the UK

Introduction

The previous section made two arguments. The first was that polarising alternatives – a characteristic feature of political discourse and debates – is not necessarily appropriate when applied either to theoretical perspectives or to educational policy priorities. The second argument was that reform strategies such as the integration of general and vocational education or the introduction of an outcomes-based curriculum are means, not ends to be defended for themselves. I want to relate these general arguments to a number of the specific reforms currently being implemented, reviewed or under discussion in South Africa, and where appropriate to contrast them with the UK experience. In particular, I shall be concerned with the introduction of the NQF, Curriculum 2005 and the debates about higher education that have followed the proposals made by the Council for Higher Education (CHE).

SAQA and the National Qualifications Framework

Establishing a single, comprehensive National Qualifications Framework is a massively ambitious project. Various kinds of qualifications frameworks are under discussion in many countries; however, there are no examples of one that has been fully implemented. The fundamental questions are, first, is the establishment of a national qualifications framework a crucial first step in creating a modern and democratic system of education and training in South Africa, and second, if the answer to this question is broadly positive, have the strategies and priorities of the South African Qualifications Authority (SAQA) been right?

The main model for establishing a National Qualifications Framework in South Africa has been drawn from New Zealand, the only other country in the world to attempt something similar. However, even without South Africa's painful legacy of divisions and neglect, and with a population less than a tenth of the size, [11] the New Zealand Qualifications Authority has encountered enormous difficulties. It has been forced to take many steps backwards from the original plan that was based on unit standards. It has had to allow the universities and the academic secondary schools virtual autonomy and has attempted to shift its emphasis from standards to the hardly less diffuse notion of quality (Smithers, 1995).

In the UK progress has been more modest. We have proposals for a national framework in Scotland – the Scottish Credit and Qualifications Framework (SCQF) – which at present are little more than an agreement 'on paper' among the key players. It is far from clear how widely it will be accepted in practice by employers or how agreements will be reached with university admission tutors over such contentious

11 A point made very forcibly by Khetse Lehoko at the Round Table.

issues as equivalence between different types of qualifications. In England there is a partial national framework up to level 3 (roughly equivalent to matric in South Africa) and criteria for vocational qualifications up to level 5 (higher degrees) under the aegis of the Qualifications and Curriculum Authority (QCA). Proposals for a separate Higher Education Qualifications Framework have been launched but are being resisted by the universities and many professional bodies who jealously guard the qualifications for which they are responsible. A Joint Forum, that brings together all the bodies concerned with qualifications in the UK, has expressed grave doubts about the feasibility of a single national framework, at least in the short term.

The examples of the UK and New Zealand and the broader international experience of qualifications frameworks (Young, 2001) raise a number of questions about developments in South Africa.

First, the most successful education and training systems as measured by levels of participation and attainment are those in Asia and continental Europe. However, they are based primarily on *institutional* rather than *qualifications* frameworks. Qualifications in these countries are closely tied to the specific institutions through which they are delivered, and progression and mobility are based on trust and working relationships developed over time by the stakeholders involved. The UK, New Zealand and South Africa have gone down a very different and riskier route on the assumption that qualifications frameworks will represent the future means of modernising systems of education and training. The assumption is that the 'institutional' model is linked to the 'old' economy, when people secured jobs for life. It is seen as too inflexible to cope with the short life of many modern jobs and the need to promote and encourage lifelong learning. It is assumed that all countries will have to develop national qualifications frameworks sooner or later. A recently launched project by the OECD on the role of national qualifications frameworks will no doubt provide further evidence about international developments. However, recent research on the nature and functions of qualifications frameworks (Young, 2001) indicates some of the dilemmas likely to face South Africa. A qualifications framework can been seen as consisting of three components:

- *a map of all the qualifications included in the framework*: This can act as a guide for users and a template for those wanting to propose new qualifications and is very much what the SCQF offers.
- *an organisation or bureaucracy*: This refers to such bodies as the occupational and subject area Boards and Committees with responsibility for registering qualifications, establishing standards, accreditation, quality assurance and monitoring of assessment. This is what is being developed nationally by SAQA in South Africa.
- *practices and agreements between users, providers and assessors*: It is these practices and agreements that underpin the trust on which the role of qualifications in progression, promotion and transfer of learning are based. They play a crucial,

though less visible, role in all qualifications systems. Without them standards and qualifications, however well designed, are likely to have very little meaning or credibility.

SAQA appears to be progressing with the first two of these components, but it is not clear how the new patterns of trust that will be needed if the claims of a framework are to become a reality will be developed. This is the politically least visible but practically most important component of a qualifications framework. The experience of the UK in the period from 1987 to the mid 1990s was of developing a bureaucracy and registering large numbers of vocational qualifications, few of which were used. The new basis of trust was not there; users either continued with old qualifications because in a pragmatic sense they 'worked', or did not use qualifications at all.

Unlike the QCA in the UK, SAQA has responsibility for registering higher education qualifications. However, with the experience of New Zealand to learn from, it is not clear that higher education qualifications, mostly from universities and already widely trusted, should have been given such a high priority from the start. In addition, SAQA has devoted much time to establishing the elements and systems needed to underpin a national framework (for example, by establishing national bodies to generate and accredit standards). An alternative approach could have been to build on existing regional, sectoral and other frameworks and to find ways of extending them to areas where no qualifications exist. Given the history of South Africa, the priority to establish the national framework and systems is understandable on the grounds that working from existing qualifications and frameworks might appear to be maintaining the divided qualifications of the apartheid era. However, trying to get the national framework in place first may not be maximising the use of scarce (human) resources and expertise. Furthermore, if the NQF is to extend from being a map for users of qualification routes, a massive extension of opportunities for and involvement of people in education and training will be required. In other words, the long-term goal of the NQF requires many more learning opportunities (and therefore many more teachers, trainers and assessors) and many more people seeking to convert their learning into qualifications. These are not priorities that can be promoted by SAQA. The wider policy question is whether there is a danger in exaggerating the role of an NQF in achieving the country's educational goals. It is undoubtedly a crucial component of a system of lifelong learning, but only one. Equally important and crucially complementary priorities are likely be the promotion of institutional capacity among providers, new ways of funding learning, and finding ways to stimulate both the private and public sectors to develop human resource development strategies and incentives for their employees to take up learning opportunities.

Curriculum 2005

The origins of the OBE basis of Curriculum 2005 appear very different from those of SAQA and the NQF, although they are now closely linked in the SAQA publicity.

Whereas the NQF had its origins in COSATU's proposals in the early 1990s for career pathways for workers, OBE arrived on the educational policy agenda much later. Although an outcomes-based curriculum has been a topic of discussion at a national level in the UK (Jessup, 1991) and Australia, and the Spady model has created some interest in a few USA states and Canadian provinces, I am not aware that any other country has attempted to develop an OBE-based curriculum. In South Africa it appears to have been adopted, initially somewhat uncritically, for two reasons:

- It was new and undoubtedly represented a 'clean break' with the old apartheid curricula, in particular its heavy content basis.
- In the form in which it was adopted in South Africa OBE has been associated with learner centredness, 'freeing teachers', and the idea that 'everyone can succeed'; it therefore appeared to fit with the post-apartheid emphasis on democratic participation and access.

In both cases, it may be seen to be an example of two of the more general problems raised in the previous section – over-politicisation of educational issues, and a polarisation of alternatives, in this case between 'content' and 'outcomes' as the basis for the curriculum. This polarisation suggests that the critical role of content in any curriculum needs to be more clearly distinguished from the particular role of content in the apartheid curriculum.

As I understand it, in Curriculum 2005 school subjects are replaced by eight learning areas within which occupational and disciplinary knowledge are integrated. This in itself is a massively ambitious and difficult task with few if any international precedents. In addition, by stressing the non-school experience and everyday life of the learner and the importance of learners being able to apply the knowledge that they learn, C2005 aims to develop an alternative to the rote learning, memorisation and passivity associated with the apartheid curriculum.

While most people would endorse the broad educational goal of integrating the everyday experience of students with what they learn in school, it appears incredibly and perhaps unrealistically ambitious. At the institutional level, it represents an attempt to reverse the whole history of mass schooling that has been based on quite opposite assumptions. For example, the assumptions of most school curricula are that:

- Learning is best organised in school timetables that bear no direct relation to the everyday life of learners.
- Subjects are ways of organising knowledge based on pedagogic practice proven by long experience.

The education of young people within most curricula is not based on freeing students *from subjects* but on freeing them *from being excluded from knowledge* and from only having access to ideology, whether political or religious. Most school curricula represent attempts to provide students with opportunities to learn through subjects such as physics, chemistry and history. This is not to deny that such curricula are not embedded in ideology, that school timetables are often designed more with bureaucratic than pedagogic priorities in mind, nor that the traditions of school subjects do not need to be open to criticism. However, it does suggest that Curriculum 2005 may have based its rejection of the principles of a subject-based curriculum more on its political associations with the divisive apartheid curriculum and its narrow and highly prescriptive content than on a more critical examination of alternative curriculum principles.

A similar point can be made in relation to pedagogy. There seems to be a need to separate the extreme distortions of the apartheid curriculum from the necessary elements of memorisation and rote learning that are a feature of any curriculum. This point is consistent with the recommendations by the Review Committee (DoE, 2000f) for a greater emphasis on vertical progression and coherence of learning. This would involve giving a greater emphasis to conceptual progression within the learning areas and less to how they are related. It may be that links between the different elements of the school curriculum and between school and non-school learning may be achieved less by the curriculum itself and more by new ways of *embedding schools* in their communities. This would of course be a radical shift from the apartheid era in the form of governance of schools and make considerable demands on local capacity. This is an example of the importance of not separating governance issues from curriculum issues and, to repeat an earlier point, that what may be needed is not a blanket critique of the previous curriculum but a separation of its educational potential from its form.

The second issue that I want to raise about Curriculum 2005 is that of its complex system of curriculum 'tools' – the 66 specific outcomes, the range statements, the assessment criteria, the performance indicators, the Phase Organisers, and the Expected Levels of Performance. This list is reminiscent of the early days of NVQs and GNVQs and other outcome-based programmes in the UK, many of which have gradually been dropped in favour of more conventional 'input' measures. It is understandable that centrally-based curriculum designers want to make what is a quite new approach to the curriculum as clear as possible to teachers, parents and students and to provide them with as many tools as possible. However, the NVQ experience suggests that the approach being adopted for Curriculum 2005 has two major weaknesses. First, teachers are likely to be overwhelmed by the new tools and end up over-specifying requirements for students in the form of tasks so that students become task-oriented rather than syllabus-oriented, and the curriculum becomes no more learner-centred that that which it replaces. Second, outcomes – especially critical outcomes that are designed to stress the importance of 'breadth of learning' – tend inescapably to remain 'generic' and lack sufficient content specificity to guarantee the learning that they seek to emphasise.

It may be useful to contrast the assumptions of Curriculum 2005 with traditional curricula. The latter are based on a number of principles:

- ❑ syllabuses linked to end of course examinations;
- ❑ a normative basis for assessment that assumes that only a given proportion of learners are able to succeed; and
- ❑ entrance tests to limit the range of abilities of students in any programme.

These are the principles of the classic socially-exclusive curriculum model that denied all but minimal education to the majority of working-class children in the UK for much of the last century. Similar principles presumably applied under apartheid in South Africa to deny access to black children. C2005 rejects each of the principles of the traditional curriculum. Outcomes linked to course assignments replace syllabuses and terminal examinations, criterion referencing replaces normative-based assessment, and programmes are open to all students. It aims, therefore, to open up the curriculum to all children and integrate it with their experience. At the same time, it tries to ensure that students actually get access to the curriculum through a complex system of specification (the tools referred to earlier).

The OBE model generates two problems. In practice, as Christie and Jansen (1999) have argued, it is and will continue to be extremely difficult for poorly-resourced schools with under-qualified teachers to deliver. Despite political support for it from the South African Democratic Teachers Union (SADTU), it appears anything but teacher-friendly in its present form. The English experience of similar approaches is that it leads to 'task completion' or 'assignment completion' as the dominant form of student activity and at best provides a way for under-qualified teachers to cope in over-size classes – the modern version of the rote learning that it was designed to replace! Secondly, C2005 could – if it goes for highly detailed specification of outcomes, like outcome-based programmes in the UK – actually de-skill the better-qualified teachers. In the case of NVQs and other outcomes-based programmes, the complexity of the range of tools led to what became known as 'box-ticking' – checking that a student had provided evidence for each outcome but with no indication of how well he or she had done. The alternative is to endorse the Review Committee's suggestions for the reduction of curriculum bureaucracy. However, the issue of ensuring the widest possible delivery and quality remain. If specification of outcomes cannot, in principle, guarantee quality, the only alternative is to see that the curriculum is a set of guidelines rather than outcomes, and to give teachers more responsibility for interpreting the guidelines. This of course involves improving the quality of teachers, their training and professional development, and is not just a question of improving the qualifications of teachers as individuals. It goes back to the implications of the epistemological issues raised in the previous section. High quality curricula as a means for acquiring knowledge are based, like high quality research, on specialist professional communities (of teachers, in the case of the curriculum) – what are known in the UK as subject associations for history, geography, languages, mathematics etc. These organisations can be enhanced to support an improved curriculum, and can provide the links between school and university teachers and between school teachers and employers. Furthermore, such associations can be encouraged to collaborate in developing ways of linking their subjects to the new learning areas.

Restructuring higher education

The restructuring of Higher Education and the Mode 1/Mode 2 debate (Kraak, 1999a) on higher education curricula have emerged as issues in policy debates in South Africa since the first democratic election. Undoubtedly the problems of restructuring higher education are far more acute in South Africa than in European countries on account of the legacy of apartheid. However, they are qualitatively similar because the best universities are not unlike European universities and share their history. It follows that comparisons in both directions are valuable. I find it useful to distinguish between *institutional* problems and *system* problems. The first type – which includes low performance, distorted curricula (this is less of a problem in European countries), the need to improve the employability of graduates, and low participation – are found in the UK as well as South Africa. The UK approach to these problems is a combination of funding incentives, subject benchmarking, quality assurance mechanisms, and competition for students. There is much debate in the UK about what these new forms of accountability will achieve other than increased levels of bureaucracy and increased pressures on individual institutions. The issue for South Africa is whether there is the capacity for such an approach and, more fundamentally, whether it should be a priority.

The main systemic problem facing all countries is to find an approach for developing a system based on mass participation and deciding whether it will be a single stratified system or a diversified dual system. There appear to be a number of models:

❑ *the USA model*

This model is based on a weak-capacity state and assumes that elite private institutions will drive up standards by generating competition for students and research funding. In the USA model weak institutions either close or continue to give poorly-valued degrees, and strong institutions (both public and private) are allowed to decide their own priorities. This is not a viable model for South Africa or the UK, though our top universities are pressing for the freedom to 'compete' on the global market. The issue, if they were given this freedom (for example, to set their own fee levels), is whether they would also continue to play their current national educational and research role.

❑ *the UK model*

This is based on medium-capacity regulation by the state and a quasi-market (there is only one private university). A single unified but stratified system has replaced the previous elitist binary system of universities and polytechnics. The regulated quasi-market allowed weak or small institutions to be merged. A number of trends are discernible in the forms of both academic drift and vocationalism. The former polytechnics have expanded in fields such as media, cultural and business studies, and at the same time all universities are focusing more on the skills their graduates need if they are to be employable. Finally, the stratification of universities – based on research funds and entry qualifications of students – into an elite group and the rest is consolidating, and intermediate (sub-degree) level programmes are increasingly neglected.

Among the uncertainties that lie ahead for the UK higher education system are (i) whether it will find ways of significantly expanding its undergraduate recruitment beyond the current proportion of 1:3 from each cohort, (ii) how it responds to the growth of 'corporate' universities, and (iii) whether the 'elite universities' will be able to maintain their traditional high standards in the face of pressures to expand and widen participation.

❑ *the continental European model*

The pattern of higher education in EU countries other than the UK tends to be based on dual systems of research-led universities and various forms of high quality Institutes of Higher Vocational Education that concentrate on teaching and research in applied areas and that develop close links with the private and public employment sector. There is much less emphasis than in the UK on the use of funding mechanisms as incentives for influencing institutional priorities. The strength of the model is that there are clear progression routes from work-based vocational qualifications to higher-level vocational programmes leading to professional recognition.

For South Africa, this model has two problems. It depends on accepting a form of division based on two types of institutions with different educational goals operating broadly on the basis of Mode 1 (disciplinary) and Mode 2 (trans-disciplinary) curricula. This might appear as a return to or continuation of the divisions of the apartheid era. Some form of binary or dual system would, however, mirror the existing divisions in the Further Education and Training Band between senior secondary schools on the one hand and technical colleges and work-based training on the other. A clearly distinct vocational strand within higher education could provide progression routes that are not based on some form of matric examination and could therefore be a way of improving the status and quality of provision in the technical colleges. The second problem is that the historically disadvantaged universities in South Africa appear completely ill-equipped to become Institutes of Higher Vocational Education even if that became policy. This would require substantial investment in the new applied sector and the conversion, merger or closure of the weak institutions.

Conclusion

In this chapter I have drawn on international (primarily UK) experiences to reflect on a number of educational policy developments in South Africa in the period 1990-2000. I have argued that both the theories that informed our critiques of the past and the policies that have been endorsed by the democratic movement were in a number of senses overly idealistic, not in the vision that inspired either the struggle for democracy or specific reforms but in their applicability as a basis for policy. This argument about idealism had a number of strands. First was the tendency to be overly optimistic about the democratic potential of economic changes, especially the demise of Fordism as the dominant mode of production. Second was the conflation of political and educational discourses and the assumption that the language of participation, integration and rights of stakeholders could apply in any straightforward way to achieving educational goals. Linked to this argument was the need to recognise the specificity of educational issues, especially those concerned with pedagogy and curriculum. Third was the importance of recognising the difficulty of achieving educational change, especially when there is such an acute lack of capacity at all levels involved in policy implementation.

From the point of view of the future of both research and policy, this leads me to two conclusions. One is the importance of a distinct space for research that is neither resourced by bodies directly involved in policy nor expected to apply directly to the improvement of policies. This is not an argument for 'research for the sake of research' – like any other public activity, research has to be accountable. The importance of an autonomous space for research is that it enables research to go beyond the polarities of critique or implementation modes. Both have their place. However, critiques are inevitably interpreted as negative and generate the need for policy makers to be defensive about their policies, and prioritising implementation is about getting things done and not asking why they are being done in particular ways.

My second conclusion is that more attention needs to be paid to the strengths that past educational models may still have for us. They are likely to have some elements that will be part of a model with quite different aims and be part of the future anyway, if only implicitly. This reassessment of past provision involves distinguishing between the ideological elements of past models that need to continue to be struggled against and their educational potential that needs to be analysed critically and built on. The argument that after six years of democratic government in South Africa it may be useful to reassess some elements of the past is difficult, because the apartheid system was like the Nazi treatment of the Jews – so unequivocally bad that the idea that it might have had any redeeming features seems inconceivable. However, in a sense some reassessment is inescapable as the past always shapes the present in some way, however much we feel that we have made a break with it. In the same way the UK cannot escape from its colonial history, the peculiarities of its social class structure, being the first country in the world to industrialise, or more recently having eighteen years of Conservative government. The issue is one of purposes and method and applies particularly, I suspect, to the debates about the curriculum that have emerged out of C2005.

There is a final point that I became increasingly clear about as I prepared and revised this chapter. There is an important aspect of globalisation that gets missed out in all the theories. The big educational questions about knowledge, pedagogy and the role of qualifications that are raised by the South African reforms are not unique or specific to South Africa; they are the difficult questions that face all of us. The debate about them needs to be global, not national, and, thanks to the Internet, it can be.

Chapter 3

Rethinking Education Policy Making in South Africa: Symbols of Change, Signals of Conflict

Jonathan D. Jansen[1]

Introduction

In this chapter, I will argue along the following lines: that the first ten years of policy making in South Africa, following official moves towards a new democracy (1990), hinged largely on the symbolism rather than the substance of change in education. I will expand this argument by drawing on published case studies of policy making from the decade 1990-2000 to develop a theoretical understanding of 'policy as political symbolism' in the context of the South African transition (Jansen, 2000a). I will conclude by using this emerging theoretical platform to explain the likely trajectory of education policy making in the next five to ten years.

The original study on which this chapter is based (Jansen, 2000a) was an attempt to chart the processes by which various education policies unfolded prior to (1990-1994) and since (1994-2000) the first national democratic elections in South Africa. In relation to this broad task, the investigation addressed several critical questions over a decade of policy production and contestation in South Africa:

- ❑ What were the major political processes and actors that shaped and influenced education policy in South Africa during the 1990s?
- ❑ Why is there such a growing distance between policy and practice in South African education after apartheid?
- ❑ Does the trajectory of education policy and politics in the 1990s suggest the likely pattern of education reform in the next century?

I will focus more closely on the second question – that is, the policy/practice problem in South African education. However, the purpose of this chapter is not to rehearse in detail the original case for understanding policy as political symbolism; this has been done extensively elsewhere (Jansen, 2000a). Rather, the more limited goal is to expand this theoretical position through a response to its critics, and then to use the theoretical argument to launch a broader discussion about the possibilities for educational reform in the future.

1 I thank Douglas Irvine, Shireen Motala, Joe Muller, Hersheela Narsee, Jane Skinner, Michael Cross, Crain Soudien, and the six critical readers for their comments.

The early 1990s and the race for policy position

Until 1990, the production of education policy in South Africa was a relatively simple matter. The state maintained control of education policy in ways that were bureaucratically centralised, racially exclusive and politically authoritarian. This pattern was firmly established at least since the consolidation of white political power following the electoral victory of the National Party in 1948 on its platform of apartheid. Despite occasional challenge to and disruption of state schooling in the 1970s and 1980s, there was only one policy player within South African education: the apartheid state. All of this changed in the momentous global and regional events that culminated in the parliamentary announcement by Frederick W. de Klerk on 2 February 1990 unbanning the liberation organisations, releasing political prisoners and accelerating movement towards the first non-racial, democratic elections of April 1994.

Since that moment in 1990, a flurry of education policies started to be developed in anticipation of the formal and legal termination of apartheid: the private sector through the Private Sector Education Council (PRISEC) and then the early National Training Board (NTB); the labour movement through the Congress of South African Trade Unions (COSATU) and the later version of the NTB; the broad democratic movement through the National Education Policy Investigation (NEPI); the self-reforming apartheid state through the Education Renewal Strategy (ERS) in two versions and A New Curriculum Model for South Africa (CUMSA); the international aid community through multiple, self-funded sectoral reports; and the non-governmental sector through a range of different programme and policy positions and alignments. All these actors jostled for position as they prepared to develop signal policy positions 'for a democratic South Africa'. This period could be described as projecting the *symbolism of policy position* – that is, contending actors seeking to establish broad symbolic positions in education policy ahead of South Africa's first democratic elections. This symbolism of position did not require detailed policy proposals, simply broad statements of intent or values – in other words, symbolic position.[2]

If the early 1990s could be characterised by the race for policy position, with enormous symbolism governing each position, then the next period could be described as the race for 'policy frameworks'.

The mid-1990s and the race for policy frameworks

In 1994, South Africa convened the first non-racial democratic elections in the history of the country. The ANC-led government of Nelson Mandela was immediately under pressure to demonstrate how it would serve the aspirations of the black majority after years of struggle against apartheid and colonialism. This period (1994-1999) is best described as a race to establish an overarching legal and policy canopy under

2 For a more detailed discussion on policy making in this period, see Chisholm (1992), Mkwanazi *et al.* (1995), Chisholm and Fuller (1996), Kahn (1996), De Clerq (1998), Kallaway *et al.* (1998), Kraak (1998), and Hartshorne (1999).

which education would be conducted in the new democracy (Samoff, 1996; Rensburg, 1998; DoE, 1999b). Nineteen racially fragmented education departments needed to be brought under one united, non-racial department. Apartheid legislation governing teachers, learners, governance and curriculum needed to be replaced. Policy and planning positions had to be specified within the context of a political system founded on reconciliation as expressed in the terms of a negotiated settlement – that is, a government of national unity (Manganyi, 2001; Nzimande, 2001). In short, official 'policy frameworks' had to be established. Based on a review of seven case studies of educational policy making in this period (Jansen, 2000a), I concluded that this period was limited to the *symbolism of policy production* rather than the details of policy implementation. To illustrate, I briefly discuss below three of the more powerful instances of policy production that offer insights into the politics of non-reform in South African education.

The syllabus revision process

In official circles, the syllabus revision process of late 1994 was presented as an attempt to alter in the short term the most glaring racist, sexist and outdated content inherited from the apartheid syllabi, which were still widely used in the aftermath of the first post-apartheid elections in April of the same year (Jansen, 1999a).

In late 1994 the new Minister of Education, Sibusisu Bengu, was approached by the National Education and Training Forum (NETF)[3] to provide political support to one of its key initiatives launched in the transition period ahead of the establishment of the new Department of Education. In this process, at least two significant political tensions shaped the first images of curriculum policy to emerge under the new government:

- the tension between preserving the core of the inherited syllabi while eliminating offensive content, and a more fundamental restructuring of the entire epistemological and value edifice of the apartheid curriculum; and
- the tension generated by the pressure for rapid completion of an essentially political process required to build short-term legitimacy for the state, and the need to conduct a more thorough and informed process of curriculum renewal over a longer period of time.

In the end, the syllabus revision process led to a minimalist, superficial reform of state syllabi, with few substantive changes to either the content or pedagogy of the 'cleansed' syllabi (Jansen, 1999a; Khuzwayo, 1999). There was a minimum of teacher development in the process, no in-depth engagement with the apartheid content, little accompanying development of new materials, and no system of supervision to ensure that the moderately changed syllabi were even used in public schools. More seriously, most of the syllabi had not changed at all despite the frenetic activity associated with

3 The NETF was a broad stakeholder forum, including the apartheid government, that intended to deal with the ongoing education crisis in the months leading to the first post-apartheid elections. For a detailed analysis of this period, see Badat (1998).

the three-month review. The mere production of alternative curriculum policies would have sufficed in this period, irrespective of the implementation possibilities (Jansen, 1999a).

The White Paper on Education and Training

In official terms, the goal of the first White Paper on Education and Training (DoE, 1995a) was to provide a generic document that framed the core values and vision of the newly established government, and in particular the ideals and philosophy of the dominant view in the state represented by the African National Congress. This document, in the view of the ANC members of government, would constitute the foundation document that guided all subsequent policy and legal action of the democratic Parliament. Much was invested, therefore, in the White Paper as the ideological steering force for education policy making and practice throughout the nine provinces (Manganyi, 2001).

The White Paper provided the first basic policy framework within which subsequent education policy making was to be understood. Understandably, the coalition government of Nelson Mandela could not expect an easy passage for the Draft White Paper through the parliamentary process. It appeared as an unedited ANC document couched in what opponents saw as militant language and setting out very radical proposals for the new system of education and training. Moreover, the National Party in particular did not see the Draft as encapsulating the spirit of national unity and reconciliation as envisaged under the Interim Constitution. An intense contestation in Parliament ensued between the ANC of Nelson Mandela and the National Party of F.W. de Klerk on the provisions and language of the White Paper (see Manganyi, 2001; Nzimande, 2001).

The political significance of the production of the first White Paper is that it provides a rare window on the process of policy making, in which establishing political authority by the dominant party within Parliament was an important goal in and of itself. That is, the White Paper served simply as the arena in which the electoral success of the ANC was translated into policy domination within Parliament. This was not a debate about how to implement the values, vision and commitments of the White Paper; it was a period in which the consolidation of political power had to become evident through the policy process (Rensburg, 1998).

The Hunter Report and the White Paper and the Organisation, Governance and Funding of Education

The Hunter Committee (named after its Chairperson, Professor Peter Hunter) was initiated by the Minister of Education in 1995 in order to generate a cohesive national framework that would govern the organisation, funding and management of education. The historical fragmentation of the education system into nineteen education departments based on race and ethnicity provided the Ministry of Education with a complex and contradictory set of procedures and legislation for governing and financing schools. New norms needed to be established to bring coherence into school governance and finance, but also to establish the legal basis for a more equitable distribution of state resources across schools. The Report of the Hunter Committee provided the framing content for the White Paper on the Organisation, Governance and Funding of Education (DoE, 1995b, 1996c).

ANC policy making was never limited to appeasement and accommodation within the education bureaucracy in Pretoria or Parliament in Cape Town. A powerful constituency included white parents of children in the public school sector. This sector of South African society held together a reasonably well-established public school infrastructure on the basis of supplemental parent resources and support. It provided legitimacy to the public school sector even though its majority occupants were being failed by the same system in the townships and rural areas of South Africa. In addition, it offered a source of ongoing revenue for public schools that the state could simply not afford to assume within the constricting base of revenue available to education under the emerging fiscal and macroeconomic policy. Nevertheless, new legislation was critical to transform the governance and financing of public schools in light of the goals of equity and democracy that were key to the framework. established by the first White Paper. To this end, the Minister appointed the 'representative' task team headed by Professor Hunter to investigate the organisation, governance and funding of schooling as critical inputs into new legislation. The task team was mandated by the Minister to see 'the widest possible public support' as the basis for its recommendations (DoE, 1995b:ix).

The political significance of this policy experience in South Africa is that it revealed the limits and politics of participation in the education reform process (Jansen, 2000a). That is, while extensive stakeholder participation was fundamental to the process, in the end the state decided on a financing strategy for schools that did not appear in the report but was based on recommendations of an external (overseas) consultant (Samoff, 1996; Tikly, 1997).

What larger story, then, do these cases tell about politics and policy in the transition? What kinds of theoretical tools are available for distilling meaning from these education policy reforms?

Theorising policy and politics in South African education

After careful interrogation of the original cases as a collective data set on education politics and policy in the transition, the following theoretical position was offered to explain the trajectory of policy development during the ten-year period, 1990-2000 (Jansen, 2000a).

The making of education policy in South Africa is best described as a struggle for the achievement of a broad political symbolism that would mark the shift from apartheid to post-apartheid society. We search in vain for a logic in policy making connected to any serious intention to change the practice of education 'on the ground'. Therefore, a focus on the details of implementation will not be fruitful since it will miss the broader political intentions that underpin policy making after apartheid. Every single case of education policy making demonstrates, in different ways, the preoccupation of the state with settling policy struggles in the political domain rather than in the realm of practice.

In short, this position explains the policy of transition in terms of an over-investment in the political symbolism of educational change. I intend to discuss and refine this theoretical position via a review of the initial thesis by six 'critical readers' deployed to engage these ideas.[4]

None of the critical readers dismiss the theoretical position of policy as political symbolism outright. In fact, they all agree that political symbolism has played some role in post-apartheid education policy making. The points of difference, it seems, revolve mainly around the weight assigned to political symbolism as explanation for policy inaction since the first democratic elections of 1994.

One of the critical readers put the case this way:

> I do agree that the political symbolism has been an important element of policy making in South Africa. It is probably an important element anywhere, and it is not surprising that it has played an important part in South Africa over the last five years given the political context. But the implication in the paper is that the Education Ministry has chosen to (resorted to?) use education policy *primarily* as a political symbol as a result of certain constraints; these constraints have resulted in the government substituting political symbolism for real 'delivery' … [emphasis in the original].

Let me start by restating what appears in the main text of the original paper. All policies have symbolic value. As I have demonstrated through studies in Namibia and Zimbabwe (Jansen, 1995, 1999d), this is particularly evident in the sphere of curriculum policy where national values and ambitions are encapsulated through representations of society in school subjects such as history, religion, geography, biology, and so forth. I do not wish to argue, therefore, that South Africa is exceptional in its use of political symbolism as vehicle for policy generation and dissemination. The wide-scale science curriculum reforms in the United States in response to a perceived national crisis following the Soviet launch of Sputnik, the rapid withdrawal of the national socialist curriculum in newly independent Zimbabwe following public protests led by

4 The identities of the critical reviewers who responded to the original paper in which I proposed this theoretical position were not known to me.

the Catholic Church, the tensions in Israel following the introduction of a revisionist Palestinian history into schools – all represent singular examples of international crises that result from the powerful role of curriculum policy as grounds for both projecting and contesting important political values, which I referred to as 'symbols'. Whether conscious of it or not, nation states invest policy with important political symbolism.

What I did argue, however, was that the over-investment in political symbolism at the expense of practical considerations largely explained the lack of change in South African education six years after the demise of apartheid. I made this argument on the basis of extensive empirical data (Jansen, 2000a), including:

- the public claims by politicians and education bureaucrats concerning the primacy of symbolic politics in education policy making between 1994 and 1999;
- the prominence assigned by politicians to policy production (the making of policy) rather than its implementation;
- the inordinate amount of attention paid to formal participation in policy processes irrespective of their final outcomes;
- the lack of attention to implementation in official policy discourses on educational change;
- the way in which policy makers invoke international precedent in the development of national education policies as part of an external legitimation of local change processes;
- the way in which international participants (mainly in the form of foreign-paid consultants) are drawn into and influence the development of national policy making as an extension of the legitimation role of post-apartheid education policies; and
- the way in which national policy positions are validated through claims to South African incorporation within the globalisation of modern economies.

Extracting these seven empirical claims from the instances of education policy making, I linked the argument to sporadic theoretical efforts in the literature to elucidate the symbolic power of policy in the politics of transitional states.

I should note, however, that the literature on this particular topic is scant given the weight of literature favouring technical analyses of education policy making. Sabatier's (1999) authoritative publication, *Theories of the Policy Process*, completely ignores the symbolic power of policy making. In comparative education another recent and authoritative account of policy processes in education, by Anthony Hargreaves and his colleagues (Hargreaves et al., 1998), completely ignores third world transitions as a site for investigating the politics of education policy making. It is this under-exploration of a potentially powerful theoretical construct that led to this particular framework being applied to education policy making after apartheid.

I am not surprised, therefore, that the bent of the critical reader positions is towards practical solutions and alternative strategies. This was not the aim of the paper. While reviewers can (and did) provide trenchant critiques of the position paper, they cannot ask for a different paper to be written. This does not mean that I dismiss the practical; indeed, in other works I have spent considerable space and time thinking about policy strategy given the constraints encountered by third world states (see Jansen, 1999b, for example). However, I believe that the rush towards solutions is often unproductive *because of* the lack of attention to understanding the factors that undermine policy change in the first place. The paper argues, therefore, for a reflective 'standing back' from the daily grind of policy making to ask what should be a fundamental question in the policy sciences: 'What's going on here?'

From a theoretical point of view, it could further be argued that a commitment to the practical at the expense of a deeper understanding of *policy inertia* is itself a preferred theory of change – that is to say, a theory (often implicit) that social problems can be fixed through technical solutions applied in a thoughtful manner. My own view is that this assumption needs to be tested, not taken for granted. The argument that 'if only there were enough resources' or 'if only there was enough capacity' then implementation would have been 'successful' is not at all supported by the extensive literature on education policy change in well-resourced contexts (McLaughlin, 1998, and the general contributions in Hargreaves et al., 1998). In other words, there is much more going on in policy development and implementation than resources or capacity. All the more reason for a 'standing back' approach that assumes that there is more to the dilemma of non-reform in the policy making process.

Perhaps the most comprehensive and recent evidence supporting the view of policy as political symbolism emerged from a study by Frederik Hess (1997), insightfully entitled *Initiation without Implementation: Policy Churn and the Plight of Urban School Reform*. From a sophisticated study of reform initiatives in fifty-seven urban school districts in the United States, Hess (1997:i) concludes that:

> … the status quo in urban school systems is largely due to political incentives which produce a surfeit of reform and insufficient attention to implementation. In fact, the continuing initiation of reform efforts *is* the status quo. The result is that successive generations of partially implemented reforms produce instability, waste resources, and alienate faculty.

Several facts are striking about the Hess study: that the lack of implementation was not due to a lack of resources; that the evidence for non-implementation spread across fifty-seven large school districts; that the data was collected on the basis of at least five different kinds of school reform; and that the data was collected through intensive methods including three hundred forty-two interviews. Against this background, Hess (1997:7,9) argues that 'reforms tend to be symbolically attractive but not to impose the costs required by significant change' and that 'the result is that policy makers have worked more diligently on appearing to improve schooling than on actually doing so'.

The reason for this extensive referencing of the Hess study is that it represents one of the very few empirical studies making a similar case to what I presented in a context where resources and capacity are not the prime explanatory variables for non-implementation. My contention is that unless policy evaluation in South Africa provides greater weight to the symbolic functions of education policy, then there is the real danger of social expectations being frustrated and theoretical progress being undermined in explaining education transition after apartheid.

To return to the question of how much weight should be assigned to policy symbolism: On the evidence harnessed through the cases, I would argue that during early transition (1994-1999) the *primary* explanation for non-change lies in the symbolic arena. Now I should be clear: this does not mean that policy formulation was 'mere words'. The notion of policy as mere words has little theoretical or practical value. As Rosa Nidia Buenfil-Burgos (2000:1) stridently argues,

> In spite of the fact that educational policies (e.g., globalising policies) do not reach schools and other educational environments exactly as they were proposed, they nevertheless leave a trace in day-to-day local educational practices. This is a position [that] … challenges the ordinary idea that policies are discourses (i.e., just words) which have nothing to do with everyday practices (i.e., reality).

Words have a purpose. Discourses have political intent. To dismiss the theoretical position of policy as political symbolism to mean the simple issuing of words is to miss the point of my thesis.

In addition, I would be remiss not to recognise the real hazards of 'practical constraints'. Another critical reader makes the point emphatically:

> In his final sentence the writer introduces the key to educational change … which I would like to have seen stressed at regular intervals throughout the text. It is not only because of stressing symbolic policy changes that the educational system has not been able to really change in a more widespread and generally beneficial manner, but because, *inter alia*, of the financial constraints on all sides.

My argument has *not* been that financial constraints are irrelevant. Rather, I have made the case for a different interpretation of the role of constraints in relation to policy choices. I have argued that it is precisely because of material constraints on policy that the state has been inclined to play up the symbolic role of policy rather than its practical consequences. However, the converse is not necessarily true: that if there were no material constraints, policy would be implemented as planned. Rich accounts of policy reform over a century of effort (see Hargreaves *et al.*, 1998) have put paid to the idea of searching for fidelity between policy and practice. Nevertheless, the room to manoeuvre in policy reform is substantially constrained by the extent to which material resources are available to educational planners.

Having said all of this, the original point of departure for my thesis on political symbolism is that politicians do not always invent policy in order to change practice. It often represents a search for legitimacy. In this regard another critical reader, in an insightful set of comments, makes the point that

> … the central policy issue which the new government inherited from its predecessor was the illegitimacy of the system as a whole. The establishment of legitimacy was no easy matter – even at the level of symbolic manipulations…. Certainly part of the contestation was about gaining influence and power but the currency of exchange was educational vision and the policy arena was thronged with gatekeepers and 'analysts' who were ready to block and discredit the attempts to construct any sort of comprehensive policy.

While I might disagree with this critical reader as to whether legitimacy was 'the central policy issue' (especially for the ANC with its overwhelming electoral mandate), I would certainly share the view that establishing the credentials of the new system required an overarching symbolic discourse about transformation (captured in key words like equity, non-racialism, democracy and redress). But this modification proposed by the critical reader (and which I accept) merely extends the argument that policy formulation was not always about changing practice, but was weighted towards important symbolic considerations that Ihron Rensburg considered strategic for the early period.

Now this does not mean that those in the planning apparatus of the Department of Education did not entrench themselves within a daily grind of policy formation. The policy mechanics, as Bruce Fuller calls them, have the task of giving implementation substance to official policy – whether they agree with such policy or not, whether they think it is implementable or otherwise. Within the sphere of curriculum policy, I have observed up close the incredible pace and stressful working conditions faced by departmental officials as they scramble to meet imposed deadlines for producing successive drafts of outcomes-based curriculum policy and planning manuals. In this regard it is useful to distinguish policy formulation goals (the Ministry as a political office) from planning implementation goals (the Department as a bureaucratic office). This distinction between political and bureaucratic functions is not, of course, absolute, especially when senior bureaucrats in government see their role as political – for example, the activists hired into senior positions in government. But the distinction does identify two orientations towards policy: one that has in mind the broader political arena within which policy is contested (Parliament, Cabinet, business and industry, civil society more broadly), and another that works more narrowly with the practitioners (teachers and principals) who are required to give expression to national policy within their classrooms. In my view, the critical readers have not always made such distinctions between the political and bureaucratic functions of policy, which partly explains the difference in reading of the original text.

Finally, the theory of political symbolism does not discount the possibility that education policies have resulted in some degree of positive change within the education system. Policies leave a trace in practice (Buenfil-Burgos, 2000). So I cannot but agree with yet another critical reader that 'I have seen little miracles of change, of new life ... though the success stories are not the work only of government'. If anything, the debate on outcomes-based education (OBE) was successful because it generated a wide public debate about curriculum and pedagogy. Furthermore, well-resourced schools were able to respond to the new curriculum through innovative changes in classroom pedagogy. But as our research has demonstrated elsewhere, these effects may have been unintended and worked largely (though not exclusively) to the benefit of schools already privileged with well-qualified teachers and a stock of inherited material resources (Maqutu *et al.,* 1999). But these uneven, unexpected, and small-site changes do not discount the observation that at a system-wide level, education remains steeped in crisis and inequality despite the flurry of policy since the first democratic elections. This acknowledgement of crisis was made, significantly, by the second ANC Minister of Education, Kader Asmal, in his *Call to Action* in late 1999. This reality cannot be explained away by the useful but limited instance of 'success stories'. The flurry of policy was replaced by a flurry of 'implementation talk' in the late 1990s.

The late 1990s and the race for policy implementation

In broad terms, politicians and bureaucrats recognise the need for and the importance of symbolic policy in the production of policy and legislation. It is clear, though, that the appointment of the second post-apartheid Minister of Education in 1999 was made in order to expedite implementation or (in political parlance) to get on with the *delivery* agenda. In other words, there is also recognition of the need to move beyond symbolic policy.

But can the current political and bureaucratic machinery in fact deliver? Can the R50,7 billion rand budget for education in fact translate into the effective provision of quality education for all twelve million learners served by 380,000 teachers in 29,000 schools? What does the Asmal Strategy suggest about the possibilities for fundamental change in an education system that, according to both the Minister and his critics, remains in a state of serious dysfunction? In short, can the Asmal Strategy take policy making beyond symbolic action?

In this section I wish briefly to point to the dominant mode of policy making in the first months of the Asmal period, and to use this as the basis for making considered judgements as to whether government will in fact be able to deliver on the delivery agenda. Thereafter, I will make some concluding remarks on the possible future of education policy and practice in South Africa.

The policy review

In education, the instrument of choice in policy making during the Asmal period is the so-called 'policy review'. I wish to describe the policy review as *a selective process intended to address those areas of government policy in which there is a perceived crisis of delivery* (see ADEA, 2000:10-28). A careful reading of the *Call to Action* (DoE, 1999a), a document that outlined the Minister's delivery plan, made clear what areas were likely candidates for policy review. One prominent candidate for review, signalled in Ministerial speeches and documents, was Curriculum 2005 or OBE[5] – a case study that usefully demonstrates the workings as well as the effects of a policy review process.

Merely to call for a policy review is to concede the possibility of failure. A review, by its very nature, carries the threat of exposure. In the case of a weak state – by which I mean a state with limited bureaucratic and political capacity to change the practice of education 'on the ground' – reviews are particularly dangerous. Unsurprisingly, the standard argument among politicians and bureaucrats alike is to pre-empt criticism of the policy review by describing it as a regular part of the policy process. However, such pre-emption simply begs basic questions about the selectivity of the reviews. After all, there are scores of policy actions apart from Curriculum 2005 that would, in a normal policy cycle, also have been candidates for review.

The policy review, in this provisional categorisation, could be described as having three functions:

- ❑ to refine policy – making minor adjustments to an otherwise effective and valued policy;
- ❑ to activate existing policy – providing implementation impetus to an accepted policy through, for example, new resource commitments; and/or
- ❑ to establish new policy – creating substantially new frames for educational practice that go beyond the scope of existing policy.

My thesis is that when a policy review effectively establishes new policy, or is perceived to establish new policy, then those with a deeply vested interest in the original policy are likely to create the political fault lines that could threaten policy implementation.

A first example is the so-called Size and Shape proposals for the restructuring of higher education, as presented by the Council on Higher Education (CHE) on request of

5 For the purposes of this discussion, I will not make a distinction between these two terms.

Minister Asmal (CHE, 2000a,b). The Minister was clear in the months leading to the review: higher education reflected the geopolitical imagination of apartheid, and was therefore irrationally organised, poorly managed and incapable of fulfilling its mandate under conditions of rising deficits and declining student numbers. In response, the CHE proposed a radical restructuring of higher education with a rigid five-class system (CHE, 2000a) followed by an equally inflexible three-class system (CHE, 2000b) for the classification of higher education institutions.

Within the Association of South African Vice-Chancellors of the Historically Disadvantaged Institutions (ASAHDI), these proposals were interpreted as a departure from the founding policy document on higher education transformation, the White Paper on Higher Education (DoE, 1997a). In the words of one of the vice-chancellors of ASAHDI, who had also participated in the policy processes leading to the White Paper, what remained was simply to implement the original policy, not to establish new policy (Mosala, 2000). The Chairperson of the National Commission on Higher Education (NCHE), the high-profile panel that prepared the groundwork for the White Paper, argued that the Task Team recommendations not only departed from the original policy but that they contradicted its premises (Reddy, 2000). Within a short period of time, a strong voice of opposition was raised against the CHE and its Task Team proposals, an opposition that included the South African University Vice-Chancellors Association (or SAUVCA, that included both black and white universities) and, solidly, ASAHDI Chancellors and many other stakeholders. It is unprecedented, in the policy making process under a post-apartheid government, that a proposed policy position has been so widely opposed among the broad constituencies aligned with the ANC.

My point in this regard is that an underlying point of contention with respect to this review of higher education was that the review constituted the establishment of new policy rather than the implementation of existing policy.

A second example would be the review of Curriculum 2005. In the months leading to the review, the Minister repeatedly pointed to the arcane language of OBE, its complex formulation and the inaccessibility of this curriculum innovation to practitioners. The appointment of a high-powered review team with a mandate to make specific recommendations for the improvement of the curriculum was inevitable. The Report of the Review Committee was comprehensive, detailed and meticulous in its analysis of the problems of Curriculum 2005 and how it could be improved (DoE, 2000f). However, the proposals created an unprecedented crisis both within ANC political circles and inside the education bureaucracy. Why? Because the sheer scope of the proposals for change were seen as displacing the flagship of the Bengu period – Curriculum 2005 – for something the Committee unintentionally tagged as Curriculum 21. This was a strategic error: the media interpreted the reference to 'a curriculum for the 21st century' as a displacement of Curriculum 2005, and all attempts to retrieve this meaning were lost on the public. More seriously, many politicians and bureaucrats considered the scope and symbolism of the proposed changes as a fundamental shift from Curriculum 2005.

The scope of the changes was certainly sweeping, removing much of the architectural edifice of the existing curriculum in favour of a streamlined, simpler and more accessible curriculum. The symbolism of the changes was not only reflected in the change of name, but in what departmental officials read as a 'back to basics' approach stripped of the ideological assertion of learner-centredness and programme-based curricula. In short, the proposed recommendations were read, rightly or wrongly, as the establishment of significantly new elements of policy – even as the Minister and the Review Team tried to stress the continuities with the existing curriculum. What made matters worse, in the case of Curriculum 2005, is that the Minister advocated the proposed changes in the public domain before it had Cabinet approval, a mistake that undermined his political standing on two fronts: within his own bureaucracy as well as with his ANC peers in Cabinet, many of whom had brought in Curriculum 2005 as the flagship political project of education.

In both cases – the review of higher education and the review of Curriculum 2005 – another factor underpinned the opposition to the review process. This factor I will refer to as *the shift towards centralising the policy process and the diminishing role of 'the stakeholder'*.

The review of policy was clearly accompanied by a centralising tendency within policy making and its implementation. This need to drive policy from the centre was always a tension in policy making, but it was clearly signalled as a preferred disposition by Minister Asmal in the so-called 'listening campaign' that led to the *Call for Action (Tirisano)* and the subsequent implementation plan. The tension has to do with an ongoing debate within government since 1994 about whether policy and its implementation should be controlled and driven centrally, or whether there should be greater autonomy vested in the provinces and other local structures for managing and overseeing delivery. There are constitutional constraints on a centrally-driven policy that limit the Ministry to 'setting norms and standards' with the provinces responsible for implementation.[6] There are political constraints on centralisation, especially in the non-ANC provinces (Western Cape and KwaZulu-Natal) where such 'interference' by the central state is interpreted as party political intervention. Minister Asmal made it clear that he wished to review these constraints under legal advice because, as he put it, 'If I am responsible for norms and standards, I am also responsible for their implementation'. The tendency towards centralisation was driven both by a need to assert control over provinces in which the ANC government perceives a lack of delivery to black South Africans for political reasons (as in Western Cape) or a crisis of mismanagement in the larger ANC-dominated provinces. In other words, there was both a bureaucratic as well as a

6 Comments made to the group of Education Policy Unit representatives during the listening campaign of late 1999.

political motivation for centralising policy implementation.

This disposition is especially evident among those working within the higher education structures in and around government. In this case, the role of stakeholders has been questioned as a methodology for driving the policy review process. As the Chief Executive Officer of the CHE has stated repeatedly, the higher education review could not be left to stakeholders to conduct.[7] While there is some logic in this kind of position (given vested interests), it does represent a departure from other kinds of consultations and reviews prior to the Asmal period in which stakeholder representation and control of these processes were central to policy making.

In the absence of stakeholders, the role of selected experts and consultants gained prominence as a mechanism for driving policy reviews and, in this process, establishing new policy. The role of the expert group, dissociated from stakeholders, was especially evident in the constitution of the two task teams – that is, the review teams for the higher education Size and Shape report and for Curriculum 2005. In relation to the latter, for example, there was much debate within and outside the teacher unions about the limited voice of practitioners (teachers) in the make-up of a review team dominated by university specialists. This specific issue – stakeholder/expert tensions – requires further analysis in another paper.

Summarised, centralisation is achieved through the dominant role of the expert group, the prominent role of the (often foreign) consultant group, and the driving role of the middle-level bureaucrat (for example, the so-called guerrilla squads for investigating tardy schools).

A major consequence of the policy review process is not only the centralisation of policy making but the dissolution of policy consensus within government and the Alliance structures.

Conclusion

The review of policy has created major dissonance and conflict, not so much between old and new bureaucrats (the primary line of fissure in the early transition), but between and among allies, different branches of government, and within the education bureaucracy itself. The role of Cabinet with respect to Curriculum 2005 is a case in point, as is its role with respect to the future of the black universities. Other conflicts generated as a result of policy reviews include the position of the powerful ANC-allied South African Democratic Teachers Union (SADTU) in distancing itself from the C2005 review, the ASAHDI Forum in rejecting the Size and Shape recommendations, the fragmentation of the departmental bureaucracy between those who see the review

7 Comments made by Saleem Badat during a Seminar on Size and Shape at the University of the Witwatersrand, 13 September 2000.

as an attack on the Bengu legacy with its 'back to basics' implications and those who see the review as streamlining what is regarded (at its core) as 'a good curriculum', and the intervention of Cabinet on details of curriculum implementation following the review.

In short, the process of policy review whose implementation logic is driven centrally and personalised with relish in the public domain by an energetic Minister, has unleashed a series of political problems. What this has led to is the consolidation of new power blocs in further frustrating implementation. The realignment of power, however, coexists with the creation of yet another layer of symbolic policies, such as the Values, Education and Democracy document (James, 2000).

Where does this leave us? South Africa is now faced with the dual problem of the lack of resource commitments and the fragmentation of political will that, together, will continue to make implementation – even if one settled for the modest goal of systemic improvements in the quality of teaching and learning in all our public schools – an unrealisable goal in the new century.

It is now clear, for example, that the Minister will face considerable difficulty and challenge, legally and politically, as the Department of Education moves to implement the recommendations of the higher education Task Team. The collision of two powerful discourses – one of 'race' (support black universities for their historical contribution and their black identity) and the other of 'realism' (close or merge black universities because of the crisis of deficits and enrolments) – is one way of describing the implementation dilemma. The black universities, backed by the SAUVCA constituency and an exceptionally poor technical report of the CHE, have been able to gain a powerful position within government and the ANC to stare down any form of combination (including closure) by the realist discourse of the Minister, his Higher Education Branch, and the CHE. On the other hand, several prominent black universities continue to march firmly towards what some CHE staff call 'the Darwinian resolution' whereby the fatal equation of rising deficits and falling student numbers (exacerbated by leadership crises) will simply close down these institutions anyway. The ongoing saga at the University of the North is not exceptional. Either way, the planned restructuring meant to create a more efficient (if not effective) system of higher education will simply not be implemented as a neat and tidy puzzle that reconfigures the apartheid higher education landscape.

This dilemma of non-implementation also holds true for the C2005 review. Even though the technical report provides a useful analysis of the problems, and the recommendations for streamlining the curriculum are sensible, the implementation of the new curriculum is unlikely to proceed. Why? Because the heavy investiture of political symbolism in C2005 in the late 1990s has meant that any attempt to change the curriculum (whatever the technical merits of such proposals) would become the subject of fierce contestation over an imagined legacy. The lines have been drawn again, between symbolic politics and grounded pragmatism. It cannot be otherwise, for symbols of change are simultaneously signals of conflict.

Chapter 4

Progressivism Redux: Ethos, Policy, Pathos

Johan Muller

Introduction

Any dispassionate review of schooling policy reform around the globe cannot fail to notice the surprisingly uniform direction it is taking. (I do not claim comprehensiveness, but have in mind the USA, the UK, Norway, Australia, New Zealand, as well as the African countries represented by the Association for the Development of Education in Africa [see ADEA, 2000].) The educational hold-all name against which all this reform (or reaction, as some would have it) is happening is increasingly given as *progressivism* – the first and only comprehensive ideology of schooling of what Ulrich Beck (2000) calls the first age of modernity. There is something richly ironic about this. As David Tyack (1974) has made clear, 'traditional' pedagogy had never bothered to name itself because it never considered that there was any alternative – it was 'the one best system', an essentially unreformable model in a world where the model and the world were indistinguishable. When the reformers did arrive, first in central Europe and then with a bang in the early twentieth century in the USA with Dewey, they did so with understandable revolutionary – or romantic – zeal, the two often meshed together.

What has to be kept in mind here is that the powerful impulse behind progressivism as an educational movement was social justice, since it was at this stage becoming clear that industrialism and mass schooling together were producing an uneducated and unskilled working class. Most of progressivism's social zeal was thus concerned with producing equitable educational outcomes for the children of the working class who were, it was now quite plain, being disadvantaged by public schooling.

As progressivism began to develop both as a theory and as a practice, it spread out over the ideological spectrum. Tyack (1974) distinguishes four important sub-variants:

- The pragmatic *administrative progressives* sought redress in the direction of scientifically-driven administrative efficiency. Ball's (1999) contemporary performative zealots are arguably the ancestors of this progressive strand rather than the post-modern functionaries Ball takes them for.
- The equally pragmatic *pedagogical progressives* (or reconstructionists) were the Deweyans proper, including both John and Evelyn Dewey and William Kilpatrick, Dewey's 'best student' and tireless advocate of the 'project method', the avatar of problem-solving learning, curricular integration and service learning, among others.

- To the left came the libertarian *educational progressives*, radical child-centred activists, who surfaced mostly in alternative schools, most notably perhaps A.S. Neill's Summerhill.
- To the left of them came the *social reconstructionists* like Teachers' College's Coutts, who attempted to marry Deweyan progressivism with socialism.

While different in both politics and pedagogy, 'All competence modes' – as Bernstein (1996:68) would call these different varieties of progressivism – 'despite their differences, share a preoccupation with the development (liberal/progressive), the recognition (populist) and change (radical) of consciousness'. Or to put that another way, progressivism was first and foremost about radical *progress*. The driving assumption – progressivism's 'most scandalous notion' – was, as Charles Simic (2000:9) has said about modernism, 'that it is possible to begin from scratch and be entirely original….' This is manifested in the pervasive chiliasm of progressivism: the original one best system was, in progressivism's founding gesture, exposed as a fraud, and the promised progressive future depended now upon a complete and total replacement of the old in all its manifestations with the new, the authentic one best system. Salvation positively depended upon a guillotine-like severance with the past.[1] To this day, this social or 'paradigm' shift is advocated by progressives in either/or terms in ways that would make Kuhn (and Lenin for that matter) wince at its romantic naïveté.[2]

There is some merit in the view that progressivism as an educational movement was an exclusively, sometimes even parochially, American phenomenon. Certainly the English did not have anything called by that name. However, their 'child-centred' movement is grown from the same stock, as were many other reforms in Europe at the time, like the Gentile reforms discussed below. There may be earlier references to it in South Africa, but in 1934 the New Education Fellowship (NEF), an international advocacy group for progressivism, hosted an enormous international conference with sessions in both Johannesburg and Cape Town. Four thousand people attended; there were three hundred formal addresses and twenty-five overseas speakers, prominent among whom was John Dewey who addressed the conference three times. The conference was opened by Minister of Education Hofmeyr and Deputy Prime Minister Smuts; the latter praised the individuality of the 'new education' which he saw as a vital bulwark against 'proletarian standardisation'.

The NEF was clearly a catholic church: Graf von Durckheim-Montmartin extolled the virtues of the Hitler Jugend for 'disciplined group education' (Malherbe, 1937:41). Eiselen and Verwoerd both addressed the conference, but so did Malinowski, Hoernle, and Monica Wilson. The tenor of progressivism was clearly evident in the framing of the

1 In this sense, People's Education was classically progressivist, as Andre Kraak (1998:2-4) shows.
2 See Spira (1998) who distinguishes between progressive and 'essentialist' education - 'student as passive', 'individual facts are taught', 'education as memorisation', and so on - as not so much a straw man as a descriptive travesty. Incidentally, Spira's panacea is 'technology-based distance learning', a method wonderfully opportune once the 'active learner' has expunged the need for any 'teacher-centred' instruction.

conference, as were some of the faultlines in the broad front. Significantly, Dewey went out of his way to distance his protocols from those of 'some would-be progressive schools and teachers' (Malherbe, 1937:25). For Dewey – as for both Gramsci and Gee, as we will see below – the new educational stress on development did not mean a completely learner-centred or activity-centred curriculum. Direction, even in these early debates, was the issue, as Dewey was at pains to point out: 'Under the alleged sanction of not violating freedom and individuality the responsibility for providing development conditions is overlooked' (Malherbe, 1937:25). More plainly still: 'But development involves a point of direction as well as a starting point with constant movement in that direction…' (Malherbe, 1937:25). Gee develops this point in an exemplary fashion below.

At this celebration of progressivism in South Africa we have to remember that universal mass education – and thus the possible flaws of progressivism – was still some way off. Mass schooling, when it did come in the form of Bantu Education, was not so much a traditional as a counter-reformative policy. No wonder, then, that the liberation movement wanted precisely that which had been denied – progressive education. This is plain in all the 'from-to' manifestos of People's Education, NEPI, the ANC yellow book, and into policy – all displaying the characteristic chiliastic certainty that everything in the first column was politically and educationally bankrupt while everything in the second column represented the inauguration of redressive social justice.[3]

But the global tide has turned, and progressivism is undeniably now passé: 'educational progressivism, in practice and in theory, is fast losing ground' (Eberstadt, 1999). Theoretically (some would say ideologically) the conceptual basis of progressivism has been directly attacked in a range of recent writing. The books by Hirsch (2000) and Ravitch (2000) have been particularly influential. Hirsch has been at pains to show that the naturalism of progressivism, from which stems the idea of the creative, active learner and the facilitating teacher, is rooted less in Dewey's pragmatism than it is in eighteenth century romanticism. As MacDonald (1998) says bitingly, 'If the child was, in Wordsworth's words, a "Mighty Prophet! Seer blest!" then who needs teachers?' She goes on derisively, 'But the Mighty Prophet emerged from student-centred schools ever more ignorant and incurious as the schools became more vacuous.' Who cares, asks MacDonald, when 'Anything But Knowledge' is the proud anti-intellectual creed of progressivism?

But people increasingly do care. Not only national but international testing comparisons have shown some striking results (with South Africa stone last on the Third International Mathematics and Science Study, TIMSS). The most charitable conclusion to be drawn is that, on orthodox measures of achievement, progressivism's predictions are not borne out. Even within the liberal progressive consensus (see Taylor & Vinjevold, 1999), it is increasingly being conceded that:

3 'For the real chiliast, the present becomes the breach through which what was previously inward bursts out suddenly, takes hold of the outer world and transforms it' (Mannheim, 1936/1991:193).

- Effective active instruction, classically proscribed by progressivism as the primary hindrance to authentic learning, makes a major difference to learning.
- The teacher thus returns, not as a facilitator or manager but as an instructional specialist.
- This means a return to the importance of content knowledge, both in curriculum stipulation and in instructional guidance. As Dewey said in Cape Town, 'The New Education needs more attention, not less, to subject matter' (Malherbe, 1937:25).

Why the *volte face*? And is it sufficient? These questions are addressed below.

The trouble with progressivism

The acknowledgement of the role of instruction in successful learning – and thus of the pre-eminent importance of the teacher and of teacher knowledge – is, as I have said, increasingly conceded by some of the leaders of progressivism, like Linda Darling-Hammond (Muller, 2000b).

In a recent communiqué (Spencer Deans,[4] 2000), the Deans of ten Schools of Education in the United States made a plea for 'moving beyond ideological divides' and listed what they feel thirty years of research into school reform in the USA has established does actually work:

- high expectations and high standards;
- curricula based on high standards;
- standards-based assessment;
- strong principals;
- stable school environment;
- parental involvement;
- teachers with content and pedagogical knowledge;
- on-going INSET; and
- micro- and macro-accountability.

This is a rather orthodox list, and mirrors the conclusions above (Muller, 2000b). The Deans are evidently trying to move the debate onto a plane where research and not ideology is the decisive factor, but it will not be so easy. They allocate positions in terms of 'liberal' and 'conservative' – a bifurcatory progressivist reflex that is obdurately diehard. Furthermore, in many quarters they themselves are seen as the problem rather than its solution. The sustained 'education school bashing', as it has come to be called, has not been on the basis of their supposed ineptitude but on the basis of their ideology – as Hirsch (2000) has said, by an 'all too ept advocacy of Romantic ideas, not by incompetence but by an all too competent rhetoric in the service of

4 The Spencer Deans are a group of deans of Schools of Education at prestigious USA universities, all funded by the Spencer Foundation.

the notion that specific subject-matter knowledge has only secondary importance.' In short, schools and departments of education are widely seen as the ideological home of progressivism.

That is almost certainly too sweeping a generalisation, and the Spencer Deans are clearly moving away from that stance. However, the contention in the field is often remarked:

> You might think progressive and traditional educational theories represent competing programs to achieve an agreed-upon goal, and that scholars would welcome signs of achievement in the same way that medical researchers welcome evidence that one cure works better than another. But you would be wrong. Inside the educational world, these two streams of thought are viewed more as alternative moral and philosophical systems, as fighting faiths. What is mere evidence in the face of such iron certitudes (Traub, 2000)?

To summarise: the 'one best system' of progressivism is under unprecedented attack. The progressives have laid claim to the moral and political high ground of social justice, but their opponents say this is just what progressivism does not deliver. The terrain is fatally politicised, and almost without fail the sides give political or ideological labels to one another. The opposition is not unified by any coherent paradigm, and it is certainly misleading to call them 'traditionalists' or 'conservatives'; Hirsch prefers the label 'classicist' that – accurate as it may be in terms of the literary canon – to my mind confuses the issue further. In the meantime, though, a steadily growing base of empirical research is pointing mostly in one direction:

> Education looks more and more like a real social science; specific instructional practices have been isolated as never before. And the outcome is pretty clear: One study after another has shown that traditional instructional methods which Chall calls "teacher centred" produce better academic results than progressive "student-centred" ones… (Traub, 2000; see also Chall, 2000).

The messy public scrap in the United States and elsewhere, edging reluctantly towards rational public debate bolstered by research results, is not particularly edifying, and the limits to furthering the debate on the basis of political position-taking have clearly been reached. What is needed is a way to recontextualise the issues that will lift discussion out of the rancours of political one-upmanship. The section that follows will examine the way that one particularly perspicacious progressive, James Gee, has dealt with some of the critiques of progressivism.

Immersion

A well-known criticism has it that progressive theories 'actually work against the new orthodoxy's supposed social justice goals of emancipation and empowerment' and that 'educational progressivism is a sure means of preserving the social status quo' (Hirsch, 2000). In the USA this point is particularly associated with the black feminist writer Lisa Delpit, and has also been made for South African progressivism (Moore & Muller, 1999; Muller, 2000b). Why is this so? According to Gee (1999), it is because progressive pedagogy effectively hides the 'rules of the game' from disadvantaged learners, leaving them without visible scaffolding on which to advance. Gee pairs the first criticism with a second, allied one, namely that the confessional strategies of progressive pedagogy causes learners to put their inner life on display, and therefore amenable to surveillance and discipline. This Foucauldian criticism is familiar from the work of Walkerdine (1988) and Gore (1997) and, for South Africa, Ensor (1995). Thus, progressivism blocks the induction of disadvantaged learners into the knowledge structure but submits them to middle-class moral regulation. On the one hand, it promotes permissiveness that generates failure; on the other, it promotes 'soft coercion' that generates social control. Taken together, these two criticisms cast progressivism in the role of a Machiavellian instrument of class control.

Where most progressives would deny this picture, Gee partly concedes the case by contending that the critique identifies the dark mirror side of progressivism, but that progressivism (or any reform for that matter) is double-edged and requires a particular kind of supplement in order to keep the virtuous side, which he claims is still viable, to the fore. To show how this might work, Gee first considers how we learn things in everyday life. We start with pattern recognition, and follow our noses analogically. However, our noses on their own will not lead us to the culturally determined pattern clusters (situated meanings) of our community. Since pattern clusters are potentially infinite, our experience requires guidance to reach the appropriate patterns; hence, 'experience and guidance (constraint, direction) are inextricably yoked'. Dewey would concur.

Learning at school is no different. Say we need to learn about 'light'. The situated meanings and pattern clusters of light in everyday experience differ from those in physics. We need, therefore, to be immersed in the physics pattern clusters, but there is also an 'absolute need for guidance (constrain, direction) as a supplement to being situated in experience'. Of course, this does not necessarily entail explicit guidance: most scaffolding, he says, is ostensive and tacit. Nevertheless, guidance is what it is, and for schooling it is the teacher who must do it.

So far the concessions to critique are modest. Progressive pedagogues, it has been argued, have always had to flout their rule of invisibility to achieve positive learning (Davis, 1996). However, in the last part of the paper Gee goes beyond acknowledging that the teacher is just another part of the scaffolding furniture. Drawing on

the Vygotskyan distinction between spontaneous (everyday) and non-spontaneous (scientific) concepts, Gee argues that one only 'gets' non-spontaneous concepts through '"overt instruction" that focuses on (a) putting things into words, (b) conscious and intentional use of new concepts, and (c) the relationship among forms and meanings'. Here the teacher breaks free from the scaffolding furniture, and becomes indispensable to direct guidance. The implication is that this is what is needed to paralyse the dark side and allow virtuous progression to flourish.
Gee presents us with three scenarios for concept learning. The first two are essentially similar, and the teacher in the second scenario (school) simply provides what the semiotic agencies of the community do in everyday life (instruction I). In the third, however, something is to be learnt (non-spontaneous concepts) which requires active intervention of a sort not found in everyday life. Instruction here (instruction II) becomes a form of direction qualitatively different to that provided by the community because 'everyday language, in creating patterns and associations, is less careful about differences and underlying systematic relations, though these are crucial to science'. Although Gee does not say it, it should be clear that instruction II requires that the teacher:

- ❑ knows more than the learner (has adequate content knowledge); but more critically
- ❑ knows the conceptual destination of the learning; and therefore
- ❑ purposefully steers the learner towards a preset goal.

With this, a number of key tenets of learner-centredness are breached, and we begin to move towards a more teacher-centred model, away from weak framing of the curriculum to far stronger framing – and thereby somewhat away from progressive pedagogy towards the more expert, purposive teacher to which the empirical school reform research is pointing.

I have made Gee concede more here than he wants to, which was merely to shore up a less 'pure' but more defensible progressivism. My argument here is that this strengthened progressivism is the lesson from instruction I but that it is not enough, as the third example makes clear. The argument for instruction II does mortal damage to the 'progressive emphasis on breaking down the boundaries between school and "life".' It is my contention that progressivism – in its stress on schooling as practice, and on pedagogy seen narrowly as teaching – loses sight of knowledge and its acquisition, which is the primary aim of learning. Put more bluntly, progressivism does not have an explicit theory of knowledge, and therefore does not have an explicit theory of curriculum or acquisition. Without it, we cannot construct a post-progressive pedagogy.

Chinese complexities

The same cannot be said for that enduring source of inspiration for the left, Antonio

Gramsci. Gramsci's (1986) starting point was that the education system – if it was to serve the cause of the new society, and as the state began to assume responsibility for public schooling – had to move away from the 'old school' towards a 'common school'. The common school was to serve the working class and through them the whole society. At the same time, Gramsci was perturbed by the proposals of the Gentile Reform of 1923, as well as by the ideas of Montessori, the 'Dalton method' (enthusiastically promoted in Cape Town by Harold Rugg's wife, Louise Kruger), and all species of an emerging progressivism. He found the reaction against the old school altogether too extreme: 'The active school [his euphemism for progressivism] is still in its romantic phase, in which the elements of struggle against the mechanical and Jesuitical school have become unhealthily exaggerated' (Gramsci, 1986:32-33). This is a surprising judgement, to say the least. Let us see how this revolutionary arrives at his pedagogical position.

The job of school is to 'accustom [the students] to reason, to think abstractly and schematically while remaining able to plunge back from abstraction into real and immediate life, to see in each fact or datum what is general and what is particular, to distinguish the concept from the particular instance' (Gramsci, 1986:38). The old school did this by weaning the pupils from folklore, which encompassed both a magical and pre-scientific view and a pre-civic view. The condition for this weaning was theoretical and practical activity (or work) on the part of the pupils. But this understanding has been elevated by the new pedagogues into an absolute, resulting in a stress on activity (educativity) at the expense of instruction. First of all, the difference between school (science and civics) and everyday life (folklore) does not disappear in the industrial era, and it remains the teachers' pre-eminent 'obligation to accelerate and regulate the child's formation in conformity with the former and in conflict with the latter' (Gramsci, 1986:36). To labour the point, 'in conflict with the latter' signals a strong discontinuity between life and school.

In a judgement whose harshness is matched only by that of the contemporary critics of progressivism, Gramsci (1986:36) goes on to say, 'If the teaching body is not adequate and the nexus between instruction and education is dissolved, while the problem of teaching is conjured away by the cardboard schemata exalting educativity, the teachers' work will as a result become yet more inadequate.' This can be paraphrased to say: if the teachers have inadequate subject knowledge, and progressivism sidelines them still further by marginalising their role and exalting that of the learners, then learning is jeopardised – exactly the conclusion of the Curriculum 2005 Review Committee (DoE, 2000f).

But what is it that the teacher must do? What kind of instruction must s/he provide? The answer comes in two parts. The first has to do with 'facts'. Just like our modern progressives, Gentile railed against teaching facts. Quite wrong, says Gramsci (1986:41): 'It is noticeable that the new pedagogy has concentrated its fire on "dogmatism" in the field of instruction and the learning of concrete facts – that is, precisely in the field in which a certain dogmatism is practically indispensable….' How so? What we learn at school, says Gramsci, is how to order facts and objects in the world. Where do the pupils get these to-be-ordered facts from? From the teacher. The good teacher informs the pupils (gives them facts) *and* shows them how to order the facts. The mediocre teacher – in the old school, at least – imparted a baggage' of concrete facts that the active pupil may learn to order by herself. Now, however, 'With the new curricula, which coincide with a general lowering of the level of the teaching profession, there will no longer be any "baggage" to put in order' (Gramsci, 1986:36). Gramsci would have been completely scornful of Gee's view that we acquire the facts of, say, mathematics by 'immersing' the pupils in maths problems in the same way as we get facts about the world through our immersion in it because, to repeat, 'There is no unity between school and life' (Gramsci, 1986:35).

Teachers must impart facts, therefore, but more importantly still they must impart a disciplined comportment to life. How is this done? In the old school, teachers taught Greek and Latin not because they wanted pupils to be able to speak those languages, but 'because the real interest was the interior development of personality … to inculcate certain habits of diligence, precision, poise (even physical poise) …' (Gramsci, 1986:37) – in other words, the mental and physical habits, 'a second – nearly spontaneous – nature' (Gramsci, 1986:38); each person needs to become the famous Gramscian philosopher, the democratic civic ideal of communism, properly considered. We teach the facts of history, not because we want pupils to imbibe facts but so that they can imbibe, almost unconsciously, 'a historicising understanding of the world and of life' (Gramsci, 1986:39). It is the almost inadvertent learning of the important comportments – 'logical, artistic, psychological experience [was] gained unawares, without a continual self-consciousness' (Gramsci, 1986:39) – that is the true pedagogical school task of the teacher; think of it as a more expansive and generous version of Gee's instruction II. The difference, though, remains striking: for Gramsci the comportments, albeit the main purpose of education, are only to be approached 'unawares' and by indirection through the teaching of facts; for the progressives the facts must fall away and the comportments become the entry point for each lesson, as we will see with Gardner below.

Progressive curriculum reform, in Gramsci's view, tackles the wrong object. It tackles the form of the curriculum instead of its content. To be blunt, Gramsci means we must throw out Latin and Greek and bring in science, maths, language and civics, but they need to be used in the same way. These are the 'relevant' carriers of the all-important mental skills in today's world. The idea that education is about the inculcation of these skills and comportments is not, should not be, the focus of education. When it does so become, then we fall foul of 'relevance' in the curriculum and vocational education – a diversification of the common school, its mission and its products. The result – and this is the crux of this whole analysis – will be a hardening and widening of class distinctions. That is precisely what the empirical studies of contemporary progressivism persistently find. This most durable of critiques of progressivism was first made by Gramsci, and no one has made it more eloquently: 'The most paradoxical aspect of it all is that this new type of school appears and is advocated as being democratic, while in fact it is destined not merely to perpetuate social differences but to crystallise them in Chinese complexities' (Gramsci, 1986:40).

To summarise: Gramsci would concur with Gee that the role of the teacher, devalued in progressivism, should be brought more to the fore. But where for Gee this role has to do mostly with shaping ('directing') the flux of experience gained through immersion, for Gramsci it should crucially provide the 'baggage', the facts, the raw material to be shaped and ordered. In other words, even Gee, in his bold retrieval of the teacher's role, conceives it in terms of skills and procedures only, not in terms of knowledge, as Gramsci does. The result is the characteristic, fatally flawed, progressive curriculum.

Anything but knowledge

> Schools are about many things, (progressive) teacher educators say … self-actualisation, following one's joy, social adjustment, or multicultural sensitivity – but the one thing they are not about is knowledge … educators will occasionally allow the word to pass their lips, but it is always in a compromised position, as in "constructing one's own knowledge" or "contextualised knowledge". Plain old knowledge, the kind passed down in books, the kind for which Faust sold his soul, that is out…. That dogma may be summed up in the phrase: Anything But Knowledge (MacDonald, 1998).

As we saw above, Gee lands himself in something of a pickle because, for instruction I, he can retain the orthodox progressive postulate that life and school – relevant everyday knowledge and school knowledge – are in principle isomorphic, whereas for instruction II this assumption has to be partly abandoned. Let us look more closely at how this key progressive postulate shapes the progressive curriculum.

The 'school subject' is the selector and orderer of knowledge in the traditional curriculum. It is an ensemble that suggests what is to be learnt and when. For progressivism this is a misleading description since it over-emphasises facts (knowledge). Rather, 'a subject is a collection of similar skills, cases, and facts that have been grouped together as an object of study' (*Engines for Education*, 2000). There are two things to note with this definition. First, it clearly prioritises skills that, from the traditional animus against facts noted already by Gramsci, we have by now come to expect. So much so, in fact, that the definition proceeds to define physics exclusively in skill terms: '"Doing physics" involves a set of skills which range from timing the wing of a pendulum to constructing particle accelerators' (*Engines for Education*, 2000).

Secondly, it turns out that this organisation of school experience is almost exactly the same as that of the 'domain', its equivalent in everyday life: 'A domain is, like a subject, a collection of skills, cases, and facts' (Engines for Education, 2000), only it is better because it will be more interesting for pupils. 'Some examples are politics, trucks, and animals.... Any of the above domains can be used as a vehicle to teach the subjects of physics, biology, or history'. So, there is nothing special about the organisation of school knowledge that cannot be improved by organising it as everyday knowledge is organised: this is the core belief of curriculum progressives. It happens to be wrong, as I shall show below.

First, though, let us examine what a radical domainal approach looks like. The most famous exemplar is that of Howard Gardner (2000). All we need to teach our children, says he, is about truth, beauty, and morality; since depth is preferable to breadth, we can teach the first through evolution, the second through Mozart's *The Marriage of Figaro*, and the third through the Holocaust. We can enter these domains through a variety of entry points derived from his theory of multiple intelligences – narrative, aesthetic, numerical, existential-foundational, interpersonal, or hands-on. It is not surprising that hands-on is a privileged mode, though Gardner does solemnly warn, 'Hands-on involvement with the Holocaust must be approached carefully, especially with children' (quoted by Eberstadt, 1999).

Gardner assures us he is a 'demon' for high standards. But how would we know? With no content stipulations, how would we know what the pupils had learnt? The truth of the matter is, the content and coverage are tacitly assumed to be in place. That is, a success can be made of this sort of under-stipulated curriculum, but only if the teacher has a well-articulated mental script of what should be covered and if the pupils come from homes where they have been well-prepared to respond to such putative freedom – in other words, only in schools by and for the middle class: 'It appears then that progressive educational ideology has come full circle. Born near the turn of the century in hopes of raising the downtrodden up, it survives now as the ideology of choice of, by, and for the educational elite' (Nathan Glazer, quoted by Eberstadt, 1999).

Putting progression back in progressive

We are back, then, to the question that originally gave rise to progressivism: What kind of curriculum and pedagogy will optimise the learning chances of the disadvantaged? So far, the empirical evidence as well as the discussions on Gee and Gramsci have stressed that a more directive teacher is certainly one place to start. But is it enough? My answer is no. The discussion in the preceding section has shown how an overriding emphasis on learning and teaching as practical activities puts the focus on what both pupils and teachers should do at the expense of what they should know. If we are not to fall back into the trap of 'facts', the question of what pupils should know translates into the following: how should the knowledge in the curriculum be organised to optimise learning?

One answer is provided by the recent report of the Review Committee established to look into Curriculum 2005 (C2005) (DoE, 2000f).

The Report begins by distinguishing between two different ways that knowledge can be demarcated and ordered: lateral demarcation and vertical demarcation.

Lateral demarcation demarcates which knowledge clusters belong together and which do not. The curriculum design and challenge here is that of *connective coherence* (integration) – of how to ensure coherent linkage between clusters. The guiding principles are contiguity, worldly relevance, and interest. The designer's job is to devise mechanisms that promote these. As we saw above, domains are issue-organisers that select knowledge units purely on the basis of interest and relevance. In C2005 these are called programme organisers. Similarly, Gardner's 'entry points' function to select knowledge units on the basis of their relevance to a particular kind of cognitive activity or skill. In C2005 these are called phase organisers. As we saw from the critiques above, as pupils traverse these relevant knowledge clusters, there is no guarantee that key conceptual way stations are reached. The progressive concession, as we saw from both the empirical research and the concession by Gee, is to bring back teacher direction. The question then arises: how does the teacher know what the key conceptual way stations are, or what kind of knowledge might be relevant to understanding them?

Here a different notion of relevance comes to the fore, namely, 'relevant to conceptual development'. Connective coherence devices are no help. For that, the second form of demarcation and ordering must be considered. *Vertical demarcation* establishes which knowledge within each knowledge cluster must be learnt, in what sequence, and at what level of competence. The curriculum design challenge here is that of *conceptual coherence* – how to ensure coherent conceptual learning progression. The guiding principle is conceptual relevance, which determines sequence, progression and pacing. Apart from allocating responsibility to the teacher, progressive pedagogy is completely silent on conceptual relevance and coherence. The Chisholm Report found that, while the mechanisms of assessment criteria, range statements, performance indicators and expected levels of performance were intended to establish sequence, progression and pacing, they were under-stipulated and did not provide the necessary guidance to either teacher or pupil. Put bluntly, there is no conceptual road map in C2005. Nor is this a simple omission; it derives from core postulates of progressivism. The preliminary evidence shows that it is the children of the poor, not the middle class, who are disadvantaged (Taylor & Vinjevold, 1999).

The Review goes on to say that different knowledge areas may have different requirements with respect to connective and conceptual coherence, and that part of the trick of curriculum design has to do with making sure that one set of mechanisms does not block the achievement of other requirements, as was the case with C2005. 'When learning areas with distinctive conceptual coherence requirements (like maths, science and language) are driven mainly by integration requirements, then the potential for conceptual progression is retarded' (DoE, 2000f:42). I will not explore this further here. My main purpose has been to put my finger on that field in which, as Gramsci (1986:41) said above, '...a certain dogmatism is practically indispensable'.

This is just what most contemporary curriculum reform has found. To quote a recent review of curriculum reform in Norway (Recent Trends, undated), 'The curriculum content is (now) precisely prescribed for each year, and with special attention to the progression-matters'. The picture is similar in Australia (Clements, undated) and in New Zealand (Education Review Office, 2000), two of our closest models for C2005. This raises the question of the criminal culpability of educational carpetbaggers who purvey for gain ideas in the developing world at the very moment that they are being discredited at home, but that's another story.

Summing up the argument made in this chapter, one could say that what is missing from progressivism is progression. The reasons for this have been variously suggested. Hirsch thinks that the Rousseauian 'natural self' in the forefront of progressive pedagogy makes progressivism recoil from any notion of progress that is not self-constructed (Stone, 1996). And if Gramsci somehow failed to persuade the left, the school effectiveness research and the TIMSS results have surely brought home the costs, personal as well as national, of keeping the self pristinely natural. A secondary reason for the omission suggested above is that there is a distinct limit to what we can say about learning and teaching without having to refer to knowledge. The progressive inclination to define all knowledge events as skills, competencies and practices precludes talking about knowledge *as* knowledge. Since knowledge breathes now so fervidly down our necks, as it probably has always done, isn't it time that we moved to a less romantic, more effective, and more socially just, post-progressive pedagogic politics and practice?

Chapter 5

Human Resource Development Strategies: Some Conceptual Issues and their Implications

Michael Young

Introduction

The link between a country's potential for economic growth and full employment and its capacity to develop the skills and knowledge of its population is now recognised by governments of virtually every country, as well as by all the major international agencies. Although in the broadest sense this link is not a new discovery, some researchers (for example Ashton, 1999) see the new focus by governments on human resources development (HRD) as a fundamental shift in the conceptualisation of the links between economic growth and the skills and knowledge of the workforce. Ashton contrasts the focus on skills as an attribute of individual and narrowly-circumscribed job descriptions, a highly specialised division of labour, and command approaches to management that were characteristic of human capital theories with the new emphasis on linking cultural, political and economic strategies in a more co-ordinated way. South Africa's new HRD strategy, *A Nation at Work* (Departments of Education and Labour, 2001), reflects this paradigm shift and shares the view widely held internationally that in the future a country's ability to achieve economic growth (and therefore to maintain and increase employment) will depend on its *human* rather than its *natural* resources. This shift reflects changes in the global economy that impact on all countries. However, while highlighting the importance of HRD issues and the increasing importance of the role of governments, the same global changes are influencing capital and consumer markets in ways that are outside the control of national governments.[1]

Comparative research is beginning to show that there appears to be no alternative in the future to a 'high skills' approach to economic growth, regardless of the extent to which this may clash in the short term with other goals such as equity and redress. At the same time, different countries are adopting very different strategies in developing a high skills approach. The differences between, for example, the countries in continental Europe, Asia and America appear to reflect a combination of historical legacies that are extremely difficult to change by even the most well-designed HRD strategy and the current political priorities of governments. This chapter considers some of the implications of the growing interest in an HRD approach to education and training policy and was written initially for the HSRC's Round Table discussion of the new South African HRD strategy. The chapter begins by exploring the issue of priorities, by

1 I am thinking of the movement of capital and the development of markets for consumer goods.

drawing on recent comparative research on the very different international strategies for moving towards a high skills economy. It goes on to consider the increasingly unquestioned assumption that HRD priorities should underpin education and training policy and the extent to which this may undermine other education policy goals, and develops the argument – often neglected by HRD strategists – that the supply of skills and knowledge is only one element of a broader HRD strategy. The chapter then moves from strategic issues to questions of implementation, and argues for the crucial importance of institutional capacity. The final section of the chapter considers some of the implications of the previous analysis for taking forward the proposals in *A Nation at Work*.

The international experience

Two general conclusions can be drawn from the international experience. The first is that approaches to HRD, despite the convergence of global economic pressures, are extremely diverse even among relatively similar countries (even those that have been successful in achieving significant economic growth). These differences invariably reflect the different histories and cultures of each country, and raise serious problems for any attempts at 'policy borrowing'. The second conclusion is that there appear to be only a limited number of strategies that provide the basis for moving to a high skill economy and that these point to the need for quite specific priorities in education and training policy.

In considering which countries might provide lessons for South Africa, it is possible to identify a number of groups of countries. There are those countries, like the UK, that do have some structural features in common with South Africa, despite obvious historical differences. Examples of such features are relatively high levels of education and income inequality, a largely voluntarist approach to the role of employers in vocational education and training that in each country has left a system of low status and low capacity, and a relatively well-developed tertiary education sector. Second, there are the 'success stories' such as Germany, some other EU countries and the countries of South East Asia, each of which represent a version of a high skill economy and which face distinct problems in the new global economic circumstances. Third, there are the 'failures' such as the Latin American countries, Russia, the Middle East, and most if not all African countries, which also have some features in common with South Africa. I will not deal further with this last group of countries except to make two points. First, they are almost all countries with substantial natural resources that they have either failed to develop (as in the case of Russia), or have exploited their natural resources without development (Nigeria, Algeria and possibly Angola, are examples). The experience of this latter group of countries lends support to the argument of those economists who state that the main condition for economic growth for developing countries is the existence of the rule of law, especially as applied to economic activities.

Researchers on the UK-based Education and Training for a High Skills Economy Project (Green & Sakamoto, 2000)[2] distinguish between four distinct national strategies among the countries they studied. They are:

- *the High Skills Society (HSS) model:* This model is represented in ideal typical form by Germany. The researchers identified its key features as: a high-quality manufacturing sector; a strong scientific and technological elite; high levels of intermediate (craft and technician) skills; relatively large differences between high and low wages; and high levels of trust based on social partnerships between the state, employers and employees. Although the researchers do not say so, my view is that there are other EU countries that represent variants of the HSS model. The major difference between these countries and Germany are the relative absence of forms of social partnership involving employers and employee organisations and the corresponding greater role for government agencies.

- *the High Skills Diffusion (HSD) model:* The ideal type of the HSD model is represented by Japan (and in a slightly different variant, by Korea). The researchers identify its main characteristics as: a high-quality manufacturing sector; high levels of intermediate skills; widely diffused high-quality general education; high levels of employee co-operation and loyalty to companies linked to a distinctive approach to management; a relatively poor-quality scientific and technological elite; and reliance on efficient large firms delivering high-quality employee training.

- *the Developmental State (DS) model:* The DS model is represented in the research by Singapore, but Taiwan has similar characteristics and the model has inspired other South East Asian countries such as Malaysia. The main characteristics of the DS model are: wage competitiveness; competent elite bureaucrats and engineers; imported specialist skills and high levels of foreign investment; improving state provision of general education and initial vocational education and training; and a strong and relatively authoritarian state. Like the HSD model, the DS model is highly dependent on distinctive features of South East Asian culture, and from a European or South African perspective appears very undemocratic.

- *the High Skills Elite (HSE) model:* This model is represented by the UK (and, in a variant, by the USA). Its main characteristics are: high levels of innovation in selective manufacturing and service sectors; high levels of capital productivity; high-quality scientific and entrepreneurial elites; weak state regulation; weak employer-employee partnerships; labour flexibility; polarisation between a high skill elite and a large unskilled labour force; a poorly diffused system of general education; and high income inequality.

2 The High Skills Economy project is a research project funded by the Economic and Social Research Council in the UK and is jointly led by Professors Phil Brown (University of Cardiff), Hugh Lauder (University of Bath) and Andy Green, Institute of Education, University of Bath. The project's initial findings are the subject of a special issue of the *Journal of Education and Work* (Volume 12, 1999).

The researchers note a striking symmetry between the four national skills profiles, the dominant competition strategies, the skill demands they generate and the patterns of sectoral competitiveness. They suggest that different high skill approaches can be divided into *polarised skill regimes* and *diffused skill regimes* and the different competitive strategies that take advantage of them. So for example, the UK produces highly skilled and creative elites for the pharmaceutical, media and financial services sectors and cheap low skilled, flexible labour for most other sectors such as car manufacture and building construction.

The researchers remain undecided about which of the regimes will fare better in the new economic climate of global economic competitiveness. The HSE model has produced high levels of employment but largely through creating low-wage, low skill jobs. The HSS and HSD models have sustained higher living standards and lower levels of inequality but are under growing strain from global economic pressures (especially in the capital market). Green and Sakamoto draw several conclusions that are of relevance to South Africa.

- There are different routes to economic competitiveness and growth with different demands on skills.
- The conditions for the HSS model are rare, so it is unlikely to be the basis for a realistic strategy.
- There is no one 'high skills' model.
- Each of the models identified is under strain in the emerging global economy.

In relation to the tension between the high skill models and the new demands of economic globalisation, neither Germany nor Japan shows signs of convergence towards a HSE model. Whereas strong employer-employee partnerships continue in Germany, Japan maintains its commitment to high levels of general education and the promotion of a common approach to citizenship.

In the UK and the USA, by contrast, although leading-edge service and manufacturing corporations remain strong the bipolarity between an elite and a low skills labour force remains, and income inequality is increasing. The problem of lack of demand for skills in the economy suggests that a strategy based on improved supply and more efficient markets for skills is not enough to raise skill levels, especially when general education is weakly diffused and increasingly driven by an economic rationale.

Although the research is based on a limited number of essentially 'developed' countries, the conclusions have a number of implications for South Africa. They suggest a number of key conditions that appear to be necessary for developing a high skill economy. These are:

- a scientific elite and sources of innovation/entrepreneurship (UK/USA);
- a relatively loyal and co-operative workforce with high levels of general education (Japan); and/or

- well-developed social partnerships and the availability of high levels of intermediate skills and knowledge (Germany).

The main factors leading to the adoption of different high skills models are associated with the history and culture of the countries concerned and it is for this reason that policy borrowing is so fraught with difficulties.[3] However, this does not mean that a country cannot move out of a 'low skill equilibrium', as shown by the transformation of the South East Asian countries. In the 1950s and 1960s the populations of these countries were characterised by extremely low levels of skill and general education.

The international experience highlights two lessons for South Africa. The first is that there is no one model for South Africa or any other country to adopt, regardless of circumstances. The dimensions by which national strategies vary include:

- the balance between the role of the state and the market;
- the emphasis on school-based or work-based initial vocational education and training;
- the emphasis on developing general education in schools or expanding access to vocational education and lifelong learning;
- national attitudes to the emergence of a bipolar skill regime; and
- the approach to inward foreign investment.

The second lesson is made clear by Ashton (1999) in a recent article commenting on the research on different approaches to a high skill economy. He makes the obvious though often forgotten point that no economies consist only of high skill jobs, however they are defined. For all kinds of reasons – some historical, some political, and some economic – all societies will have a balance of high skill and low skill jobs. The issue is the relative proportion of these jobs and the opportunity of those in low skill jobs for moving out of them.

HRD and education and training policies

In a sense, the promotion of a country's human resources is such an uncontroversial idea that it seems almost perverse to question it. It appears to be part of a progressive move away from the Fordist era of mass production when the main efforts of employers were directed to replacing human labour with machines. The idea of an HRD strategy recognises that in today's economies it is the skills and knowledge of company's employees that create its wealth, and that the efforts of management must be on enabling them to realise their potential rather than trying to replace them with machines. A point of no less importance is that new information-based technologies – unlike the old machine-based technologies – do not lead to increases in productivity primarily by displacing labour but by enhancing its capacities. The HRD

3 The UK experience of attempting to 'import' Japanese management methods and the German dual system for vocational education are two examples.

view of employment is symbolised by the famous words of the Chairman of Toyota who said, 'We want the *gold in their heads*' [my italics], and less starkly by the director of a multinational bank. In explaining why they gave such a high priority to their HRD strategy he said, 'It is our staff that provide our added value and give us our competitive edge'. The idea of HRD appears well-suited to the demands of the global 'knowledge economy' and not surprisingly is readily welcomed by educationalists not only because it appears to endorse the need for more education but because it provides a possible link between the idea of a high skill economy and the educational goal of the personal and intellectual development of all students.

However, it is worth digging a bit deeper into the origins of the idea of HRD, into what is involved in the growing use of HRD language in business, into the extension of its use to public sector organisations,[4] and into its further extension to be a framework for national policies for education and training. I want, therefore, to distinguish between:

- the business origins of the idea of HRD and its link to new approaches to production and the delivery of services,
- conflicting interpretations of HRD, and
- the application of an HRD approach to the staff of educational institutions and to the labour force generally in national educational policies.

A number of issues arise from the business origins of HRD. First, interest in HRD undoubtedly reflects the emergence of knowledge economies, the growing numbers of 'knowledge workers' and the recognition of the strategic importance of the capabilities of a company's workforce for its ability to compete in global as well as in national markets. Company HRD strategies lead to the transformation of the traditionally marginal roles of Personnel staff involved in training and recruitment, and HRD directors become as important as directors of marketing, production, and R&D. Second, the new emphasis on HRD is undoubtedly related to another aspect of global economic change – the growing competitiveness of markets as companies in even such traditionally localised service sectors as retail, hospitality and office cleaning become targets for takeover by multinational corporations. The increasingly strategic role for company HRD policies leads to an increasingly tight link between their investment in training and development and the contribution this investment makes to the profitability of the company.[5] Third, HRD priorities are inextricably linked to how a company organises work, its form of management, and its decisions on how to compete in markets. Ewart Keep (1999) makes a distinction between companies that compete primarily on *price* (when HRD is viewed as a cost to be kept down), and those that compete on the *value* and *quality* of their products (when HRD is viewed as an investment that enables a company to be more competitive).[6] These two views

4 For example, in the UK universities Personnel Officers are being renamed Directors of Human Resources.
5 An example of this in the UK is the extent to which specific business priorities determine whether or not a company recruits apprentices.
6 The difficult problem facing governments is how to promote the latter.

of HRD parallel *human capital* and *skill formation* approaches to education and training. Whereas the former focuses on individual skills and knowledge and relates education and training to its rate of return in terms of wages and salaries, the latter adopts a much broader approach that Brown (1999) has expressed as 'developing the social capacity [of a nation or a company] for learning, innovation and productivity'. The skill formation approach involves a different set of priorities that are not easily expressed in traditional kinds of objectives and targets associated with measures of individual skills and qualifications.

There are two questions in relation to the skill formation approach that may need further consideration. First, its emergence does reflect certain changes in the global economy and is expressed in the strategic approach of leading edge firms. However, in a country like South Africa that still has to create the basic skill formation infrastructure, it may apply only to a small section of the economy. Second, skill formation approaches are often associated with the 'leap frog' theory that claims that a developing country can, with massive investment in information technology, miss out the mass production stage of industrialisation. Is this realistic in South Africa, or elsewhere? I doubt it. This kind of leap frog theory fails to address two issues. First, IT investment even in highly industrialised countries creates relatively little new employment (and therefore, in practice, relatively little economic growth). The second issue is that in a country like South Africa there is still an enormous quantitative absence of production for a population of forty million and more. IT does not lay telecommunications cables, build houses or roads, provide cars and buses, TVs or furniture or clothes, or run supermarkets where they do not exist. Another problem associated with the idea of skill formation as a 'social capacity' is that there is little in the research literature to suggest how it might be measured. One research direction worth pursuing in South Africa might be to follow up the Department of Labour initiative in introducing Investors in People as a strategy for improving the human resource capacity of firms.

There are a number of reasons why a human capital or a skill formation approach is likely to be dominant in a particular country and it is likely that a mix of the two is the most realistic goal for South Africa. The balance is clearly linked to the culture and history of the private sector and assumptions about the role of the state.

A Nation at Work (Depts of Education and Labour, 2001) represents the increasingly global trend for governments to locate their entire education and training policies – from early childhood education to universities – within the context of a broader HRD strategy designed to achieve certain economic goals. However, it is one thing for a company to develop an HRD strategy for its own employees in relation to its goal of increasing profits from successful competition. There are quite other implications of extending this logic to a nation's education and training policy. Because the idea of HRD ties *means* (employee's skills and knowledge) and *ends* (how these skills and knowledge are used to achieve particular goals), it cannot be straightforwardly applied to national education and training strategy. There are a number of reasons for this. First, nations are not companies – they have much more diffuse, contradictory and competing goals that are resolved politically, not by the market and what is profitable. HRD approaches treat ends such as skill shortages and economic growth as givens, when there can be very different kinds of growth and very different ways for a country to resolve skill shortages. Thus, HRD strategies can foreclose debates about ends. Second, national goals for education and training are broader than those concerned with the competitiveness of the national economy or individual companies. For example, democratic citizenship, personal development and cultural enrichment are all goals of education policies and though they may well have indirect links with productivity and economic growth in the long term, this is not their primary aim. Third, the idea of HRD assumes a close fit between certain forms of expansion of education and economic growth. However, it may be that long-term goals such as higher levels of general education and greater equality are better achieved if education policies are not tied too closely to economic goals. In the UK there has been much emphasis by government on the direct economic benefits of education to the country and to individuals. This 'economic' rhetoric appears to be influencing the educational decisions of sixteen-year-olds who are opting for business and media studies rather than the sciences and foreign languages that are seen as requiring more studying with no immediate economic payoff. In other words, it may be in a country's long-term interests if their students do not give too much emphasis to the short-term economic goals of their educational choices.

Components of an HRD strategy

A national HRD strategy is undoubtedly important for achieving economic growth. However, an approach to HRD that focuses only (or largely) on the supply of skills in the labour force is likely to have limited effect and can even be counter-productive by unjustifiably raising people's hopes for employment (or better employment). Governments are often reluctant to tackle other reforms that are no less important for economic growth. Examples of such reforms are statutory training rights for young employees, income distribution and investment priorities, all of which shape the demand for skills. The reason for this reluctance is that these reforms are difficult to introduce and may come up against significant opposition from employers. In discussing the components that might be involved in developing an effective HRD strategy, I will draw on a paper produced by the International Labour Organisation (ILO, 2000).

The ILO paper, like *A Nation at Work*, identifies the different sectors or stages of education and training that an HRD strategy needs to include. They are:

- basic skills of adults,
- initial education of young people (including early childhood education),
- further and higher education and training, and
- continuing education and training and work-based learning.

However, it also stresses that education and training reforms are primarily *supply* factors, and that unless they are integrated into measures for changing the *demand* for a better-educated workforce they will not on their own generate employment or growth. The ILO paper refers to the following elements of an HRD strategy that need to be addressed in promoting the demand for skills:

- creating incentives for partnerships between employers, trade unions, civic and other local organisations;
- improving the capacity and skills of workplace trainers and assessors;
- extending the role of 'licence to practise' in labour markets;
- reforming investment conditions and the capital market;
- reforming corporate law; and
- developing strategic conditions for attracting foreign investment.

In other words, the ILO paper recognises that better human resources in the narrow sense of improving the qualifications of the labour force are inadequate on their own. They need to be seen as a component of a broader strategy that links improvements in the supply of skills and knowledge to new kinds of demand for human resources. It is these latter changes that are difficult to achieve. These difficulties have two aspects, one cultural and one political. The cultural issue refers to deeply-held assumptions by employers (but also in the society generally) about the potential capability of their employees. Such assumptions vary from elitist cultures such as the UK that still have low expectations of the education potential of the majority[7] to those countries like Japan which assume that the vast majority of the population are educable to what in South Africa would be matric standard. The political issue refers to the legacy of neo-liberal economics and a distrust of Keynesian demand-side interventions, that still shape government policies. An unresolved tension remains between a 'voluntarism' that assumes that employers should be left to decide their own HRD policies and the reality that the 'short-termism' of many employers makes this unlikely.

In the UK this neglect of demand issues by the present government is rationalised as an up-to-date version of Keynesianism. The government contrasts its policy of investing in education and training with the old-style Keynesianism that supported public investment to stimulate demand and with the neo-liberalism of Thatcher that left both supply and demand for skills up to the market. However, researchers such as Keep (1999) have increasingly questioned whether the traditional weaknesses – especially in relation to vocational education and training – are being addressed. Keep also argues that a supply-side approach leaves unchanged the lack of demand for skill by large sections of industry and services in the UK.

Locating national HRD strategies within a broader historical context can lead to an excessive pessimism that implies that countries are forever trapped in their past. Given South Africa's recent political history, this would be peculiarly inappropriate. It is

7 A recent survey estimated that seven million adults have problems with reading and writing.

therefore important to remember that the difficulties identified have been addressed in the past by a number of both European and Asian countries that now have highly qualified labour forces. The point of identifying the constraints of history is to be realistic about what is possible in a short time, but to remain optimistic rather than pessimistic about longer-term possibilities.

Implementation as a key element of an HRD strategy

The question of implementing an HRD strategy cuts across the earlier discussion of goals and components. *A Nation at Work* appears to follow the UK approach in concentrating on objectives, monitoring current provision, and targets. It gives far less attention to the process of implementation and the new activities that would be involved in achieving the targets. In the UK, there has been a major focus on target setting at all levels and all sectors. Implementation has occurred not in accordance with an explicit strategy but almost by default (intentionally or not) and as a result of other policies such as those concerned with funding. Two processes can be identified that relate to how institutions are funded. First, if student numbers are part of the funding formula for institutions such as Further Education Colleges, this will generate institutional competition for students in quasi-markets as the main mechanism by which targets are reached (or not). Second, if institutional funding is linked to the achievement of qualifications, this will also effect the achievement of targets if they are measured in terms of qualifications. One consequence of neglecting the need to improve the capacity of institutions is that fiscal rather than educational priorities come to dominate as educational institutions come to see themselves as businesses struggling for financial survival. This lack of attention to improving the capacity of institutions may explain why in many cases in the UK targets are not reached. In the UK in the 1990s, we have had a proliferation of targets and new systems of monitoring linked to League Tables on various outcome measures. However, there is evidence that the actual quantity and quality of skills being generated, as measured in terms of qualifications obtained, has not changed much. Two examples of this trend are (i) the proportion of young people continuing in full-time education after the age of sixteen has changed little since the early 1990s, and (ii) the numbers achieving 'technician level' qualifications through work-based programmes has remained at about one in three overall and is extremely unevenly distributed across sectors. Another possibility is that a disproportionate emphasis on targets can drive up the number of qualifications achieved but not necessarily improve standards or levels of knowledge and skill.

My general argument here, which draws on the UK experience, is that although a national Human Resources Strategy needs a framework of targets and a system of monitoring, a focus on implementation – and in particular the importance of improving institutional capacity and creating new forms of partnership – is also crucial. This balance between elements within a strategy needs to apply at national level (both in government and in national sectoral organisations), at regional level (involving new capacities and new relationships between provincial governments, providers such as schools, colleges and private training organisations, employers and other stakeholders), and at the institutional level (involving new relationships between providers and local employers, parents and community organisations).

I can only speculate as to where the major focus of HRD initiatives should be in South Africa, but some lessons from the UK experience may be useful. In the UK, a major responsibility for promoting and developing work-related skills and knowledge has been placed by government on what are extremely weak employer-led organisations for the different industrial and service sectors (the National Training Organisations, NTOs, which have some similarities to SETAs in South Africa). The dilemma for the government is trying to remedy a major national weakness in work-related skills through organisations that are themselves a symptom of that weakness. These weaknesses are most marked when there is no tradition of links between professional associations and intermediate jobs and skills, as in many of the service industries.

A Nation at Work does have a section (paragraph 2.4) on implementation that concentrates on two elements – planning and collection of data in relation to twenty-five key indicators. My argument in this section has been that, though these elements are important, they are only a framework for a strategy. In other words, they deal with the goals to be achieved and whether they have been achieved, but not with the changes in institutional practice that will be necessary to achieve the targets. *A Nation at Work* refers to the 'support of five pillars of Human Resource supply' but these are expressed extremely generally. One refers to the 'demand for skills' but nowhere is there any reference to how this will be achieved except that like the other pillars it will need 'specific intervention programmes.'

A Nation at Work argues that the first two elements of the strategy – macroeconomic policy and industrial policy – are 'relatively well developed' and states that it is concerned with the third. The problem seems to be the separation of the three policy strands so that although demand is referred to there is no strategy for linking supply to how incentives will be created to generate new demands. In the UK policies, supply is supposed somehow to transfer into demand, which it does not; without other changes it can only expand supply and potentially lead to credential inflation.

Conclusions and some comments on *A Nation at Work*

In this chapter, I have attempted to set the decision of the South African government to launch an HRD strategy in a broader international context. I have suggested that the economic pressures from globalisation have made human resource development increasingly attractive for governments as an approach to education and training policies. Several main conclusions follow from the international experience. First, even if it is accepted that there is no alternative to a strategy geared to a high skills economy, there is no one model to follow and any choice involves a set of priorities. Second, while an important focus for education and training, HRD goals remain only one such focus; in the long term goals not linked so directly to current economic demand may be equally important. Third, HRD strategies stress the importance of co-ordinating education and training with policies that address demand-side issues. However, in practice and for reasons I have alluded to, policies for developing the demand for skills can easily be relegated to the margins of national strategies. Fourth, targets and monitoring are an important part of the framework of any strategy. However, as the most visible side of a strategy and as a mechanism that gives government control of how public funds are used, targets and monitoring can be over-stressed to the neglect of the more difficult institutional changes and new practices that will be needed. This chapter has, therefore, stressed the central role of institutional capacity at every level in implementing the strategy.

These conclusions have a number of implications for the debate about how *A Nation at Work* is taken forward. First, there is need to make explicit the kind of future high skills economy that *A Nation at Work* is seeking to achieve and therefore the kind of priorities that follow. For example, are there existing sectors such as tourism and hospitality or new sectors such as information services that need to be identified and given priority? Second, should the strategy concentrate on developing general education in the school system (like Japan) or on establishing partnerships between providers of VET and social partners (as in Germany)? I have suggested that *A Nation at Work* does not have a clear strategy for promoting demand given the emphasis on increasing supply, and that it identifies a set of targets but not the kind of institutional changes needed to achieve them. This is partly a political issue. Targets and monitoring systems can be put into place relatively quickly without enormous costs or big changes in attitudes. Institutional change is slower and more resource-intensive. It is not surprising that the latter is given less emphasis. However, there are two features that successful systems – such as those in Germany, Japan and the Nordic countries, which differ in many other ways – have in common. These are a high level of institutional capacity and a high level of trust among stakeholders. Both are issues that have been neglected by countries like the UK and the USA that have relied on innovation and competition. It is difficult to see the latter route being viable for South Africa.

Chapter 6

Policy Ambiguity and Slippage: Higher Education under the New State, 1994-2001

Andre Kraak

Introduction

This chapter traces the contextual and discursive dynamics that have shaped higher education and training (HET) policy formation in the period 1990 to 2001. Although this was a period of significant policy and discursive contestation, much of the differences in position on HET were muted by the consensual politics of the early 1990s. Concerned with bringing to an end the on-going cycles of violence between contending parties in the South African conflict, the newly-elected African National Congress (ANC) government under the leadership of Nelson Mandela made national reconciliation the number one state priority. The call for reconciliation sought to forge unity and common agreement on what constituted the central tasks of social reconstruction and transformation. Seven years later, this sense of unity has receded and real differences over HET policy have come to the fore. The initial sense of common purpose attained during the Mandela era has given way to significant policy critique and division among the ranks of HET civil servants, institutional stakeholders and policy analysts. This chapter suggests a number of causal factors that have underpinned these policy divisions. These are:

- Contestation has occurred over the extent to which *globalisation and the forces of economic modernisation* should be ceded a major role in the reconstitution of post-apartheid HET.
- *Stakeholders* during the past decade have articulated competing views on the importance of equity in HET transformation and the way in which redressing the injustices of apartheid in higher education should proceed. These contestations were never resolved during the 1990s, but rather postponed to reappear in the first years of the new millennium.
- Contestation over the status of *institutional differentiation* in a new HET system was never resolved in a definitive sense in either the reports of the 1996 National Commission on Higher Education (NCHE), or in any of the later policy documents and legislative tracts.
- There has never been the unanimity or the political will across government to *activate an 'interventionist' or 'developmental'* state along with its associated instruments of state planning, co-ordination and steering.

This highly volatile terrain has thrown up three identifiable discourses that have had significant influence on the unfolding of the sequential steps of policy making, policy implementation, and policy adaptation and retraction. Each of these discourses, however, has impacted differentially – at certain historical moments having significant influence, at other times receding. These three discourses can be labelled as:

- a 'high-skills' or 'economic rationalist' discourse;
- a 'popular democratic' discourse; and lastly
- a residual 'stratification' discourse.

The interplay between these discourses and the unfolding politics of the day can best be understood by a categorisation of the period into five identifiable although overlapping phases:

- *the pre-'taking of power' phase*: By 1989, the possibility of a negotiated settlement had dawned. The politics of the anti-apartheid movement shifted from mass struggle to 'preparing to govern'. The period 1989-1994 witnessed the mobilisation of the entire anti-apartheid movement behind the task of forging new policy propositions across the entire gamut of human existence. It is during this period that 'popular democratic' and 'economic rationalist' discursive tensions began to emerge, but were muted by the consensus-building dictates of the day.

- *the legislative era*: The 1994-1997 period witnessed significant education legislation being enacted by Parliament, culminating in the passing of the *Higher Education Act* in October 1997. The content of this legislation reflected a particular 'settlement' between the above-mentioned competing discourses.

- *the policy implementation phase*: This period overlaps with the legislative era described above (beginning with the transfer of power in April 1994), but became amplified after the passing of the *Higher Education Act* in October 1997 to the present. It is a period when the limits of state power began to surface and when policy idealism in education was inevitably mediated by the structural constraints and political limits facing the new state.

- *a vacillating state, the era of policy doubt and retraction*: The complexities of governance in the new state begin to emerge, particularly in the period 1999-2000 when the Council on Higher Education (CHE) Task Team on Size and Shape deliberated. During this period the discursive tensions and political difficulties reached a high point, resulting in significant policy doubt, retraction and reversal.

- *the National Plan, February 2001*: The release of this policy document sees the state reaffirm its support for the key policy principles contained in the 1997 *Higher Education Act* and a new determination to implement them.

Policy ambiguity and slippage are the key outcomes of this circular interplay between discourse, state power and history.

Competing discourses in the pre-'taking of power' era

The policy implications of settlement

This chapter argues that the evolution of education policy discourse in South Africa has been profoundly shaped by the dramatic contextual developments of the early 1990s, both in South Africa and in the world at large. In making this point, the analysis applies the concept of settlement that has been borrowed from the Australian literature on the social compact formed in 1983 between the Australian Labour Party government, big business and the labour movement. Sedunary (1996) defines 'settlement' as a framework of compromise in which contradictory interests are reconciled to their perceived mutual benefit and in which attendant ideologies delimit the grounds of action and conflict.

Such political settlements are provisional. Their emergence is tied to contemporaneous historical conditions. They are many-sided, and may have conservative or progressive manifestations that arise at different historical moments. Fundamentally, they are about reconfiguring the relative roles of market and state in the regulation of society. They also impact on the arena of cultural politics, in the struggle over meaning and discourse (Sedunary, 1996).

Webster and Adler (1999) provide a similar analysis of settlement in South Africa. They suggest that the political compromise forged between 1990 and 1994 has the potential to provide a mutually beneficial 'class compromise' in the double transition of consolidating democracy alongside economic reconstruction: 'A compromise requires a mutually shared sense of stalemate. It also requires parties to accept that the costs of not compromising outweigh the benefits to be had from standing firm' (Webster & Adler, 1999:2).

What, then, were the conjunctural determinants of this compromise and settlement in South Africa? A watershed moment in this process occurred in 1989, with dramatic events within South Africa but also world-wide. This was the year in which the communist Eastern Bloc regimes collapsed, signalling a massive symbolic defeat for all left-wing movements across the globe. This was also the year in which the ailing apartheid regime surrendered to the idea of a negotiated settlement in what was rapidly becoming a civil war. A negotiated settlement did not only represent an end to war. It brought with it a necessary moderation of the key political propositions of the opposing parties in the South African conflict. Ideological allegiances and the associated social and economic policy propositions of the national liberation movement shifted dramatically from left-socialist formulations to what at best can be described as social democratic and at worst neo-liberal thinking.

This watershed moment set the stage for the way in which the anti-apartheid movement began 'preparing to govern'. The politics of reconciliation and consensus-building were most forcefully entrenched by the establishment between the National Party and the ANC of the Transitional Executive Council (TEC) in the period immediately prior to the elections of April 1994 and, more importantly, by the post-election formation of the Government of National Unity (GNU) that consisted of the ruling ANC and the two leading opposition parties, the National Party and the Inkatha Freedom Party.

From an educational vantage point, three additional ingredients helped shape the discursive terrain in the early 1990s. The first was the emergence of a 'high skills' thesis – a concept borrowed from the British literature on education and economic change. There has never been unanimity, however, in the international or South African literature on globalisation's impact on education, and a considerable body of writing – strongly influenced by the work of key Australian educational critics – has coined the term 'economic rationalism' to describe, in more pejorative terms than the high skills thesis, this economically-driven process of educational restructuring. Secondly, a 'popular democratic' discourse was present throughout the 1980s and 1990s, borrowing from the radical traditions and values of the anti-apartheid struggle. Thirdly, and more recently, there has been the re-emergence, albeit in a more contemporary wrapping, of an older discourse – stratification thinking – that was dominant in educational planning in the apartheid reform period. Each of these contending discourses will now be examined.

Economic rationalism and the high skills thesis

The process termed 'globalisation' has undoubtedly been the key trigger in the emergence of economic rationalist discourse and the high skills thesis. This is because globalisation poses massive new challenges for the education and training systems of economies across the world. Globalisation arose as the outcome of three simultaneous developments in the advanced economies of the world:

- the demise of Fordist production regimes and the onset of global economic crisis in the mid-1970s;
- the advent of information technology in the early 1980s, and in particular its facilitation of the internationalisation of finance capital; and
- the rise of innovative forms of work organisation in the early 1980s, now referred to as 'flexible specialisation' or 'post-Fordism'.

The new economic system that emerged from these three developments is characterised by high-quality export manufacture aimed at specific consumer niche markets. Innovation is at the heart of this new system – the ability to continuously reinvent products and add value to existing designs through reconfiguring new information and knowledge about product and process.

One of the most central adjuncts of globalisation has been its new education and training demands – for example, the need for a highly skilled labour force that is able to employ the new technologies and add value to existing goods and services. However, it is not merely specialised skills that are needed; more well-rounded and diverse skill competencies are in demand. Enterprises require entire labour forces that are able to adapt to unpredictable and volatile global product markets and rapid technological change. They require broad problem-solving skills to anticipate flaws in production. It is the ability to retool and respond quickly to rapidly changing market conditions that is highly valued.

In short, globalisation has imposed new conditions on competitiveness that have to do with attaining higher quality manufacture and higher productivity, both on the basis of a more highly skilled workforce. The challenge of attaining these new conditions of economic competitiveness led a group of British economists and educationalists to posit the theory of a low skills or high skills equilibrium (see Finegold & Soskice, 1988; Finegold *et al.*, 1990; Finegold, 1991; Young, 1992; Brown, 1999; Keep, 1999; Lauder, 1999). It is a 'social market' or 'social democratic' argument about the necessity for educational reforms to interlock with macro-economic, industrial and labour market reforms such that their *combined impact* had a better chance of meeting the new conditions for global competitiveness – the attainment of high-quality manufacture through a highly skilled and highly productive workforce. The high skills thesis sees educational reform as constituting one component of a necessarily larger set of socio-economic reforms. It posits the argument that the attainment of successful reform in one institutional sphere (for example, education) is conditional on parallel changes occurring at other institutional levels (for example, in the macro-economic, labour market and work organisation environments).

Finegold *et al.* (1990) argue that in countries such as Britain the interlocking of particular neo-liberal educational and economic policies has produced a low skills equilibrium. They argue that the network of self-reinforcing institutions and social policies that interact to perpetuate such a low skill economy include: the state and capital's lack of long-term human resources planning; an emphasis on the production of low cost, low skill products; the absence of a successful export-oriented, competitive manufacturing strategy; unco-ordinated state policies in the spheres of economic growth, industrial policy and education and training; and finally, a divisive qualifications structure that limits mobility between education and training institutions, thereby hindering the necessary process of continuous skills upgrading. In such a scenario, single reform innovations (such as increased investments in education and training) will not be sufficient to break the self-reinforcing cycle of a low skills economy. Real change will require a reversal of most of the above conditions to produce a new, self-binding high skills economy.

The high skills thesis was very influential in the development of ANC macro-economic and educational policies in this early period (1990-1994). However, it was not the only theoretical interpretation of the education challenges posed by globalisation. Other significant international contributions to the South African debate have been the writings of Australian (Taylor *et al.*, 1997), American (Slaughter & Leslie, 1997) and other writers who have coined the term economic rationalism to depict, in a pejorative sense, a discourse that in their view has acted to subordinate educational policy reforms within a larger project of macro- and micro-economic restructuring.

These two literatures are significantly different in their interpretation of globalisation. The Australian literature is a left-critical discourse about globalisation, dismissing much of its impact as the neo-liberal or neo-right subjugation of the educational process to the dictates of the market and the accentuation of existing social inequalities in education. In sharp contrast, the high skills thesis is more concerned with promoting the development of a new set of complementary social, economic and educational policies (the high skills road) that would allow countries to adapt to globalisation on more beneficial (essentially social democratic) terms.

Both of these literatures influenced the education policy making process in South Africa. However, the economic rationalist discourse remained merely oppositional, whereas the high skills thesis has been very influential in fundamentally shaping the content of the early education and training policies of the ANC and its ally, the Congress of South African Trade Unions (COSATU). The central propositions of the evolving South African variant of the high skills thesis were:

- *linking education, labour market and macro-economic restructuring* within a single, integrated programme of socio-economic reconstruction;
- *promoting the idea of a 'developmental' state* to 'steer' the implementation of such an integrated programme of complementary reforms; and
- privileging the idea of a *unified and integrative education and training regulatory framework.*

The evolution of this high skills discourse is different from the conditions that pertained in countries such as Australia. It arose out of the policy processes of the mass democratic movement and was formalised by the ANC as official education and economic policy in the run-up to the elections of April 1994. It arose out of a strategic view adopted by the anti-apartheid movement regarding the most optimal way of taking power and adapting to globalisation on terms beneficial to the working class and the poor. This is in sharp contrast to the more traditional corporatist partnerships struck between the state, capital and labour in Europe and in Australia during the 1980s. This unique social democratic trajectory requires closer interrogation.

The construction of a South African high skills discourse

linking educational reform with macro-economic and labour market restructuring (1990-1994)

The first coherent ANC macro-economic policy framework in the post-1990 period was termed *Growth through Redistribution* (ANC, 1990a,b; Erwin, 1990; Kaplan, 1990; Kaplinsky, 1990, 1991). Drawn up in collaboration with COSATU-aligned economists, it was the precursor to the more influential *Reconstruction and Development Programme* (RDP) that was formally published in March 1994. *Growth through Redistribution* posited the argument that the goals of equity (basic needs provision and redistribution) and economic growth (the increased export of value-added goods) were compatible within a single, comprehensive plan for social reconstruction. The RDP comprised the integration of four key reconstruction programmes: meeting basic needs, developing human resources, building the economy (making it globally competitive), and democratising the state.

> The RDP is based on reconstruction and development being parts of an integrated process. This is in contrast to a commonly held view that growth and development, or growth and redistribution, are processes that contradict each other.... In this view, development is a deduction from growth. The RDP breaks decisively with this approach.... The RDP integrates growth, development, reconstruction and redistribution into a unified programme (ANC, 1994c:6).

ANC-linked economists argued that this relationship between growth and redistribution constituted a *singular* process that contrasted sharply with the dualistic approaches of industry and the previous government who both saw growth as a separate and necessary prerequisite for redistributive activities (Gelb, 1991:30). The ANC emphasis on a singular process relied heavily on the notion that economic growth was achievable through an extensive and rapid redistribution of wealth, income and resources (Gelb, 1992:25).

Occurring in concert with the work done by these ANC economists on *Growth and Redistribution*, COSATU launched its own programme, the *Reconstruction Accord*, in March 1993. The *Reconstruction Accord* was premised on the fact that new social relations of production between capital and labour were essential for economic renewal. There had been a growing realisation within COSATU that current global restructuring directed towards higher value-added production, a higher science and technology content in production, and export-oriented economies could not be avoided. These global requirements for growth would necessarily have to be achieved through agreements with capital, but on terms beneficial to labour (See COSATU, 1993a, 1993a; Erwin, 1992:23).

COSATU was also concerned with bolstering state power and promoting a deal between a future ANC government and the organisations of civil society that would commit the state to a programme of 'fundamental transformation to the benefit of workers and the poor' (COSATU, 1993b:1). The *Reconstruction Accord* had five central pillars. These were:

- ❑ *A democratic political solution*: The new government must be effective and strong to implement a programme of economic reconstruction and development. Trade unions, through co-determinist structures, would be able to influence state decision-making.
- ❑ *Education and training for all*: There would be an integrated education and training system administered by a single national department, and a career-pathing system based on the linkage of workers' skills to pay and grading structures. Unions would be enabled to play a central role in the restructuring of work in areas such as health and safety, new technology, investment and work organisation.
- ❑ *A programme of job creation.*
- ❑ *A social wage package to end poverty.*
- ❑ *A programme to extend socio-economic rights* (COSATU, 1993a:4-7; 1993b:5).

Both the *Reconstruction Accord* and the RDP emphasised the notion of an integrated package of policy reforms linked together in a single coherent plan for social reconstruction. The RDP consciously sought to link economic policy to other policy domains, most particularly employment growth and labour market reform, education and training (ET) and human resources development (HRD), public works programmes and youth training schemes (see ANC, 1994c:81).

Two other policy texts in this period emphasised the need to link education reform to macro-economic and labour market reforms in pursuit of a high skills future for South Africa. These were the National Education Policy Initiative (NEPI) reports on *Human Resources Development* (NEPI, 1992) and the concluding *Framework Report* (NEPI, 1993). These documents adopted Finegold's concept of a low skills and high skills equilibrium to compare the former government's education and training policies with those of the incoming ANC government. These reports depicted the former government's proposals for an *Educational Renewal Strategy* (DNE, 1991, 1992) and a *National Training Strategy* (NTB/HSRC, 1991) as reinforcing a 'low participation, low skills' system. In contrast, the NEPI *Human Resources Development and Framework Reports* both proposed a high skills equilibrium alternative based on a high skills development path requiring: a strong state; a strong civil society; consensual government characterised by vigorous social partnerships between state, capital and labour; a clear economic growth path; and good-quality basic education and high levels of educational attainment (see NEPI, 1992:36,67; NEPI, 1993:25).

the developmental state

Another central policy tenet of this time was the ANC's emphasis on the need for an 'enabling state'. The RDP base document noted that 'neither a commandist central planning system nor an unfettered free market system can provide adequate solutions to the problems confronting us' (ANC, 1994c:78). Alternatively, the ANC advocated an enabling state that was 'slim' but that could intervene strategically while carefully marshalling its scarce resources. State intervention would be selective and targeted, based on sectoral planning. However, where the state chose to intervene, its intervention would be pervasive and far-reaching (Erwin, 1990:38; Gelb, 1991:31). The enabling state would also intervene decisively in the development of an export orientation (as occurred in the successful newly-industrialised countries). This would entail the training of highly skilled technicians and engineers, developing a local R&D infrastructure and technological capacity, and targeting specific sectors and industrial clusters for the development of beneficiated products that could compete on world markets (Kaplinsky, 1990:24; Kaplan, 1991:187,196; ANC, 1992:66).

privileging the idea of a unified and integrative ET regulatory framework

The high skills argument world-wide has a political predilection towards the idea of a single, unified and integrated regulatory framework, primarily as a response to the pressures of globalisation, the massification of the education and training system, and the emergence of new forms of knowledge production. This predilection is reflected in the shift away from the divided, elite education and training systems that characterise the past and present towards the more open and unified ET system essential in the future (Gibbons *et al*, 1994; Scott, 1995).

Adrienne Bird and Gail Elliot (1993a,b), with strong input from British educationalist Michael Young (1992), were instrumental in developing these ideas further in two discussion documents published by the ANC in 1993. They proposed a 'unified, multi-path model' of education and training built around a nationally integrated curriculum with a single qualifications structure. Learners would be required to complete a given number of modules. Some modules would be 'core' and compulsory while others would be optional and could be selected from a bank of vocational and academic modules. The precise content of these core and optional modules would be determined by the 'multi-path' context in which learning was done – whether in the school classroom, the factory training centre, at night-school, or by correspondence. The essence of this unified model was its flexibility and credit accumulation properties. These ideas acquired hegemony within the ANC and became official government policy with the publication of the *White Paper on Education and Training* (DoE, 1995a) and the passing of the *South African Qualifications Authority Act* in 1995.

Radical-progressive and popular-democratic educational discourses

The second significant discursive development in the 1990s was the consolidation of 'radical-progressive' propositions on educational reform. This discourse derives historically from the People's Education movement of the 1980s, led largely by the National Education Crisis (later Co-ordinating) Committee (NECC). People's Education was primarily a political movement that viewed the school classroom as a central site of struggle against apartheid. However, in the period 1985 to 1990 it also came to represent a fledgling radical pedagogic alternative to the Bantu Education that had been imposed by the apartheid state since the mid-1950s. Some of the central propositions of People's Education included:

- the democratisation of education through the participation of a cross-section of the community in decision-making on the content, quality and governance of education;
- the negation of apartheid in education by making education relevant to the democratic struggles of the people;
- the achievement of a high level of education for everyone;
- the development of a critical consciousness; and
- the bridging of the gap between theoretical knowledge and practical life (Levin, 1991:3).

People's Education became an educational pedagogy encompassing the development of critical thinking, inter-disciplinary curriculum content, learner-centredness, participatory teaching methods, community involvement, and the desire to link the focus of formal education with the world of work.

Many of the ideas of People's Education were only tentatively developed by the late 1980s, primarily because of the heavy state repression of NECC structures during this period but also because the very concept of People's Education was imprecise and open to multiple interpretations. Further development of these ideas did not take place during the negotiations era. This later period witnessed a widespread abandonment of the egalitarian language of People's Education. In its place arose an expert-led, multi-stakeholder policy making process that prioritised other discourses – primarily the high skills discourse described above.

Some of the pedagogic concerns of People's Education were subsumed within the adaptation of outcomes-based education (OBE) to South African conditions. Because of OBE's highly technicist and behaviourist origins, its implementation in South Africa after 1995 served to depoliticise the radical pedagogic traditions inherited from People's Education. However, the political concerns associated with People's Education were resurrected within an oppositional discourse around the concept of equity. It represented a call for fundamental social and institutional transformation to eliminate the inequalities imposed by apartheid education. This had a broad appeal among the majority of students, staff and ex-graduates of the previously disadvantaged (largely black) institutions. They argued passionately for a radical upgrading and transformation of these institutions to bring them on par with the historically privileged (largely white) institutions. Because of this radical, moral and political genesis, the discourse is termed 'popular democratic'.

The demands for equity on the one hand, and the demands of the high skills discourse around economic development on the other, were seen by certain analysts in the education policy debates of the early 1990s to contradict each other. Analysts such as Badat *et al.* (1994) maintained that equity was not an inevitable consequence of development, and that policies for equity did not necessarily lead to development. They argued that international experience had shown that favouring one goal would jeopardise the other. They advocated pursuing the two goals as parallel rather than correlative objectives. They asserted that the tension between equity and development had to be recognised, and that in order for both objectives to be achieved they needed to be planned for separately. Badat *et al.* made a case for a balanced approach that accommodated both equity and development, and recommended that this should be the basis of a framework for a reconstructed higher education system in South Africa.

These discursive tensions – between equity and development – remained throughout the policy making period from 1990-1997. The new state's response was cautious, wishing not to be seen to be privileging one fundamental demand over the other. Following the logic of Badat *et al.*, the new state sought to balance these dual imperatives in HET policy:

> ... the South African economy is confronted with the formidable challenge of integrating itself into the competitive arena of international production and finance which has witnessed rapid changes as a result of new communication and information technologies. These technologies, which place a premium on knowledge and skills, leading to the notion of the 'knowledge society', have transformed the way in which people work and consume. Simultaneously, the nation is confronted with the challenge of reconstructing domestic social and economic relations to eradicate and redress the inequitable patterns of ownership, wealth and social and economic practices that were shaped by segregation and apartheid. (DoE, 1997a:9).

The 1997 White Paper, *A Programme for the Transformation of Higher Education* (DoE, 1997a), commits itself to a programme of redress. It notes that the Ministry of Education's commitment to changing the composition of the student body would be effected through the targeted redistribution of the public subsidy to higher education. It asserts that the relative proportion of public funding used to support academically able but disadvantaged students must be increased. The White Paper also states that ensuring equity of access must be complemented by a concern for equity of outcomes.

Increased access must not lead to a 'revolving door' syndrome for students, with high failure and dropout rates. In this respect, the Ministry is 'committed to ensuring that public funds earmarked for achieving redress and equity must be linked to measurable progress toward improving quality and reducing the high drop-out and repetition rates' (DoE, 1997a:22).

A residual discourse of the old order: stratification thinking

The final discursive influence on HET policy over the past decade is that of 'stratification thinking'. This is a residual discourse – a contemporary expression of a much older discourse that has strong roots in the education policies of the previous government. Three definitive influences in the development of stratification thinking in South African education and training are:

- the adoption of a trinary system of HET in South Africa by the Van Wyk De Vries Commission of 1974;
- the explicit stratification of the post-school system proposed by the De Lange Commission in 1981; and
- the proposals of the *Education Renewal Strategy* of 1991.

The trinary model proposed by the Van Wyk de Vries Commission of Inquiry into Universities in 1974 maintained that universities should concentrate on the teaching and research of the basic fundamental principles of science, that technikons should concentrate on the application of scientific principles to practical problems and on technology, and that colleges should provide vocational training (DNE, 1995:10). This fairly rigid differentiation of function between institutions has been maintained to this day. In a 1995 report, the state acknowledged that the 'present system was to a large extent characterised by rigidity and inflexibility, with each sub-sector and institution largely working in isolation. This situation was not only inhibiting as regards the articulation of learners, but at the same time it hampered the essential exchange of expertise' (DNE, 1995). The report continued to argue that the trinary divide was problematic because universities were also involved in professional or career training, that technology was increasingly more dependent on links between disciplinary and inter-disciplinary knowledge, and that the technikons had in any event moved well beyond their 'application of technology' mandate by offering courses in business, commerce and the social sciences and by acquiring the right in 1993 to offer degree programmes (RSA, 1993b; DNE, 1995:12,19; see also Committee of Technikon Principals, 1995:5).

The 1981 De Lange investigation into the *Provision of Education in the Republic of South Africa* (HSRC, 1981a) provided the second significant moment in which stratification thinking was applied to the reform of the South African post-secondary education system. De Lange's proposals were driven by the desire to maximise student mobility across the key institutions of the post-secondary sector (colleges, technikons and universities), and in so doing to maximise the production of high-level skills that were in short supply. De Lange was concerned with the rigid boundaries defined between these institutions. The Commission proposed a major institutional change to resolve this problem – the introduction of the Five Year College, based on the Taiwanese experience. The Five Year College proposal was geared strategically to addressing the severe skill shortages at the middle and high person-power levels. Students would be enrolled after having completed Standard Seven (today's Grade 9). The benefits of such intensive education and training at an early age, according to De Lange, were that pupils would be enabled 'from puberty onwards to acquire the system of values appropriate to their careers at the middle level' (HSRC, 1981b:26).

De Lange's Five Year College idea was quickly forgotten in the controversy surrounding the refusal by the De Lange Commission and the apartheid state to support a single, non-racial system of education. However, the idea was not lost entirely. It was resurrected in the *Education Renewal Strategy* (ERS) published by the Department of National Education in June 1991. The ERS proposed a similar innovation – the Edukon.

The Edukon proposal formed part of a larger set of rationalisation reforms that aimed to impact on the post-secondary and tertiary education sectors. These reforms incorporated a dual institutional strategy of both downgrading and upgrading the character of universities, technikons and technical colleges. Such institutional reordering had become imperative, according to the ERS, for several reasons: overlaps and duplication in the large number of instructional programmes on offer at universities, technikons and colleges; a lack of definition about the differing emphases of these institutions; and the need for more cost-effective education (DNE, 1991:36-39).

Institutional downgrading would entail shifting many programmes from universities downward to technikons, especially all university-level diplomas and certificates. It would also entail a shift downward of many technikon programmes to technical colleges (DNE, 1991:36,58). Institutional upgrading would entail the following changes: raising the status of certain universities into centres of excellence as post-graduate institutions; technikons offering some degree courses in technology; and technical colleges being upgraded into colleges of further education – to be known as Edukons (DNE, 1991:54,60,61).

Edukons were viewed by the ERS as important institutions capable of facilitating greater flow between the post-secondary and tertiary sectors. Edukons would have a number of functions. They could offer the academic bridging courses that are currently placing a huge burden on universities and technikons. They could also offer 'transfer credits' for study at universities/technikons, as well as various vocational programmes (DNE, 1991:54,60,61; DNE, 1992:37).

While the Edukon concept had merit, a number of serious problems were associated with these proposals. Much of the proposed institutional downgrading proposed by the ERS was a response to the problem of 'risk students' (those with E aggregates), whom the ERS wanted to phase out of the costly university route. It was felt that these (largely black) students should be channelled through more cost-effective alternate routes to post-secondary study such as the Edukon.

The limits of institutional stratification thinking

Later sections of this chapter will look at a more recent set of proposals – the recommendations of the Task Team of the Council on Higher Education (CHE) that investigated the Size and Shape of HET in South Africa (CHE, 2000a, 2000b). It is historically significant that the CHE proposals on institutional typology are similar to those of the ERS and the De Lange Commission. The purpose of making this comparison is not to stigmatise and discredit the CHE proposals through an association with the apartheid regime. Institutional stratification ideas were widespread across the globe during this time, particularly with the adoption and expansion of binary and trinary systems of post-secondary education and training in the 1960s and 1970s. However, by the late 1980s South Africa stood out from HET developments in the rest of the world in three critical ways. Firstly, the social consequences of stratified and therefore exclusionary education and training systems were more severe in the South African case because it was overlaid by a system of racial discrimination. Secondly, the technikon and college sectors have tended to remain behind in comparison with the 'institutional creep' evident internationally, that has seen polytechnics elsewhere compete with universities on an equal basis in terms of research and post-graduate output, the qualifications of staff, and partnerships with industry (see Goedegebuure, 1992:187). Lastly, the more recent stratification proposals in the South African context (the 1991 ERS and the 2000 CHE proposals) perpetuate rigid binary and trinary divisions that fly in the face of the new knowledge and skill demands of globalisation.

The original premise of the trinary divide – the strict separation of institutional functions, the development of basic science and its application to social contexts in the form of technologies, and the training of workers in lower level vocational skills – has become obsolete. Gibbons *et al.* (1994) and Scott (1995) argue that this is a consequence of the emergence under globalisation of a more interactive dynamic between science and technology (S&T) than that allowed by the traditional binary-trinary divide. They argue that S&T policy in the 1970s saw science being rallied to the needs of technology and national economic development in a linear, sequential and hierarchical conception of S&T. Scientists at universities pursued basic science research in isolation from the context of technological application, leaving the latter task to the technicians trained by polytechnics and employed in industry. This approach is now obsolete, with a shift to what the authors term an 'innovation and technology interchange' phase from the early 1980s to the present – the aim being to hitch the scientific enterprise to industrial renewal and competitiveness. This has led to the blurring of the distinction between science and technology, and therefore between the essentialist roles of universities and polytechnics. It has also led to the growth of a plethora of formal and informal industry-science-technology partnerships, with university and polytechnic scientists acquiring increasing familiarity with the workings of industrial enterprises:

> ... the notion of technology transfer ... cannot any more be understood as a transmission of knowledge from the university to the receiver easily and usually with almost no follow up. Instead it is no longer like a relay race, in which the baton is passed cleanly and quickly from one runner to the next. Technology transfer looks more like a soccer game in which the university is a member of a team. To score it needs the aid of its team mates. The ball is passed back and forth constantly among the players who may include businesspeople, venture capitalists, patent attorneys, production engineers, and many others in addition to the university faculty. This is why it has been suggested that technology interchange is a more appropriate phrase than technology transfer (Gibbons *et al.*, 1994:87).

In this dynamic environment of technology interchange, the distinction between university-based and technikon-based scientists and technologists has become less important. Given all of the above, it therefore becomes problematic for the CHE to resurrect, at the start of the twenty-first century, the idea of rigid structural differentiation. The specific proposals of the CHE will be examined in more detail in a later section of this chapter.

The legislative period: mapping out the new HET policy framework

The most influential policy formulation exercise in the HET arena during the 1990s was undoubtedly the National Commission on Higher Education. The next section will highlight five key pillars of the new HET framework proposed by the NCHE and, in large part, accepted by government in the 1997 *Higher Education Act*. What is most significant about the five pillars is that they deal with issues central to the concerns of the high skills discourse. This is evident in three critical ways. Firstly, the central thrust of the NCHE recommendations and the 1997 Act is to make HET institutions more responsive to socio-economic priorities. Secondly, the NCHE and the Act promote a 'planning and co-ordination' imperative which seeks to more effectively steer the total system – using financial, performance and other incentives – in directions consonant with national macro-economic and labour market priorities. Lastly, the NCHE proposes a variant of a unified regulatory framework in its recommendation for a 'single co-ordinated system of HET'. All three recommendations are central to the high skills thesis.

The five pillars of the new South African higher education policy framework are: a single nationally co-ordinated system of HET; a planning and co-ordination imperative; increased access and raised participation rates; increased responsiveness to societal and economic needs; and programme differentiation and the development of institutional 'niche' areas.

A single nationally co-ordinated system of HET

The key recommendation of the NCHE in 1996 was that 'higher education in South Africa should be conceptualised, planned, governed and funded as a single co-ordinated system' (NCHE, 1996b:89). The need for such a proposal arose because of what the Commission perceived to be an absence of any sense of 'system' in South African higher education. Three major systemic deficiencies were noted:

- There was a chronic mismatch between higher education's output and the needs of a modernising economy.
- There was a strong inclination towards closed-system disciplinary approaches and programmes, which has led to inadequately contextualised teaching and research. The content of the knowledge produced and disseminated was insufficiently responsive to the problems and needs of the African continent, the southern African region, or the vast numbers of poor and rural people in our society.
- There was a lack of regulatory frameworks, due to a long history of organisational and administrative fragmentation and weak accountability. This inhibited planning and co-ordination, the elimination of duplication and waste, the promotion of better articulation and mobility, and the effective evaluation of quality and efficiency (NCHE, 1996b:2).

The 1997 White Paper on HET raised similar concerns. It argued that the current system of provision was too fragmented, unco-ordinated, supply-driven, and insufficiently responsive to national priorities (DoE, 1997a:18). Significantly, the policy formulation process in HET has identified the resolution of these problems in the creation of a 'single co-ordinated national HET system'. All of the HET policy texts argue that a new regulatory framework is needed that will co-ordinate the HET band as a single coherent whole, applying uniform norms and procedures with sufficient flexibility to allow for diversity in addressing the multiple needs of highly differentiated learner constituencies.

The importance of planning and co-ordination

At the heart of the first key pillar of the new HET policy framework – the idea of a single nationally co-ordinated system of HET – is a strong emphasis on state co-ordination that will strategically 'steer' the system via a regulatory framework of financial incentives, reporting and monitoring requirements (particularly with regard to key performance indicators), and a system of programme approval. In line with the constitutional notion of co-operative governance, the central state's role is to manage the system in co-operation with other role players and not through prescriptive fiat or other interventionist mechanisms. The state will govern through a 'softer' regulatory framework, that seeks to steer the system in three important ways:

- through planning requirements, which will encourage institutions to outline a distinctive mission, mix of programmes, enrolment targets and overall institutional plan;
- through the use of financial incentives, which are aimed at encouraging institutions to reorient provision to address national, regional and local education and training needs and priorities; and
- through a set of reporting requirements regarding performance indicators dedicated to measure, in the spirit of greater institutional accountability, the extent to which the institutional plan and national priorities are being met. In so doing, these performance indicators are very influential in shaping the allocation of the next cycle of financial awards.

Two types of 'plan' are advocated in the HET policy texts. They are:

- *a National Higher Education Plan*: The NCHE argued that a National Higher Education Plan is pivotal to the goal of effective co-ordination in HET. The Plan would be developed on a rolling three-year basis. Its aim would be to establish a programme mix that is 'broadly in line with emerging national and regional needs which will require system-wide and institutional planning processes able to co-ordinate the overall shape and size of the system' (NCHE, 1996b:112,119). The first such National Plan was released in March 2001.

- *Institutional Plans*: On the basis of guidelines provided by the National Plan, HET institutions would be required to devise three-year rolling plans that would include institutional mission statements, proposed programmes, indicative targets for enrolment levels by programme, race and gender equity goals, and proposed measures to develop new programme areas (DoE, 1997b:19). Such an institutional plan would be expected to 'take into account the unique or distinctive mission of the institution, and be informed by student demand, by labour market requirements, by societal equity and development needs and by the new demands of knowledge production in the context of technological innovation and globalisation' (DoE, 1998c:3).

The final moment in the planning process will be the attainment of approval for institutional plans that will lead to the allocation of funded student places to institutions for approved programmes in particular levels and fields of learning.

Increasing access and participation rates

An earlier section of this chapter has already discussed the demand for equity in higher education. This demand constitutes the third key pillar of the new HET policy framework. The call for increased access and higher participation rates for blacks in the HET system is a response to apartheid's inequities in education, as well as a response to globalisation's growing pressure for a more highly skilled future workforce.

The NCHE noted these massification imperatives by arguing that the emphasis on increased participation signified a shift away from a higher education system that 'enrols primarily middle class students into elite professional and scholarly pursuits, to a system characterised by a wider diversity of feeder constituencies and programmes' (NCHE, 1996b:76; DoE, 1996b:18-19).

Responsiveness

A fourth key pillar of the new HET policy framework is the emphasis on 'increased responsiveness', indicating a shift away from 'academic insularity, a closed system governed primarily by the norms and procedures of established disciplines, towards an open higher education system which interacts more with its societal environment' (NCHE, 1996b:76). This new emphasis on responsiveness takes two forms. The first is responsiveness to community needs, which is usually incorporated into the outreach programmes, service learning, and the community-sensitive curricula and research programmes of HET institutions. The second form is socio-economic – greater 'responsiveness' to the demands of economic growth and technological development. The NCHE noted that this new form of responsiveness was leading to dramatic changes within HET, particularly with regard to new forms of knowledge production. Knowledge production has become an 'increasingly open system in which a number of actors from different disciplines and from outside higher education participate. The value of knowledge is assessed not only on scientific criteria but also on utilitarian and practical grounds' (NCHE, 1996b:125-126; see also DoE, 1996b:35, and DoE, 1997b:31).

There is significant evidence of the growth of these new forms of trans-disciplina ry research and knowledge production in the South African HET system, with more and more applied research and consultancy work seeking solutions to some of South Africa's most acute social and economic problems. The new HET policy framework seeks to encourage this greater responsiveness to community and socio-economic need.

Programme differentiation and institutional 'niche' areas

Even though the NCHE proposed a single co-ordinated system with strong homogenising tendencies and central planning imperatives, the Commission was at pains to emphasise the need for on-going institutional diversity and flexibility regarding boundaries. The Commission argued:

> The wide array of higher education programmes makes the boundaries of higher education difficult to define. So do conceptions of lifelong learning, the recognition of prior learning and articulation and transfer between further and higher education. All pre-suppose a continuum of learning that makes it extremely difficult to draw hard boundaries around higher learning....The Commission's view [is that] in the medium to long term, global and South African conditions are likely to push the single co-ordinated system towards a more responsive, dynamic and "fuzzy" relationship between institutions and programmes rather than towards a new binary or stratified system....The Commission [therefore] believes that the primary challenge of a state policy on higher education is not firstly to try and specify the exact system (for example, a stratified, binary or unified structure) but rather to place greater emphasis on obtaining systemic coherence and ensuring diversity through a regulatory environment. The regulatory environment will have several tasks: firstly, to create the conditions that enable optimal levels of co-operation and responsiveness; secondly, to establish a single, co-ordinated national system of policies and procedures to steer the entire higher education system in directions consistent with key economic, social and cultural goals; and thirdly, to facilitate in an orderly fashion the diversity of programme offerings (NCHE, 1996b:85,102-103,165).

The new system will ensure diversity in terms of institutional missions and programme mixes. This should evolve in 'terms of a planned process based on the recognition and pragmatic consideration of current institutional missions and capacities on the one hand, and emerging national and regional needs and priorities on the other' (NCHE, 1996b:167).

Differentiation of mission in a future system will be based on programmes, not institutional types. In the past, learner mobility was restricted by the rigid boundaries that separated the differing institutional types (colleges, technikons and universities) and by the terminal qualifications on offer. Diverse course provision was constrained by a bureaucratically managed, unresponsive and supply-led system of higher education provision. In contrast, the new National Qualifications Framework (NQF) – that was formally established by the *South African Qualifications Authority (SAQA) Act* of 1995 and that bears a strong resemblance to the 1993 proposals by Bird and Elliot for a unified qualifications structure – attempts to resolve all of these constraints by allowing progression and diversity through its credit accumulation and transfer capabilities. The NQF espouses a philosophy of lifelong learning that envisages learners enrolling for modular components of programmes at differing sites of provision and at different moments in their learning lives. These learners will accumulate a flexible combination of credits over time that will eventually earn them the award of a qualification.

Differentiation within a single nationally co-ordinated system will, therefore, be based on institutions developing programme niche areas – centres of excellence – that provide them with a distinct character different from that of neighbouring institutions. This form of differentiation will not be entirely *laissez-faire* and market-driven, but will be linked to government HRD planning and funding strategies and, ultimately, to the needs of the labour market and the country's future economic growth path.

Beginnings of the policy implementation phase

The third historical period under review is the period during which the new ANC government took control of the organs of state power in April 1994. One of the most immediate tasks facing the new leadership in the field of education was the dismantling of the homeland regimes and the apartheid system of education and the creation of a single, national and non-racial education department. This has been one of the new government's greatest educational accomplishments.

Even though the new phase of governance has a seven-year history, the implementation of new HET policy only started much later, after the passing of the *Higher Education Act* in October 1997. The implementation phase, therefore, has been relatively short – just three years. However, the time that has passed since 1994 is very significant because it is during this seven-year period that the true limits of state power really surfaced. Policy propositions prior to this realisation were idealistic and unmediated by the structural and political constraints of the day. These limits on power have inevitably reverberated into the way in which initial policies are now being re-interpreted and implemented.

The current limits on state power have arisen as a consequence of four problems that emerged during this seven-year period. These problems are:

- fiscal restraint and a shift towards conservative macro-economic policy;
- a weak regulatory regime in higher education;
- an unforeseen proliferation of market forces in higher education; and
- the amplification of policy doubt

Each of these problems will now be briefly discussed.

Fiscal restraint and a shift in macro-economic policy

One of the most significant and earliest shifts in ANC policy occurred in June 1996 with the release of the Growth, Employment and Redistribution (GEAR) strategy as the government's official macro-economic dogma, displacing the RDP from its earlier status as the party's social democratic orthodoxy on economic policy. The significance of GEAR was that it privileged the attainment of monetary policy objectives such as the reduction of the state's fiscal deficit and inflation rate at the expense of other important features of the RDP's broad socio-economic platform of policies – particularly those elements in the RDP and *Growth Through Redistribution* doctrine that were premised on co-ordinated market policies, a developmental state, and those strategies that prioritised the provision of basic needs (DoF, 1996). Work by Webster and Adler (1999) highlights the genesis of this shift from what the authors term the 'Left-Keynesian' framework of *Growth Through Redistribution* and the RDP to the conservative macro-economics of GEAR. The roots of this shift lay as far back as November 1993 with the formation of the Transitional Executive Council when ANC officials, along with representatives from the apartheid government's Department of Finance and Reserve Bank, negotiated a secret deal with the World Bank to secure an $850 million loan. In return, the ANC (as the future government) agreed to maintain existing monetary policy, prioritise inflation reduction, contain government expenditure, and desist from raising taxes – the key premises of the future GEAR strategy. Webster and Adler (1999:15) show how these two tendencies – Left-Keynesianism and macro-economic conservatism – ran parallel to each other from 1993 onwards, but with the former having a significant influence over the latter. For example, the initial COSATU *Reconstruction Accord* was redrafted by the ANC in its preparation of the April 1994 RDP election manifesto to include strong references to the new monetarist principles. By June 1996, with the publication of GEAR, this conservative macro-economic framework was the new ANC economic orthodoxy, having effectively neutralised COSATU and Communist Party opposition to these shifts.

The impact of GEAR on the policy debates in the HET sector was also severe. Along with the publication of the government's Medium Term Expenditure Framework (MTEF) in 1997 (that laid out government's intended expenditure patterns and priorities over a three-year period), the impact of these tight fiscal policies meant that the HET sector was unlikely to be allocated more financial resources than before. Total education expenditure has stabilised around 21.3 per cent of total government expenditure. Higher education has consumed 14 per cent of this allocation (Cloete & Bunting, 2000:66). These percentages are very favourable in comparative terms. Exceeding them would be extremely difficult for government to afford or justify.

These limits on state intervention filtered through to HET even during the policy formulation phase. Perhaps the most contrasting feature between the White Paper of 1997 and the 1996 report of the NCHE was the former document's fiscal realism:

> What is not clear, however, is what increases in participation rates for black students, and overall, are possible within the foreseeable future in the context of the government's macro-economic framework and fiscal policies.... It is unlikely that the recent trend of public expenditure growth rates in this sector can be sustained over the next decade, given other pressing social needs.... Despite national fiscal constraints, and the government's commitment to fiscal discipline, the central role of higher education in developing high-level skills and competencies essential for

> social and economic development requires sustained financial investment in the higher education system. Substantial additional costs are associated with greater student participation, redress of current inequities, and the restructuring of existing programmes. These costs will have to be met from a strategic mix of funding sources. These will include system and institutional efficiencies, a greater volume of private contributions, and increased, redistributed and tightly targeted public sector outlays (DoE, 1997a:21,45-46).

A significant shift in focus has therefore occurred – already present in the policy making period of 1997 but amplified later – that higher education transformation could only be brought about through the attainment of greater institutional efficiencies and cost-effectiveness and the redistribution of these savings to targeted transformational interventions. However, as Cloete and Bunting (2000:64) point out, the state has failed to increase the amount allocated to redress through earmarked funding in the 1995-1999 period, and is therefore unlikely to be able to afford a dramatic increase in the near future. The subsidy block grants to institutions still dominate about 88 per cent of government allocations, while the level for earmarked funding has remained relatively stable since 1995 at 12 per cent. In short, fiscal restraint (and lower economic growth rates than initially forecast by GEAR) seriously constrained government's ability to act positively in terms of redressing the inequities inherited from the past by the HET system.

A weak state and weak regulatory regime in higher education

The role accorded the state has changed considerably since the transfer of power to the ANC in April 1994. Prior to this watershed moment, the dominant view of the state within ANC ranks was that it should be a 'developmental state', making strategic interventions to overcome the limits of the market in steering economic and social development in directions consistent with socio-economic priorities.

However, the actual experience of state power has been somewhat different. A more realistic awareness of the weakness of the state has materialised in the post-apartheid period. Netshitenzhe, a prominent ANC intellectual, argues that the weakness and fragility of the state arises

> from the political compromises made, most significantly the reconciliation of both race and class relations that underpinned the settlement in 1990. This compromise has limited the new state's powers to act decisively. South Africa's re-entry into the global economy has also weakened the new state primarily because of the power of financial markets and their "susceptibility to subjective manipulation" (quoted in Kraak, 2001:101).

Capacity problems are perhaps the most limiting factor of the new state. Young and inexperienced 'new guard' cadres entered the state alongside remnants of the 'old guard' without sufficient transfer of the tacit knowledge about state governance from the old to the new. In addition, sufficient policy 'adhesion' has not occurred satisfactorily within the state apparatus. Significant levels of policy doubt exist (discussed in more detail in a later section), particularly with regard to certain policy platforms such as an integrated education and training system, the incorporation of senior secondary schools within the FET band, higher education's incorporation within the NQF and SAQA, and a single, national and co-ordinated HET system; these have not acquired the full support of the civil service.

Two other structural features have limited the power of the state. Firstly, the old apparatuses of the state have remained largely unchanged. For example, the Departments of Education and of Labour were not integrated as expected from the policy texts. This decision has had serious ramifications, most importantly the failure of the new state to discard the political fiefdoms and territorial modes of working that characterised the divide between 'education' and 'training' in the apartheid state. In addition, few meaningful linkages have been established between education, the key economic departments (the Department of Trade and Industry, for example) and the science department (the Department of Arts, Culture, Science and Technology). These divisions within the state continue and seriously hinder the development of a comprehensive and well co-ordinated human resource development strategy for the country. They weaken the possibilities for attaining 'co-ordinated social market' policies founded on the idea of a developmental state – the short-lived RDP being the best example of failed cross-sectoral attempts at policy co-ordination.

Lastly, state power has been considerably weakened by the dissolution and incorporation of the 'Bantustan' and homeland regimes into the central state alongside the simultaneous devolution of power to nine provinces. The first process acted to incorporate an inefficient, bureaucratic and often corrupt Bantustan and homeland civil service within the new central state. The latter process acted to devolve the powers of the developmental state to nine provinces, two of which are governed by opposition parties less committed to official education and training policies.

In short, all of these factors have acted to limit the state's ability to act decisively across all social policy domains, including education and HET.

An unforeseen proliferation of the power of market

A further contributing factor in the decline of the state's role has been the misreading (during the policy formulation process) of the power and speed of the market and individual choice in HET, that together have led to significant changes in the institutional landscape of higher education.

Three related factors have contributed to these changes. Firstly, institutions have been forced to seek new sources of income, given government's refusal to increase their subsidy allocation. Some have enthusiastically taken up government's call for greater responsiveness in meeting priority socio-economic needs. These needs have been interpreted by HET institutions via market signals of what skills are in demand in the labour market. Such changes are occurring in a very uneven way, with some institutions more adept at developing their distinctive programmes and niches than others. As a consequence, a new HET institutional landscape is in the making. Cloete and Bunting (2000) provide a fascinating overview of some of the institutional shifts that are beginning to emerge as a consequence of increased market responsiveness. They identify four new archetypal responses to differentiation:

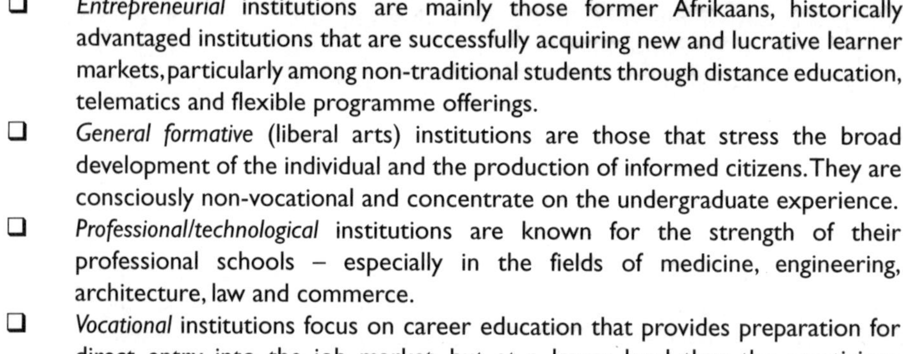

- *Entrepreneurial* institutions are mainly those former Afrikaans, historically advantaged institutions that are successfully acquiring new and lucrative learner markets, particularly among non-traditional students through distance education, telematics and flexible programme offerings.
- *General formative* (liberal arts) institutions are those that stress the broad development of the individual and the production of informed citizens. They are consciously non-vocational and concentrate on the undergraduate experience.
- *Professional/technological* institutions are known for the strength of their professional schools – especially in the fields of medicine, engineering, architecture, law and commerce.
- *Vocational* institutions focus on career education that provides preparation for direct entry into the job market, but at a lower level than the prestigious professions (Cloete & Bunting, 2000).

These descriptions, although tentative, suggest that significant shifts are already taking place in response to market forces that are unassisted by government regulation and steering. These shifts are not necessarily responses to national socio-economic priorities, but often are merely forms of opportunistic competition between institutions trying to capture key market niche areas.

The second yet related market factor in reconfiguring the institutional landscape of HET is student choice, triggered by a greater variety of both public and private institutions open to students of all races and languages. Institutions that previously did not enrol large numbers of African students but that are now successfully doing so are the formerly white Afrikaner institutions and the technikon sector – both of which have received significant increases in African enrolment since the late 1990s. Together with an emerging private higher education system, these institutions have succeeded in poaching African students away from the historically disadvantaged institutions.

Third, student enrolments have fallen dramatically over the past five years – from a high of 605 000 in 1996 to a low of 564 000 in 1999. Reasons provided for this decline include the high cost of tuition fees, the dramatic drop in the number of matriculants with university exemption certificates, the perceived decline in the quality of public HET, and the consequent growth in private and international HET in South Africa (see Cloete & Bunting, 2000).

All of these market factors – responsiveness, enhanced student choice, and declining total enrolments – have combined to create dramatic shifts in the institutional landscape of HET. The changes have also impacted unevenly, triggering expansionary and contractionary effects across the system. Table 6.1 illustrates the uneven impact of these changed enrolments on the institutional landscape:

Table 6.1 Changes in Total HET Enrolment: 1995 compared to 1999	
Historically White University (Afrikaans)	36 000
Historically White University (English)	4 000
Historically Black University	-22 000
UNISA	- 21 000
Historically White Technikon	15 000
Historically Black Technikon	12 000
Technikon SA	-20 000
Total Change	**4 000**

Source: Cloete & Bunting, 2000:23

It is precisely this dramatic and unregulated institutional differentiation that led the government to appoint the CHE Task Team to investigate the Size and Shape of a future HET system. Interestingly, the key recommendations of this investigation have sought to stem the unregulated reconfiguration of institutions by restricting the shifts to three rigid institutional types. Whereas the Cloete and Bunting typologies are defined in terms of programme or niche differentiation, the CHE has proposed a stratified model of institutional differentiation.

An unsure state and the amplification of policy doubt in HET

The amplification of policy doubt in the past two years has also contributed to the weakening of state power. In the July 1999 to February 2001 period, the state appeared unsure of its direction, vacillating between two diametrically opposed frameworks – a 'single co-ordinated' or a 'stratified' system of HET.

Earlier sections of this chapter highlighted the influence of the high skills thesis and popular democratic demands and their careful cohabitation in new government legislation. Earlier discussion also noted a third discourse, stratification thinking – a residual set of ideas from the old order. The key dynamic that occurred in this current historical period – the late 1990s into the new millennium – has been the dramatic turnaround in the influence of these three discourses. This occurred primarily because the discursive balancing under the persuasive call for settlement never fully succeeded. While it had the effect of forcing these very different discourses into unresolved cohabitation, it also distorted the eventual outcomes in later years. For example, the high skills argument never acquired the position of orthodoxy needed for its successful implementation. This was in part a consequence of the muting of the social and economic demands it expressed. Left-wing critics such as Wolpe (1994) opposed much of what he saw (pejoratively) as an economic rationalist discourse because it privileged the renewal of a new form of capitalist exploitation – globalisation. However, Wolpe and others who opposed the high skills thesis weakened its appeal without providing an alternative theorisation of the education-economy nexus.

Wolpe's opposition to the high skills route was joined by a different set of propositions – not necessarily left-wing and anti-capitalist – that emanated from within academe and that saw the changes suggested by economic rationalism as the commercialisation and privatisation of higher education (see Subotzky, 2000; Jansen, 2000b; Orr, 1997; see also the Australian papers referred to earlier in the text).

However, this failure to privilege the high skills route was not only the failing of the policy formulation process or of the Department of Education. It was compounded by the glaring absence of a coherent set of economic growth, industrial, and human resources development policies that would have given support to the high skills imperative.

Underpinning all of this policy slippage was the significant shift in macro-economic policy from the social democratic platforms of the *Reconstruction Accord, Growth Through Redistribution* and the RDP to the more conservative monetary policies of GEAR. Ironically, this shift confirms the scepticism of left critics who have questioned the political orientation of the high skills thesis. The regularity of the accusation that a neo-liberal economic rationalism underpinned much of the HET policy framework rose sharply in the wake of the demise of the high skills thesis after GEAR's launch in June 1996.

Likewise, according to its proponents popular democratic discourse was not satisfactorily incorporated within policy. Under the persuasive call for settlement, the new state had in essence signed away the possibility of strong redistributive action to redress the institutional inequalities created by apartheid. Expressions of equity and redress in the policy and legislation were, as a consequence of settlement, merely ameliorative and not substantive. In response, popular democratic discourse formed the basis of an emerging oppositional movement to the ANC government's new policies on HET. The equity and redress voice outside of the official policy arena grew stronger and more strident in the period under review, as one after another of the historically disadvantaged institutions succumbed to crisis, driven mainly by growing institutional debt, mismanagement, poor leadership, and on-going staff and student protest. This dissident discourse – vocally articulated by the Vice-Chancellors and Deputy Vice-Chancellors of most historically disadvantaged institutions (HDIs) – argued that many of the problems experienced by HDIs after 1994 were due to the absence of any substantive programme of radical redress for these institutions.

The final outcome of this interplay between discursive tension and state incapacity in HET has taken three forms:

- ❑ There was no explicit pursuit of a major programme of institutional redress – fiscal constraint and conservative macro-economic policy disallowed this.
- ❑ There was no explicit pursuit of the high skills route that was predicated on a massified and unskilled workforce – fiscal constraint, the dramatic decline in HET enrolments, and a lack of consensus over the validity of the high skills route disallowed this.
- ❑ The new state did not use any of its envisaged planning and co-ordination levers – lack of capacity disallowed this.

Lurking behind the imminent demise of both of the high skills and popular democratic discourses lay the residual arguments from the old order about the utility of stratification in resolving educational problems in post-secondary education and training. The next section will show how this residual discourse was resurrected – albeit temporarily – in the period July 1999 to February 2001, partly as a consequence of the presumed non-viability of the other two discourses in shaping HET policy and implementation.

The consequence of all of this discursive tension was that there was no strong binding consensus forged across all HET constituencies in support of the official policy enacted by the new government. It was a period characterised by a lack of policy adhesion.

A vacillating state (July 1999 to February 2001)

The historical roots of a residual discourse on stratification

An earlier section has already described the historical influence of stratification thinking in South African educational reform in the 1980s and early 1990s. This section will show that such thinking was never entirely displaced from the domain of educational policy discourse, including the policy formulation processes led by the new government from 1994 onwards.

The most explicit display of stratification thinking emerged during the consultation processes of the NCHE. Opposition to the NCHE proposal for a single co-ordinated system of HET based on *programme* rather than *institutional* differentiation did emerge. It had to do with the insecurities of the HDIs that they would be disadvantaged yet again because of their lack of capacity to respond creatively to new programme offerings. Their insecurities are evident in the minutes of a meeting between the NCHE, the Committee of University Principals (CUP), and the Committee of Technikon Principals (CTP) on 1 June 1996 (NCHE, 1996c). The minutes refer to the terms 'flexible' and 'functional' differentiation, that were catch-phrases used during the NCHE deliberations to signify a 'unified' and a 'stratified' system, respectively. Severe tensions and differences of opinion over differentiation had been evident in the NCHE and between the NCHE and CUP prior to this meeting. A compromise position was to emerge on differentiation at this meeting. The compromise was premised on a middle-ground formulation that supported functional differentiation in the short term to medium term, but that was not principally opposed to a transition to flexible differentiation in the longer term. Professor Balintulo (then at the University of Durban-Westville) made it clear that elements within the HDI Forum (a committee of Vice-Chancellors from the HDIs) leaned toward the middle position. The logic of this support was based on the following arguments:

- The HDIs would be outmanoeuvred by the historically white institutions (HWIs) if flexible differentiation were imposed immediately. The HDIs simply did not have the capacity and experience to bid for flexible programme arrangements as effectively as the HWIs. Hence, in the short term, the HDI Forum insisted that the status quo should remain.
- There was no principled opposition to flexible differentiation in the longer term, especially once the HDIs had received capacity-building and redress support to enable them to bid competitively and flexibly for programmes across the full spectrum (NCHE, 1996c).

The interim *Discussion Document* of the NCHE, released in April 1996, elaborated on these divisions between supporters of functional and flexible differentiation. It reported that elements within the technikon sector had made submissions that argued strongly for the retention and reinforcement of the technikons as a distinct sector with a unique mission within higher education. The case of the technikons' support for functional differentiation rested heavily on:

> ... the need to ensure an appropriate mix of graduates and diplomates to meet South Africa's broad human resource needs. The view that the current mix is skewed in favour of university graduates, and the proposition that "career education" is best ensured and protected within a higher education sector dedicated to this purpose, have been put forward. The argument is for the retention of functional differentiation with an altered balance to enhance the technikon's role.... Technikons would have a delineated function in the offering of career and vocational education (incorporating experiential learning, and via programmes designed in conjunction with the relevant "employers" grouping) and in development and product-related research. Universities, in contrast, would focus on general formative education, intellectual preparation for professions, and basic and applied research. This broad functional differentiation would determine the location of new programmes linked to emerging needs, and there would be a phased orderly reassignment of existing programmes mislocated in terms of these broad criteria where this is required. In practice, this would mean universities and technikons taking responsibility for different programme types and levels on the single qualifications framework (NCHE, 1996a:55).

Under flexible differentiation, in contrast, differentiation would occur in terms of institutional missions and programme mixes. It would evolve in terms of a planned process based on emerging national and regional needs and not the inherited sectoral location of the institution (NCHE, 1996a:56-57).

The final report of the NCHE, released in mid-1996, fudged these differences by adopting the middle-ground position referred to above. The NCHE resolution reads:

> The Commission's task is not to propose a unified, binary or stratified institutional structure for the single co-ordinated system, but to recommend a set of transitional arrangements that will hold while national and regional needs are clarified, planning capacities are developed and institutional development proceeds. The Commission believes that the system should recognise, in name and in broad function and mission, the existence of universities, technikons and colleges as types of institutions offering higher education programmes. But these institutional types should not be regarded as discrete sectors with mutually exclusive missions and programme offerings. The new system will evolve through a planned process which recognises current institutional missions and capacities, addresses the distortions created by apartheid, and responds to emerging regional and national needs. At a later stage in this evolution, it may be decided whether the new system should retain the distinction between universities, technikons and colleges, change the nature of the distinction, and increase or decrease the number of institutional types (NCHE, 1996b:15-16).

The Commission saw their proposal for a single co-ordinated system of HET as occupying the middle ground in an often-heated contestation over differentiation. In this formulation, the concerns of those supporting functional differentiation could be reconciled with the arguments for greater flexibility. The NCHE conceived of its proposal as pragmatic, providing a continuum along which the system could gradually move, from 'functional differentiation' towards a truly single system with softened boundaries (NCHE, 1996b:283).

Nonetheless, the dissenting voice remained. In the final 1996 report of the NCHE, Brian Figaji, Rector of Peninsula Technikon, published a minority report that expressed opposition to Colleges of Further Education encroaching onto HET turf by offering career and vocational education at HET level. More significantly, Figaji also opposed the notion of differentiation being based on programme rather than institution. His view was that if any institution could offer any programme, it would 'negate the current institutional missions and educational cultures' of existing institutions such as technikons: 'The result of this scheme is going to be "academic creep" at an unprecedented scale with vocational and career education once again sidelined in favour of the higher status "academic" programmes' (NCHE, 1996b:318).

Figaji has since led the call for opposition to the notion of programme differentiation. In a 1999 lecture, he warned against the dangers of a policy framework that inevitably would push institutions towards convergence and homogeneity – exactly the opposite of the differentiation desired by policy. In his speech, he again repeated the case for a 'higher education system with different institutional types such as colleges, universities and technikons, each with its own distinct mission and programme' (Figaji, 1999:15).

The dissent around differentiation, along with other factors such as the negative impact of market forces on the institutional landscape of HET, the inability of government to manage the key planning levers, and the lack of policy adhesion within the state itself, were all precursors to the turnaround in policy that occurred in the period July 1999 to February 2001.

The proposals of the CHE

The launch of the Size and Shape Task Team was a response to a call by the new Minister of Education, Professor Kader Asmal, in July 1999 for the review and reform of the institutional landscape of HET. The Task Team was set up in January 2000. It published a draft discussion document in April 2000 and a final report in July 2000 that articulated a distinct set of recommendations to the Minister regarding the reconfiguration of the HET institutional landscape.

The point of departure for the Task Team was the existing HET policy framework. However, the Task Team argued that this framework on its own was not sufficient. Events since the passing of the *Higher Education Act* in 1997 necessitated a rethink on certain issues. The Task Team argued that while the 1997 Higher Education White Paper provided a powerful and robust framework for the transformation of higher education, it did not and could not anticipate a number of conditions and developments that had since emerged. These included:

- institutional responses that exacerbated the inherited fragmentation and incoherence of the system and the inefficient and ineffective utilisation of resources;
- competition between public institutions around programme offerings and student enrolments that overshadowed co-operation and led towards homogeneity and sameness in an environment of declining enrolments;
- the pace of change in instructional modes at various institutions;
- weaknesses and capacity problems in national and institutional planning processes that in the short term compromised the efficacy of these instruments to steer and regulate higher education;
- inadequate senior and middle-level management capacities within the system;
- the diversification of funding and sources of revenue and the extent to which state funding had become an increasingly limited instrument for steering and regulation of higher education;

- the excessive marketisation and commercialisation of higher education;
- the decline in students with matriculation exemptions; and
- the lack of adequate regulation of private higher education that could have adverse consequences for a vibrant public higher education sector (CHE, 2000b:33-34).

These conditions, the Task Team reported, threatened important policy goals and required an immediate response. South Africa could not continue to function on the basis of an inefficient, fragmented and unplanned set of institutional roles.

The recommendations on differentiation

The recommendations made by the Task Team were controversial and to a large extent in conflict with the essence of the new HET policy framework. At the heart of the Task Team proposal was the promotion of a highly diversified HET system premised on institutional differentiation rather than programme differentiation as advocated in all of the previous policy texts. The Size and Shape report proposed a new three-tiered institutional landscape. The three institutional types were defined primarily by prescriptions imposed on their core teaching and research functions:

- *A bedrock HET* institution was defined as a dedicated undergraduate teaching institution with limitations imposed on the extent and spread of its postgraduate and research programmes. Its key function was to provide high quality undergraduate teaching to a wide constituency of learners.
- *A comprehensive institution* has significant postgraduate and research capabilities, with its primary function being the production of new scientific knowledge and the training of the country's future cadre of high-skill graduates.
- *An extensive Masters and limited Doctoral institution* was defined as an in-between institutional structure with greater resources available than the bedrock campuses, that could offer extensive Masters programmes, but with similar limitations to those applicable to the 'bedrocks' in relation to Doctoral programmes and knowledge production functions (research).

Support for the CHE proposals

Support for the CHE's three-tiered model did emerge, unsurprisingly, from the technikon sector. This sector, particularly through its mouthpiece organisation, the Committee of Technikon Principals, was notably enthusiastic about the key components of the CHE proposals. In its formal response to the Task Team report, the CTP gave the key proposals its full support:

> The CTP welcomes the report of the CHE Task Team on Size and Shape. There are many areas of dysfunctionality in the Higher Education sector and the reconfiguration of this sector is long overdue. The CTP sees

> the report of the Task Team as the beginning of a necessary process which will eventually result in a more streamlined and cost-effective Higher Education sector, which will provide and promote quality career education and research, and relevantly-educated and appropriately-skilled human resources for the development needs of a transforming South Africa and the changing world (CTP, 2000:1).

With regard to institutional typology, the CTP gave approval to the more 'flexible and acceptable three-tier system which most institutions would find easier to engage with' than the five-tiered structure which the CHE *Discussion Document* of April 2000 had proposed (CTP, 2000:2). On differentiation, the CTP noted, 'There is a strong argument for differentiation and diversity in the Report which the CTP fully supports, because it would facilitate more effective responses from institutions to the various social needs of the country' (CTP, 2000:2).

The CTP was particularly encouraged by the Task Team support for the idea of a University of Technology. It saw this recommendation as a way of putting technikons in South Africa in 'line with the rest of the world where such institutions are called Technical Universities, Institutes of Technology or Universities of Technology' (CTP, 2000:3).

Opposition from stakeholders

The CHE recommendations, as could be expected, also triggered strong opposition from key stakeholders in HET, particularly from the South African Universities Vice-Chancellors Association (SAUVCA, formerly the CUP), which argued:

> The essence of [the] SAUVCA submission concerns firstly, a rejection of the three-tier system proposed by the CHE Report and a renewed call for an appropriately regulated policy environment which allows for negotiated mandates for differentiation based on programmes.... The CHE report principally anchors its key implementation proposal upon a three-tier, externally-imposed institutional typology to achieve system differentiation that is flawed on both educational and strategic grounds.... The core three-tier institutional typology is conceptually problematic as it establishes artificial dichotomies between research and teaching as well as between undergraduate and post-graduate provision. Further, it introduces pre-determined, unhelpful grading and ranking of institutions within imposed status-bound hierarchies which will be viewed negatively by employers, staff and students. It will further entrench the infamous South African HAI/HDI discourse ... [and] destroy the pockets of research developed to date which will in turn depress the culture of scholarship in the "bedrocks" and trap [staff] in de-motivating environments (SAUVCA, 2000:1,5).

SAUVCA's opposition to the proposals was essentially two-fold. First, there was concern that the three-tiered system would simply replicate the racial differentiation imposed by apartheid education. Secondly, the proposals were seen as a reversal in policy orientation, away from the single co-ordinated system emphasised in earlier policy texts towards a classical social stratification model of provision.

Conclusion: The National Plan

The release of the Ministry of Education's *National Plan for Higher Education* in February 2001 provides the final moment of policy slippage, although in a more desirable direction. At the heart of the National Plan is a reaffirmation of the key principles of HET policy as contained in the White Paper of 1997 and the Act of 1997. The National Plan also firmly rejects the rigid structural differentiation of the CHE report, although it adds a new element in the on-going policy debate about institutional differentiation.

The Plan reaffirms three key policy goals. These are:

- to increase participation rates from the current 15 per cent to 20 per cent over the next ten to fifteen years;
- the need for equity in HET provision, and requires institutions to set equity targets specifically in areas where black and women students and staff are under-represented; and
- the commitment to a single co-ordinated national system that is simultaneously diverse.

The document adds two further riders to the process of institutional restructuring: It aims to formulate a plan for a new institutional landscape through mergers and regional collaboration by December 2001. Secondly, it proposes the retention of the binary divide between technikons and universities for at least the next five years, primarily to limit the extent of institutional creep and the drift towards programme uniformity (DoE, 2001:1,14-15).

The tendency towards uniformity of provision, according to the Plan, 'is worrying'. There has been little evidence of attempts by institutions, it argues, to identify unique institutional strengths and niche areas, either existing or potential, that would differentiate between institutions:

> In fact, other than the broad distinction between universities and technikons in terms of the career-oriented and technological focus of the latter, there is little else to distinguish between and within the aspirations of the university and technikon sectors. It would not be an exaggeration to suggest that many institutions aspire to a common "gold" standard as represented by the major research institutions, both nationally and internationally (DoE, 2001:50).

The Plan identifies three determinants of the tendency towards uniformity. These are: the absence of planning capacity at institutional level to identify unique niche areas; the lack of a strong regulatory framework designed to ensure diversity; and the highly competitive and imitative behaviour of institutions as witnessed in the past decade (DoE, 2001:51).

The solutions to these problems do not lie with the CHE's proposed rigid system of structural differentiation 'which introduces an element of rigidity which will preclude institutions from building on their strengths to respond to social and economic needs' in unique and differing ways (DoE, 2001:54). The solution lies in a return to mission and programme differentiation as outlined in the 1997 White Paper that would allow institutions to define a unique developmental and programme trajectory for themselves in a way that would not 'lock them into a predetermined institutional structure' as would be the case with the CHE proposals (DoE, 2001:54). The tendency towards uniformity will be restricted by levers, sanctions and incentives built into the 'planning grid' proposed by the National Plan, that would limit provision in areas that were duplicative or inefficient in the use of scarce resources.

However, the most significant element in the National Plan with regard to institutional differentiation is its concern that the programme distinctions between technikons and universities – career-oriented versus general formative and professional degree programmes – have been dramatically eroded. Technikons have gradually increased their degree offerings both at undergraduate and postgraduate levels. This has led in turn to a number of technikons requesting a change in status to become 'universities of technology' (DoE, 2001:57).

The Ministry's response to these developments has been to attempt to halt this erosion by retaining the binary divide between technikons and universities for at least the next five years as 'two types of institutions offering different kinds of higher education programmes' (DoE, 2001:57).

There has always been ambiguity on the question of the binary divide (as discussed earlier in this chapter), and the 1996 NCHE report and 1997 White Paper proposed a careful and balanced approach to the issue by speaking of a gradualist continuum of provision with the distinctions between colleges, technikons and universities retained in the short term and with shifts to a single system with permeable boundaries in the long term. The decision by the Ministry to retain the binary divide for five years is therefore in line with previous policy formulations. Yet it is clearly also a response to the demands by technikons for their distinctive contribution – career-oriented tertiary provision – to be retained. The rejection of the rigid structural differentiation proposals of the CHE is clearly a response to the widespread opposition to those proposals from the university sector. The Ministry's National Plan, therefore, has attempted to straddle the middle ground. The Department, however, is remaining silent (as did the NCHE) on the strategic desirability of a strong binary divide in South Africa. What this defensive position fails to take into account are the new education and training demands of globalisation, as was so clearly outlined by Gibbons et al. in an earlier section of this chapter – demands that act to differentiate less between the institutional typologies of university and technikon but that emphasise a higher level of education and training competencies across all tertiary institutions. The extension of a rigid binary divide in South Africa will have the effect of delaying the technological upgrading of many technikons. These institutions are not currently comparable with the former polytechnics in the United Kingdom and Australia, who through less severe functional differentiation as well as institutional creep compared favourably with the university sector in those countries in terms of research and graduate output, qualifications of staff, and linkages with industry. Their recent upgrade into or incorporation within universities and 'universities of technology' were logical responses to the higher-level technological requirements of globalisation – something that many of the current South African technikons are not in a position to achieve.

The ultimate assessment of the National Plan, however, lies with its strongly articulated commitment to implement policy, and in particular to implement the levers, sanctions and incentives that will steer the entire system in the direction of a diverse yet single co-ordinated national system of HET. The document asserts strongly that the framework outlined 'is not open for further consultation. The focus must now be firmly on implementation' (DoE, 2001:13).

The Ministry, through its Plan, has begun to articulate a determination to act decisively to bring out the desired reforms. Institutional 'voluntarism has failed to encourage these objectives'. The only way to make any real headway is through 'direct state intervention and stronger signals from government' (DoE, 2001:81). Key areas requiring state intervention include: a reduction in the total number of institutions in the country through mergers; instituting stronger and more cost-effective forms of regional collaboration; attaining greater efficiencies across the entire system; and implementing the new funding and programme planning levers that will steer the system in the desired directions as of January 2003.

The National Plan is the final moment in the on-going cycle of policy development, adaptation, reinterpretation and slippage that has characterised the past decade. It is a positive development in that it reasserts the policy fundamentals that acquired widespread stakeholder support in the mid-1990s and that have as yet to be implemented. It puts an end to the institutional rigidities and stratification thinking proposed by the CHE. It displays greater policy maturity, acknowledging the 'implementation vacuum' that has existed since the passing of the Act – due largely to the capacity constraints of both the national Department of Education and the HET institutions (DoE, 2001:8). It displays a new determination to carry through the implementation of key policy objectives.

This realignment of direction is a necessary but not sufficient condition for the revival of the high skills thesis and for an improvement in our future economic prospects in a rapidly globalising economy. Alongside the consolidation of a massified and nationally co-ordinated system of HET provision, the high skills route will also require a return to the co-ordinated market policies implicit in earlier ANC economic texts, particularly a renewed commitment by government to link educational policies to a wider basket of macro-economic, industrial and labour market reforms. Only when these complementary policies are implemented simultaneously and interlock in a virtuous circle of economic growth will a high skills equilibrium materialise. The jury is still out on the viability of this option.

Chapter 7

Reflections from the Inside: Key Policy Assumptions and How They have Shaped Policy Making and Implementation in South Africa, 1994-2000

Ihron Rensburg

In preparation for the important Round Table discussion for which the precursor to this chapter was written, I pondered for some time the question: What is the most appropriate methodology for offering useful reflections on the policy and implementation process from a viewpoint within the state bureaucracy? Does one recount all the policies and their implementation, successful or otherwise? Does one provide insight into a limited set of key policy moments? Or does one offer a reflection on key policy assumptions that framed the development of policies and their implementation? I selected the latter approach, principally because I believe that future development and implementation processes can be informed by the elucidation and elaboration of some of the most critical assumptions and by debating these more widely

First, it is important to situate the current moment. Essentially two policy periods characterise the last six years. The first of these periods, 1994-1999, overlaps with the period of governance of the first democratically-elected government and accounts for the first five years of policymaking and implementation. This period was marked by:

- a considerable emphasis on state building and system development that comprised creating new post-apartheid governance institutions such as the one national and nine provincial departments of education, and the development and promulgation of policies, laws, regulations, and national norms and standards;
- symbolic change statements and announcements to signal the transition to a new order while managing the fears of national minorities;
- critical systems change programmes such as the equitable distribution of teachers across all schools and the development and implementation of a new post-apartheid outcomes-based curriculum beginning in the early school grades (DoE,, 1999b, 2000a).

The second period, beginning mid-1999 and continuing to the present, is marked by an overall governmental shift in emphasis to accelerated policy implementation focusing on service delivery to the poorest citizens (Mbeki, 1999, 2000). In education this focus is now reflected in the elaboration of policies, laws, regulations, national norms and standards, and their elucidation into targeted and implementable education programmes such as the *Tirisano* programmes and the review and streamlining of key policy decisions made during the first period (DoE, 1999a, 1999c). During this period there appears to be a reduced appetite for state building and system development type activities such as White Papers and other policy papers.

It is against this background that I will now discuss several critical assumptions – as problematic as they have turned out to be – that have framed and shaped our programme of education change. The intention of this contribution is not to lament but to unveil, from a perspective within the state, issues that will be critical as the country takes the next steps in policy development and implementation. Also, it is important to observe that in contemporary South Africa we are faced in many respects with a difficult and alarming situation that is pitting the emergent state against the mass media and other contemporary public commentators. Consequently, many of the ideas and much of the analysis that some of us within the bureaucracy may offer simply falls on deaf ears. In that respect one hopes that the conversations precipitated at and by the Round Table may lead to a more substantive discourse in the public education policy domain.

Identity changes: from national liberation struggle to national reconstruction and development

Let us then turn to the first of these fundamental assumptions. Few of us fully understood how our anti-apartheid and national liberation struggle identities would be integrated into our new identities as national public service managers. Moving to a state building programme clearly requires a whole new set of predispositions – an analytical frame associated with creating and occupying, as some will suggest, the high ground of a new state in which one no longer represents only the interests of the majority of the people (and of course the national liberation struggle), but in which one is now clearly engaged in a process of state building. I will elaborate below some of these policy moments to demonstrate the somewhat contradictory nature of the programme that was embarked upon in the last six years.

This development is worth noting particularly in the case of curriculum change. Note that the development, design and implementation of the new curriculum has its theoretical and epistemological roots, ironically enough, not within the new and emerging state – although it is now legitimated by it – but within the anti-apartheid and national liberation struggle. Its elaboration into a change programme, however, has its roots in the emerging state. Let me demonstrate the challenges brought upon us by the assumption of our new identities. As senior state bureaucrats, we were charged with the duty and determined to turn an anti-apartheid and national liberation struggle framework and concept model for a post-apartheid curriculum into a change programme. This often brought us into sharp conflict with a range of actors: the mass media, the former ruling class and now the opposition bloc to government, contemporary public commentators, policy analysts, and even some of the ruling parties' own allies. The mass media, always interested in eye-catching headlines and less interested in the complex and painful process of post-apartheid reconstruction, would focus attention on poor policy implementation. Former ruling and now opposition parties would beat the drum of sliding quality and standards as we aggressively pursued the achievement of our equity goals. Contemporary public commentators and policy analysts were less interested in the mechanics and detail and conflict that went with post-apartheid policy making and system development than in the impact of these on real classrooms. At the same time, allies of the ruling party were keen on seeing the immediate rather than the deferred impact of government's progressive policies.

It is worth noting here that state building and systems development are about selecting policy options based upon the best available information, and elaborating these into change programmes. It seems to me that many of our contemporary critics, policy analysts and even some allies of the ruling party might still be trapped in the pre-1994 moment – the pre-policy selection debate – and are not adequately interrogating the post-apartheid identity changes in which policies have to be selected and elaborated into change programmes.

Notwithstanding these observations, it is difficult to conclude definitively that our conversations about curriculum change in South Africa in the last four or five years have resulted in a deeply epistemological debate about curriculum change between those seeking fundamental change and those engaged in a deep philosophical debate. It is only in the last nine to twelve months that I personally can discern an awakening and a positing of some of the future directions and alternatives to Curriculum 2005, our flagship post-apartheid outcomes-based curriculum transformation programme. Much of the critique until now has focused on the strategy of our curriculum change programme and on problems with its implementation, not on its epistemological and theoretical foundations. The more recent criticisms have shifted focus to the underlying foundations and organisation of that programme. It is clear that a substantive part of these criticisms are valid, and that they will be considered as we refine the programme's organisation and structure and refocus its implementation. For example, some of the criticism is now assisting us to streamline the unnecessarily complex design features of the curriculum, to achieve a better balance between horizontal curriculum integration concerns and the vertical conceptual progression of learners within a learning area, and to reduce the complexity and unnecessary jargon of the national curriculum statement.

Some criticism has not been helpful, however, such as suggestions that implementation was not well thought through. Any review of the period of implementation must take account of the dramatic impact of massive over-expenditure on salaries in 1997/98. Unanticipated, this wreaked havoc on planning, resulting in meltdowns in expenditures on teacher development, subject advisory services and learning support materials. Other areas also suffered, including expenditure on early childhood development, special education, adult basic education, and building maintenance. A further criticism focused on the impact of the new curriculum statement on subjects such as history and geography, since they were now integrated within the new learning area called human and social sciences. This line of critique seemed to be misplaced, since the design of the curriculum in question focused on the compulsory general school education band (Reception Year through to Grade 9). The point here is that the educational and curriculum goals of compulsory general education differ from that of the further education band that follows. Critique must therefore be focused first on the fundamentals – viz., what are the goals of compulsory general school education? – and then go on to examine the technical aspects of design features of the curriculum. I return to this matter below.

I wish to turn next to what can be loosely organised under the question, what holds the national education system together? This question arose recently in an education policy conference that reflected on the Commission for Higher Education's recommendations on the future size and shape of our higher education system. I wish to elaborate on this matter here, precisely because it lays bare several other assumptions that have informed our education change programme.

National, provincial and institutional: a three-tier education system?

Let me open up this line of reflection by asking a question: Given the assumption during the 1993/94 period of a unitary national state as the driver of post-apartheid reconstruction and development, do we now have unfettered national competence in the education change programme in South Africa? Put differently, do we have unfettered provincial or institutional (school, college, university, technikon) competence in the education change programme in South Africa? What is the balance or distribution of roles, responsibilities and powers between the national, provincial and institutional levels of governance in education? Are these levels in alignment with each other? Note that in respect of the institutional level, significant roles, responsibilities and powers have been assigned to all institutions. Part of the analyses of the emerging state in South Africa must focus on who leads change, in education and across the board. While the policy domain of higher education has traditionally been confronted with finding an appropriate national response to the leadership and public accountability roles of the state and those of institutional autonomy and academic freedom, this matter has now emerged with some force in relation to schools and colleges. This was unforeseen, and is now affecting quite substantively the leadership role of the state in education change. Add to this dimension the somewhat unplanned for influence of provincial governments in general and further education policy and change, and the question arises even more forcefully: Who leads, and how is that leadership exerted in South Africa? And what does this mean for those leading and managing change at each of these three levels?

Unfunded policy mandates: policy, programmes and the fiscus

A particular manifestation of this phenomenon is the set of problems that have emerged around budgeting and policy – *viz.*, unfunded policy mandates. This matter was precipitated sharply when several provincial governments massively overspent, particularly on personnel costs in 1997/98. To elaborate, work in the first five years assumed unfettered national competence so our state building and system development included the development of a wide range of necessary post-apartheid education policies, laws, regulations, national norms and standards, and programmes. Yet, (especially but not only) because of the massive provincial overspending referred to above, many of these policies and programmes remain unfunded or poorly funded and therefore were slowly or poorly implemented.

It is important to insert into the discussion at this point a related and critical policy assumption that did not materialise during this critical period. All senior managers worked for most of the first five years on the assumption that their substantive post-apartheid state building and system development programmes would be accompanied by an expansionary rather than an austere macroeconomic and fiscal framework that would free considerable resources for South Africa's reconstruction and development programme (ANC, 1994c). However, government's controversial Growth, Employment and Redistribution strategy (GEAR) replaced its Reconstruction and Development Programme (RDP) as the macroeconomic and fiscal policy framework (DoF, 1996). Many senior managers publicly and privately contested the new framework, introducing a significant lag between policy announcement and policy implementation. It was only much later, with the introduction of the *Public Finance Management Act* in 1999, that the stick was introduced to bind senior managers to the new macroeconomic and fiscal framework. Clearly then, the impact of post-apartheid education change was limited by inadequate consideration of implementation, especially the three-tier education system. It is this policy weakness – bringing policy and programmes in line with budgets – that is a substantive focus of attention during the second five years of democratic governance.

The interpreters: human capacities that lead and implement change

Let me next turn to policy assumptions about our human capacities to interpret and implement the post-apartheid education programme. In this area a whole set of assumptions have informed the programmes of the last six years, assumptions that are significantly out of line with the *de facto* situation. While pre-1994 education planning was shaped by the assumption of a national unitary government and a centralised education policy, planning and financing mandate and capacity, the post-1994 Constitution laid the basis for a new challenge. It created an education authority comprising one national and nine provincial departments. The consequence of this largely unforeseen situation is wide-ranging competencies and varying abilities to plan and implement education change programmes across our national education system. I am suggesting that this is in part the outcome of inadequate early appreciation of the post-apartheid governance regime and its human capacity requirements.

Human capacity in terms of staffing needs at the policy development, policy making and policy implementation levels is one thing; the ability to interpret and lead in this new policy regime brought upon us by the Constitution is another. During the first five years there were varied interpretations of this new and somewhat unexpected policy regime among senior managers in national and provincial government. Furthermore, the vast majority of these senior managers come from an anti-apartheid and national liberation movement whose culture was one of democratic centralism, with an emphasis upon centralism rather than localised voluntarism. This experience and culture clearly impacted upon the interpretation of the new policy regime. Having made this observation, it is difficult not to conclude that what we have seen during the first five years is a kind of voluntaristic interpretation of the new policy regime as well as a voluntaristic engagement with policy development and policy implementation among senior managers. Some individual senior managers have explored more substantively than others the spaces between national, provincial and institutional mandates and competencies. Some managers have simply taken for granted that provincial systems have unfettered competencies; other managers have simply assumed the opposite – viz., that the national system has an unfettered mandate and competencies in policy development, policy making and policy implementation. Witness the decentralised roles anticipated for schools in the *South African Schools Act* of 1996, and the centralising role of Curriculum 2005 (see below). I am suggesting that if there is one area that is worth exploring, then that is the role of senior managers as interpreters of the new policy regime. I am also suggesting that part of the weakness of the emerging South African state is precisely this: the absence of adequate and consistent leadership – not prescription – in policy development and policy implementation. So once more the question arises: What holds the system together?

Democratic institutional governance or autonomous and atomised schools and colleges?

Let me illustrate this point further through the *South African Schools Act* of 1996. I am suggesting here that we should ask the same question in relation to the 28,500 schools and colleges – viz., what holds the system together? What binds them into a national system? And similarly, do school governors and school managers have unfettered mandates and competencies? The *South African Schools Act* allocates substantive roles, powers and responsibilities to school governing bodies (SGBs), especially those declared as Section 21 schools. Note that those able to take on Section 21 duties are in the main those schools that were classified as Model C schools before 1994, were the best resourced, and served in the main our white communities.

The original intent with the *South African Schools Act* was to continue where the anti-apartheid and national liberation struggle left things in 1993/94 – viz., the creation at school and college level of Parent-Teacher-Student Associations (PTSAs). These PTSAs were originally created in the 1980s as organs of people's power and as an alternative to the apartheid state's school committees. They were to act as centres of localised power that would operate independently of the apartheid state and would lead an anti-apartheid education for liberation (1980/81) and People's Education (1985-92) programme.

The irony is that we have recreated PTSAs in the new system, and we have SGBs and therefore schools that can function independently of the post-apartheid state and outside of its policy imperatives. Specifically, in respect of the Section 21 schools that are principally the elite public schools and that serve communities in the upper quintile in terms of socio-economic status, we can ask: to what extent are they part of the national system and national education project? Similarly, we can ask about the schools that serve our people in the bottom four quintiles in terms of socio-economic status. To what extent are SGBs (and therefore schools) functional in respect of the policy objectives of democratic governance and participation? To what extent do they share and understand national education imperatives and the national education project?

This matter is especially relevant in the light of Micheal Young's argument about the need to shift emphasis from overarching policy and systems development matters to support for and a focus on institutional change as an alternative route for building and expanding participation. But how do we apply this proposition to the situation in South Africa where enormous powers have been transferred to these institutions? Until now the majority of Section 21 schools have displayed little enthusiasm for promoting open access, admission and participation by the majority of learners. In fact, they have preferred to put up new walls and to substitute race-based admission policies with policies such as high school fees, stringent admissions policies, exclusionary language polices and watertight geographical feeder zones. This matter aside, though, how do these schools and colleges become part of the national education project when we have already scripted for them roles ranging from semi-autonomy to full autonomy within the national schools and colleges system?

I am suggesting that one of the lenses through which we can reflect on the last six years is precisely by analysing each of these policies and laws and posing questions in the manner that I am suggesting. Critically, as Micheal Young cautions us, we should undertake this while being careful not to create a polarisation, an either-or scenario.

From teacher unionism to a new teacher professionalism in the service of education transformation?

I turn next to our assumptions about the role of teacher organisations in the national education change programme. An important assumption was that teacher unionism would give way to a new post-apartheid teacher professionalism, and that this would occur in an autonomous manner. The national teacher organisations, especially the left-of-centre and militant South African Democratic Teachers Union (SADTU), was expected to undergo autonomous identity transformations. To be fair to the situation of teacher unionism in the pre-1994 period, teacher professionalism and teacher unionism – certainly from the point of view of SADTU – were never separable; they were one (Rensburg, 1996). A pre-1994 defence of teachers was assumed consistent with the People's Education project. It was assumed that the natural leap forward into the post-1994 period would see teachers take on the new challenge of education service in post-apartheid reconstruction and development. It was assumed in designing, developing and implementing the post-apartheid curriculum that teachers would on their own, autonomously, take ownership of that curriculum project and that they would give it flesh, would give it life.

I posed this question four years ago (Rensburg, 1996), and I pose it again at this point. Have we left our comrades behind in the anti-apartheid and national liberation trenches? Have we left SADTU behind as a particular union that now represents two out of three teachers in South Africa? What are the causes of such a development? How do we bring them back on board again?

So these are some of the questions about the assumptions we have held about the continuity of education struggles and post-1994 education reconstruction and development. I suggest that this approach of exploring, elucidating and elaborating policy assumptions offers a useful, productive, and developmental approach to understanding continuity and breaks in policy development, policy making and policy implementation. Such an approach does not call for a superficial dogmatic support of government policy and implementation. The conversation between government and SADTU has until now not opened up these questions and their solutions.

Policy commercialism or policy leadership in analysis and research?

Until now I have argued that education systems are held together or torn asunder by their own establishments, by their own systems of governance, by their national and provincial (or state) systems, their schools and colleges, governing bodies, teachers, and the leadership of teacher organisations and unions. I wish to expand this thesis by arguing that there is another social partner that plays a critical role in holding the system together – *viz.*, its education policy leadership. I wish especially to challenge my colleagues who are practitioners of education policy analysis and research. I wish to suggest to them that in analysing, researching, and evaluating our collective efforts of the last six years, we have not helped our post-apartheid mission. Just as our teacher unions and the new bureaucrats in the education administration are facing identity transformation, I suggest that policy analysts and researchers are also faced with continuity and change as they face the post-apartheid education project. I would suggest that policy analysis and research has moved from providing a service to the anti-apartheid and national liberation movement, to a post-1994 policy commercialism. Its focus has shifted to competing for short-term research projects, to fund-holding on behalf of the state, and to shoot-from-the-hip criticisms of the policy directions of the emerging state. Important as these roles may be, policy research and analysis has moved away from its pivotal role in education transformation and change. In effect it has become follower rather than visionary, looking backward rather than anticipating the troubles ahead.

I am arguing here that in South Africa policy analysis and research has drifted alarmingly away from what I wish to call a conversation, a debate, the elucidation and elaboration of a theory of education transformation, at systems and institutional levels. It is an enormously important conversation that we are engaging in here about pure and applied research. Yet we do this without applying these thoughts and findings to our education change programme. I am suggesting that the policy commercialism that dominates public policy research in South Africa is useful only in the short run. In the medium to long run, it may turn out that we have taken wrong directions in policy making.

Let me be more specific and illustrate this concern. Critics of Curriculum 2005 (DoE, 1996a) constantly make the fundamental error of collapsing the specificities of general and further education and training as they critique post-apartheid curriculum policy and implementation (see DoE, 2000f, and Chapter 2 of this book). As I outlined earlier, it is vitally important to examine the purposes of compulsory general school education prior to undertaking an analysis of its design features. Failure to do so can result in misplaced analysis, and can lead to the offering of false solutions that may be incompatible with the underlying purposes of curriculum in this band of learning. Let me elaborate further.

Often one is confronted by a critique that does not make the distinction between the teaching of chemistry in the first ten years of schooling (compulsory general education) and in the last three years of schooling (post-compulsory further education and training). For example, do we teach physical science, meteorology, astronomy and sociology in general compulsory education as we do in further and higher education? What is my point? My point is that across the globe in general compulsory education there is a particular approach to knowledge, to the organisation of the curriculum and therefore to knowledge acquisition, knowledge production, and so on. Therefore, it should not be surprising that South Africa decided to develop a curriculum for compulsory general school education that comprises eight learning areas. The critique does not help the policy makers because it is flawed to the extent that it does not pose the critical questions through the lens of general compulsory education. It focuses upon the design features, rather than on the underlying purposes and deeper epistemological debates about knowledge and its implications in compulsory general school education and post-compulsory school education. And so, I suggest, the questions being posed by the critique are of acute relevance to further education and to higher education. Let me be even more precise. Do we have a discipline focus, a subject focus in those eight learning areas? Or do we have an integrated cross-curriculum organisation of knowledge and therefore of learning and teaching? These are clearly some of the questions that are occupying our minds as we take the next step to refine our curriculum for general compulsory education. (See DoE, 2000d and 2000f, for subsequent decisions of Cabinet and the Council of Education Ministers.)

I am suggesting that current debates – such as those about post-apartheid curriculum change – are many a time fatally flawed. The key challenges facing us over the next decade, therefore, are to strengthen and build our policy leadership, to sharpen our analytical capabilities, and to build up robust policy institutions.

A focused programme with top priorities or a reshuffle of the cluttered education agenda?

As noted above, during the first five years we focused our attention on state building and system development, including the establishment of new education departments and overarching policies, laws, regulations and national norms and standards. Strangely, this period did not see us distil top priorities for post-apartheid education reconstruction and development. Accordingly, most senior managers and officials have worked on the assumption that their individual responsibilities and line functions were top priorities. This situation has resulted in considerable policy and programme overload on the system, as individual national and provincial managers and officials separately arrive in school districts with bags of policies and programmes that are not always consistent with each other. Clearly this situation could not endure for it did not offer integrated and coherent programmes in support of school and school district development. Many of these programmes of the early years were developed largely from the perspective either of the national Department of Education or the provincial department of education.

South Africa's education system has now moved closer to a distillation of priorities as announced in *A Call to Action: Building an Education and Training System for the 21st Century* (DoE, 1999a). This analysis identifies nine priorities to be implemented within five national programmes. Currently these programmes are being implemented within more than fifty projects. Note that while the country is moving towards some kind of prioritisation the focus in these projects remains largely at the level of general system as distinct from the institutional level. What it is still not offering us is a set of institutional and geographic targets through which we can shift the education system dramatically forward. In addition, these projects are being implemented within an unrealistic resource frame. In this respect, the argument of Micheal Young in this volume for an institutional focus rather than a system-level one offers an enormously important framework for our future work.

There are other policy assumptions that I wish to introduce to stimulate discussion. However, because of time and space, I shall simply note these:

The simultaneity of transformation and the maintenance of the system: To illustrate, the post-apartheid education transformation programme in the period immediately following the democratic breakthrough in 1994 comprised many critical activities, including the dissolution of the nineteen racially-based and ethnic-based departments of education, the establishment a new national department and nine provincial departments of education, the equal distribution of teaching posts across 27 500 schools, and the development of a new curriculum for compulsory general school education. Each of these activities on their own required high-level human resource planning, management and implementation capacity to be successfully accomplished. These activities were being undertaken against the background of an existing system. It was unimaginable to contemplate shutting down schools and colleges so that we could focus all our attention on the immediate post-apartheid reconstruction priorities. We had to ensure that schools and colleges continued to offer the best services possible; salaries had to be paid, as had water and electricity bills. Schools and colleges had to be managed and governed, teachers had to teach, and professional support services had to be made available. These apparently contradictory programmes exert pulls in both directions within the organisation and draw considerable and unanticipated resources. Yet they have to be addressed simultaneously within considerable fiscal constraints. To illustrate again, the desire to map a new further education and training system for South Africa's high schools and colleges must be pursued side by side with attempts to raise the validity, reliability and international comparability of the senior certificate examinations. This requires old and new bureaucrats to work together – the former are in general more skilled in maintaining systems and the latter in building new post-apartheid systems.

The unanticipated and unplanned for shift from a mass-based, social, anti-apartheid movement to a top-down, technocratic, post-apartheid education change programme: Virtually all of the post-apartheid education reconstruction policies have their nascence in the anti-apartheid and national liberation movement, and were expected to receive popular support. However, with the weakening and even the death of some key social movement organisations – as their leaders assumed new roles in the building of the post-apartheid state – popular participation in social change has declined. Change has become technocratic and depoliticised. A case in point is the absence of substantive meetings of the African National Congress education alliance where policies are debated and hammered out before being advocated and defended on the streets. Significantly, with the decline in leadership capacity within social movement organisations of the left during this period, power has shifted inexorably towards the executive arm of government. While this has meant that decision-making had fewer hoops to jump through, it has left the new bureaucrats naked and on their own against the consolidating positions of education neo-liberals and the mass media. (See further treatment of this subject in Rensburg, 1996.)

In conclusion, I trust that this contribution has opened rather than closed the possibility for a thoughtful, provocative and frank discussion about education policy development, policy making and policy implementation in the brief period since national liberation in 1994. It is more urgent now then ever to consider what holds the system together and to act on this. Also, it is now time to set national education priorities and to shift the focus of our post-apartheid education change project to the introduction of specific, circumscribed, visible and institution-level change programmes that once again mobilise our people behind them.

Chapter 8

Macro-Strategies and Micro-Realities: Evolving Policy in Further Education and Training

Anthony Gewer

Introduction

Further Education and Training (FET) is located at the intersection of a range of policy and legislative imperatives, all aimed at addressing the compelling human resources development needs of the country to compete in an increasingly global economy. This sector comprises a diverse array of education and training provision, both public and private, the majority of which currently takes place in senior secondary schools and to a lesser extent in the technical college sector. FET is therefore a complex system, through which government must reconcile the need to create access to education and training for the mass of the population, while at the same time ensuring that all learners receive equitable education and training provision across the system.

FET sits at the crossroads between general education and training and higher education, as well as providing access to the world of work. In this way, FET has the potential to offer a wide variety of both initial and second-chance opportunities to diverse learners – those that are school-going, out of school, employed and unemployed (DoE, 1998a).

At the heart of FET policy implementation is the push to transform public FET colleges[1] to become key drivers of the system. In doing so, FET colleges are being positioned to respond to current macro-strategies for human resources development, in particular the Skills Development Strategy of the Department of Labour (DoL, 1997). At the college level, however, the challenges facing the Department of Education in delivering on this are immense, and are complicated by a lack of cohesion in the policy environment. The policy frameworks guiding this transformation are rooted in traditional institutional divides at all levels of the system, and this impacts on the capacity of colleges to transform. The historical divisions between education and training have been perpetuated despite earnest attempts early in the 1990s to bridge this divide.

Thus, the FET system is currently plagued by high levels of fragmentation at both institutional and curriculum levels. The institutionalised education and training divide that has been a historic feature of this society continues to persist, and the matriculation

1 The terms 'FET colleges' and 'technical colleges' are used interchangeably in this chapter.

certificate continues to be viewed as the primary indicator of the performance of the system. The formal schooling system is in the process of addressing the backlog created by apartheid education while at the same time improving the system of delivering to learners. Technical colleges, on the other hand, accommodate a significantly smaller number of students, and their performance is not given the same amount of national exposure. The impact of this on the ground is that colleges continue to get a significantly smaller portion of government's attention, and, in operationalising policy, expectations are not effectively balanced against the resultant realities.

Setting the policy scene

The period 1998-2000 has witnessed a flurry of activity around Further Education and Training. Immediately following the publication of the Green and White Papers and the promulgation of FET legislation, all in 1998, the Department of Education laid out a forceful agenda with pressing timeframes in its *National Strategy for Further Education and Training, 1999-2001* (DoE, 1999d). Although there have been significant delays in the realisation of the objectives within this strategy, the compression of policy development and implementation strategies during this period reflects the strategic role that FET is expected to play in meeting government delivery imperatives with respect to skills development and job creation.

The evolution of education and training policy that has informed and complicated this agenda provides important insights into the nature of policy shifts in a transforming socio-political environment. Following from the policy ideals of the early 1990s, where the talk was of education and training as a 'single entity within a single system' (NTB, 1994), the current FET policy environment is characterised by distinct Departments of Education and Labour, that continue to differentiate their roles along conceptions of supply and demand.

The National Training Strategy Initiative (NTSI) laid the foundation for an integrated framework for education and training (NTB, 1994). This report followed on from an earlier report of the National Training Board, under the apartheid government in 1991. The first NTSI had begun to put in place a process of raising the profile of vocational training, but allowed the labour market to determine what form such training should take (through devolving training to Industrial Training Boards). In particular, it did not address the disparities in training provision and opportunities for blacks and whites. The revised National Strategy Initiative, which was influenced substantively by the ANC-COSATU alliance, sought to provide the basis for equity and redress, and represented a critical departure from the market-led focus inherent in the first NTSI document to a macro-institutional framework (Kraak, 1997). The report laid the basis for a state-driven transformation process that was aimed at democratising education and training through mass access and demand-led programme provision. It reflected the tensions inherent in the need to address the developmental needs of the country with respect to socio-economic upliftment, while inevitably responding to the pressures of the global economy (Groener, 1998).

The revised NTSI outlined the environmental factors that needed to be in place to achieve this framework for integration, including a coherent governance structure with integration at all levels. Along with other early policy initiatives, the NTSI supported the idea of putting in place a single Ministry of Education and Training to ensure integration at all levels of governance, and therefore to ensure cohesion in policy development (see ANC, 1994a,b). The creation of two distinct ministries for Education and Labour in April 1994 forms the basis for the complexity in policy development and implementation (King, 1998; Jansen, 1999c). In FET – which straddles the two ministries in such an integral manner, perhaps more than other education and training strands – this complexity is particularly stark. This is because the traditional divide between formal schooling and industry-related education and training continues to operate along the lines of the respective roles of the two departments. The Department of Education maintains responsibility over formal schooling, while the Department of Labour oversees the development of strategies for skills development in industry. It is in the context of technical colleges that this divide may become blurred, in that technical colleges have traditionally straddled Education and Labour.

Current FET policy continues to place a significant emphasis on overcoming traditional and historical barriers between education and training, through seeking to develop an interlocking system that allows optimal mobility on a programme level but retains some of the previous institutional differentiation.

The key vision of the second NTSI was the creation of a National Qualifications Framework (NQF), where learning is expressed in terms of nationally accepted outcomes, representing a combination of knowledge and skill. The NQF was viewed as the vehicle for creating the opportunity to equalise the education and training playing field, through an emphasis on flexibility and articulation. In essence, the vision for the framework was that it should allow learners of different ages to access high quality programmes in a variety of institutional settings, through a variety of different modes, and to progress towards qualifications at a pace with which they were comfortable. It should break down traditional notions of time-driven curriculum and face-to-face teaching, and should encourage curriculum innovation in response to community and industry demands.

White Paper Four emphasises the programme-based focus of FET that seeks to 'overcome outdated divisions between "academic" and "vocational" education, and between training, and will be characterised, not by the "vocationalisation" of education, but by a sound foundation of general knowledge, combined with practical relevance' (DoE, 1998a:30).

In order to achieve this, FET policy provides the basis for putting in place a system that is governed by a nationally co-ordinated regulatory framework, that has as its unifying characteristic the NQF. The policy framework calls for co-operation, both intra-governmentally in the form of co-operative governance and between government and other stakeholders (DoE, 1998a). The implication underlying this is that FET exists within a broader strategy for human resources development, necessitating a paradigm shift in notions of learning, and providing a vibrant environment for all stakeholders in the provision of education and training. Owing to the large number of stakeholders that are involved in the provision of FET programmes – including government, public and private providers, communities and employers – the success of FET will be determined by the extent to which the involvement of these stakeholders is not undermined by overly restrictive and rigid frameworks. The challenge facing policy makers is the creation of an enabling environment for creativity and innovation, while still fulfilling government's basic obligation of delivery of education and training to all citizens.

Mechanisms for realising FET policy imperatives

Legislated institutional differentiation

The institutionalisation of FET policy is established in the *Further Education and Training Act* (RSA, 1998b), that provides the basis for establishing public and private FET institutions. The Act empowers the MEC 'to declare any institution providing further education and training programmes as a public further and education institution' (RSA, 1998b:10). The Act goes on to stipulate that 'no public school which offers further education and training programmes may be declared a further education and training institution …. until after a date determined by the Minister…' (RSA, 1998:10). This stipulation raises a central challenge to the emerging FET system. Following on White Paper Four (DoE, 1998a), that classifies senior secondary schools as an 'unresolved policy issue', the Act requires senior secondary schools to continue operating according to their current status – thus being subject to the *South African Schools Act* (RSA, 1996b). This disallows any changes in governance or funding regulations.

It is clear that this policy framework creates the basis for viewing colleges and schools as clearly distinct institutions that will potentially serve different functions in the FET system. While the legislation does not rule out schools becoming FET institutions at some time in the future, it is critical to begin to analyse the unique characteristics of the institutional contexts in FET colleges that support policy demands.

Technical colleges have been prioritised as a key focus of policy implementation, especially from the perspective of institutional restructuring. The implementation of FET policy is located within the move towards the merger and declaration of technical colleges as FET institutions (DoE, 1999d), in line with the *Further Education and*

Training Act. This legislation sets the foundation for the restructuring of the institutional landscape for FET. The national Department of Education has released a set of draft criteria against which such FET institutions will be declared. The *Draft Criteria for Declaration of FET Institutions* (DoE, 2000b) outlines the optimal form that colleges should take once the process of transformation is complete and includes areas of governance, management and administration, quality assurance, resources and learner support. The criteria speak to the need for efficient administration systems, self-assessment on the part of colleges, and sufficient resources (financial, human and physical) to manage an effective institution.

Besides the singular criterion of size (minimum two thousand Full-time Equivalent students), the extent to which colleges will be expected to prove themselves against these criteria seems questionable. What these criteria do achieve, though, is to alert colleges to the levels of planning and accountability – especially with respect to issues of redress, access and equity – that will be expected of them. They have set the tone for elevating the status of FET colleges by preparing the path for gradual autonomy and sustainability. They will form central components of the strategic plans of the colleges, against which their performance and funding will be judged.

The declaration of FET institutions is a provincial responsibility. A college achieving this status implies that it will become progressively more autonomous in its governance and management structures, have greater flexibility with respect to programme offerings and staff establishment, and become more responsive to industry and the community through flexible learning delivery. However, it will also mean the college will become subject to programme-based funding, that will be determined by institutional target-setting and reporting. While the norms and standards for such funding will be determined nationally, it will be the role of the provinces to monitor and support colleges in accounting for the achievement or non-achievement of targets. These mechanisms are designed to force colleges to become more accountable and relevant in their service delivery.

Operating in tandem with the declaration process, is the process of merging FET colleges. The Department of Education seeks to significantly reduce the number of technical colleges throughout the country in order to promote better efficiency in resource utilisation and greater learner participation. The merger process will result in 'mega' institutions in each province comprising clusters of current institutions. It is expected that the process of merger and declaration will happen simultaneously in order to set up the landscape for equitable distribution of financial resources and to provide a basis whereby weaker and stronger institutions can engage each other in the challenges of transformation.

One intended fundamental outcome of this transformation is that colleges will locate themselves better to respond to the needs of the labour market. The Skills Development Strategy (DoL, 1997) provides for multi-level plans – skills plans at national and provincial levels, sector skills plans in each of the twenty-five delineated sectors, and workplace skills plans. The Department of Education requires each provincial education department to come up with a strategic plan for regional FET transformation (DoE, 1999d). In the development of their strategic plans, colleges will need to combine these various plans in identifying the education and training needs of their constituencies.

A second fundamental outcome is that all programmes offered by colleges will need to be aligned to the National Qualifications Framework, and the majority of these programme offerings should be registered within the FET band. Through programme-based funding the Department of Education will provide incentives for comprehensive planning and quality delivery, by putting in mechanisms to monitor learner achievements and by requiring colleges to set targets for improving delivery.

The legislative framework is an important mechanism for defining the functional differentiation of FET colleges and schools. The question is whether this institutional differentiation implies a fundamental shift from the notion of an integrated framework for education and training. The framework suggests that colleges are being positioned to take on a particular response to social and economic demands. The difficulty inherent in this process, however, is that in order to achieve this colleges will require significant investment and support. Colleges continue to be the responsibility of the Department of Education. However, in shifting their focus significantly to becoming delivery agents of the Skills Development Strategy, there is a critical imperative for intra-governmental co-operation between Education and Labour to ensure that colleges are sufficiently resourced to achieve this strategic objective.

Changing the landscape

The particular characteristics of technical colleges arguably place them in an advantageous position, allowing the state to address issues of skills development, while continuing to address the crisis in the schooling system. The demand-led, programme-driven agenda guiding the transformation of colleges provides the basis for justifying a non-interventionist steering role of the state, while school transformation, being largely supply-driven, requires higher resource investment. The policy framework positions colleges to address issues of economic demand at the level of the interface between education and work, requiring a greater level of responsiveness to the external labour market. Implicitly it forces colleges to achieve accountability, as their service provision will be subject to labour market scrutiny. This will ensure their sustainability in an increasingly competitive education and training sector, necessitating the provision of programmes that adequately equip learners for the broad challenges of the workplace.

In order for colleges to reach this goal, there are a number of significant challenges that face government in addressing the historical factors that have relegated colleges to second-rate institutions. The range of programmes being offered by colleges is limited predominately to national programmes that are theory-based, largely because the staff establishment posts in these colleges are subsidised by government on the basis of student enrolments in these particular programmes. In addition, historically advantaged colleges serving predominately white students were given certain levels of autonomy,[2] and these have therefore been able to build up large resources that allow them to innovate with non-formal programmes that may have a more practical base. Many colleges, both previously advantaged and disadvantaged, also benefited from apartheid structures as they were able to service parastatals, mining companies and others with artisans and apprentices. This allowed them to accumulate physical resources, such as workshops, for practical training. There are a number of colleges, however, especially those that were established in disadvantaged areas to provide skills training for black students, that are poorly-resourced and continue to offer a narrow range of programmes.

The *FET Act* seeks to equalise the institutional landscape by providing all colleges with 'progressive autonomy' and ownership. The merger and declaration process will bring together previously disadvantaged and previously advantaged colleges into unified institutions with the belief that these will enhance the capacity of the colleges to respond to labour market demands, enhance access for a larger range of learners, and provide a more efficient and higher quality service to learners. It is envisaged that such mega-institutions will become multipurpose campuses, will seek to overcome current duplication of programmes, and become more dynamic in their ability to innovate with programme development.

While technical colleges are well located across the country to provide access for learners, in urban, peri-urban and rural environments the disparities in location between urban and rural colleges will be a critical determining factor with respect to sustainability. For a number of colleges in well-established urban regions of the country, the merger process and the achievement of autonomy will be a relatively painless and positive process due to relatively stable regional economies where there are clear opportunities for job creation and employability. For colleges in areas of 'jobless growth' – where there is a general decline in the primary sector production that sustained the economy of the country through the twentieth century, such as agriculture and mining – colleges are in the position of having to adjust their focus towards small business development in order to ensure that the current crisis of unemployment and poverty can be addressed. The task facing these colleges is an onerous one, and the danger exists that such colleges will be thrown into the wilderness without a compass or map. Therefore, as colleges become autonomous and are forced to retreat from dependency on government control, the need for systematic

2 The historical differentiation of 'state-aided' and 'state' colleges was predominately rooted in apartheid philosophy. Therefore, state-aided colleges were established to serve white learners and were given more autonomy, while state colleges served non-white learners and were given no autonomy. Although some provinces have now dropped this distinction, the historical inequities persist.

planning for the utilisation and sharing of resources in the most appropriate manner to address both regional demands and national priorities will become a necessity.
The imperative of planning is critical in this context. Successful college mergers should be informed by an intensive process of strategic planning that incorporates socio-economic profiles, labour market information, and skills plans – for particular sectors and for each province as a whole. (Sector and provincial skills plans are required by the Department of Labour.) As such, mergers are fundamentally geared towards enhanced positioning of colleges with a strategic understanding of the role of the newly-merged college as a centre of learning for local and national economic growth. Without this focus on planning, the potential of merged colleges to meet economic and social demands is limited by a lack of clear understanding of needs. This undermines the college's ability to overcome duplication of programmes, achieve quality or promote employment.

The merger challenge is underpinned by the fears and anxieties associated with such exercises. At the political level, the necessity of ensuring the sustainability of such institutions for the purpose of the political agenda requires that the process of merger be conducted very carefully. The merging of colleges involves not merely the sharing of physical resources, but also requires a reorienting of organisational cultures and mindsets. The potential exists for many historically disadvantaged colleges to be overshadowed by larger and better-resourced historically advantaged colleges. The solution to this dilemma may be that, from the point of view of driving change, historically disadvantaged colleges may receive a political push to be the leading institutions within the merger process. This will necessitate that these colleges receive significant support in order to meet this challenge. It also requires that sufficient focus is given to building the transformation agenda into historically advantaged colleges, so that the notion of equal partnership becomes a reality. All of this is a complex and time-consuming process that will not be completed in the near future. In operationalising the forceful policy agenda for mergers it is important not to overlook these complexities if sustainability is going to be achieved.

Funding incentives

As expressed in the Green Paper, the government sees itself as playing a 'steering' role, both at national and provincial levels, focusing not on a prescriptive approach through centralised planning, but rather through an inclusive and consultative strategy that will ensure accountability and facilitate quality. Kraak (1999a) summarises this 'softer' approach as comprising three key components: planning requirements, financial incentives, and reporting requirements. These components provide the basis for ensuring that providers of education and training, especially public providers, are putting in place internal systems for monitoring of performance and quality, with a focus on public accountability and institutional sustainability.

Traditionally, the range of programmes being offered in colleges has been limited by outdated syllabi, overemphasis on theory in isolation from practical experience, and a preoccupation with enrolling as many students as possible regardless of the learner's aptitude or interests. These parameters for programme offerings have largely been determined by national criteria for funding of staff establishment posts in colleges. FET policy puts in place the mechanism for nationally-determined formulas that focus on the programmes that lead to appropriate qualifications, which are registered on the National Qualifications Framework.

As colleges have always been dependent on government funding for survival, they have continued to offer national programmes with little regard for innovation. Colleges have been locked into a restrictive choice of programmes that can be offered, and these have not been subject to any external quality assurance. Colleges, therefore, were not held accountable or penalised on the basis of poor programme delivery and the poor results that arose.

Current policy demands that the range of programmes being offered in FET institutions be determined by a sound analysis of the needs of the community and regional economy, coupled with national priorities (DoE, 1997b). Government requires colleges to develop strategic plans, including targets, against which such formula funding will be awarded. The implication of this is that college provision will become subject to external monitoring, and this will determine the level of support received from government. Such funding will be the domain of provincial departments, and the programmes to be funded may vary from province to province. In addition, a certain percentage of funding in colleges will ultimately need to be sourced from external funding.

It is through such mechanisms that government seeks to instil in FET institutions a culture of responsive programme delivery. FET institutions must become more sophisticated about the way they collect information about the outside environment and combine it with internal data to inform programme development. Such programmes will be developed and offered in response to an identified need. By implication, FET institutions will be forced to align their programmes with the needs of commerce and industry, achieving a better balance of theory and practice and including a substantive focus on practical workplace experience to properly equip learners for future employment.

The new funding framework also requires that all FET programme offerings be aligned with the NQF and be subjected to external quality assurance (DoE, 1998a). Such programme offerings will need to comprise registered unit standards and should lead to registered qualifications. Implicitly, therefore, the Department of Education funding regime forms the foundation for orienting FET institutions to outcomes-based education and training. Furthermore, the capacity of FET institutions to access funding from the National Skills Fund or the Sector Education and Training Authorities, will be based on programme accreditation. Therefore, funding becomes a significant motivating factor in the transformation of curriculum into an outcomes-based framework that meets the requirements of the NQF.

Curriculum reform

The NQF provides the vehicle for overcoming the traditional divide between education and training, by creating 'an integrated national framework for learner achievements' (RSA, 1995). The NTSI formed the basis for early debates around integration and established a credit-based system, comprising units of learning that combine to form qualifications (NTB, 1994). Such units of learning should comprise statements of outcomes, aligned to endorsed standards and reflecting an integration of knowledge and skill, referred to as 'applied competence' (DoL, 1997). From the perspective of FET, the changing nature of 'skills' training through an applied competence model should create the basis for bringing vocational education more into the realm of building 'thinking' learners, a realm that has traditionally been associated exclusively with academic education.

The units of learning comprise three different types: fundamental, core and elective. When combined these units should provide a holistic learning pathway that brings together the fundamental competencies of communication and mathematics, with a defined set of outcomes that result in a qualification. It is possible for learners to acquire the same outcomes and qualifications through different programmes (SAQA, 2000b,d). However, the NQF places the responsibility on providers to develop and deliver curricula and programmes based on these outcomes and qualifications.

The range of programmes currently being offered by technical colleges is largely limited to national programmes (examined by the Department of Education) that are theory-based and reliant on rote learning for the purpose of examination. According to aggregated data, programmes in technical colleges fall into two fields of learning – Business Studies and Engineering Studies – with Utility Industries representing a growing but not yet comparable field (Powell & Hall, 2000). The vast majority – 93 per cent – of learners are enrolled in these formal, theory-dominated programmes. Certain colleges have introduced some practical, non-formal programmes, such as those registered by Industry Training Boards (ITBs),[3] but this only accounts for 7 per cent of learners (Powell & Hall, 2000). The current programme range indicates a clear predominance in colleges of theory to the exclusion of practical, work-based application. Despite the specific role of FET colleges in providing vocationally-oriented education and training, there is currently no requirement for colleges to expose learners to practical experience in a workplace or work-related environment.

Technical colleges have not been required to engage significantly in curriculum and programme development, as this has traditionally been provided by the Department

3 Now reformed and broadened into Sector Education and Training Authorities (SETAs).

of Education. In addition, beyond meeting the requirements of the ITBs for certain non-formal programmes, no mechanisms have been put in place by the Department of Education to subject colleges to external quality assurance. FET policy requires colleges to align their programmes with the NQF, in order for these programmes to be nationally recognised and funded. This necessitates that colleges are able to identify the appropriate outcomes and qualifications and to engage in curriculum and programme development processes. It also implies that colleges will be subject to external quality assurance via the various sector quality assurance bodies through whom these programmes will be accredited.

Curriculum reform provides a key lever to achieving transformation in FET colleges, by instilling a demand for high quality, nationally accredited programmes aimed at holistic development of the learner. For colleges, developing programmes in line with the NQF necessitates a fundamental mind-shift. It requires that colleges identify clear programme needs, so that the programmes that are being offered are appropriate to the target learners. It requires that colleges overcome imbalances between theory and practice, where practical experience is necessary for the achievement of programme outcomes, and focus fundamentally on the integration of knowledge and skill, so that learners are optimally prepared for economic activity. Finally, it demands that colleges become accountable for programme provision, which will ultimately have an impact on the level of funding they will be able to access.

For the Department of Education, however, the challenge of curriculum reform is located in whether the achievement of parity in generalist and vocationally-oriented FET qualifications is possible or desirable. The social value attached to the national matriculation results is indicative of the primary focus placed on enhancing access to learning based on general knowledge, with less emphasis on the need to provide practically relevant education and training. Transformation at programme level needs to be understood in this perceived role played by learning institutions. Schools continue to be the primary pathway to higher education institutions, while colleges have been identified as the key providers of skills training for the workplace.

The Department of Education provides a clear indication of the desire to bridge learning in these two institutional contexts under the NQF:

> The Ministry seeks to transform the separate and distinct areas of learning in schools and colleges, to an integrated approach to education and training. Through the integrated approach, the FET curriculum will be brought in line with the principles of the NQF, which will guide the development of relevant curricula, qualifications, unit standards, programmes and assessment strategies consistent with the outcomes-based approach (DoE, 2000e).

The implication of this is that curriculum reform in schools should be governed by the same requirements that guide curriculum development in other FET providers. However, the Draft Curriculum Framework (DoE, 2000e) clearly orients the accumulation of credits in schools to a whole qualification rather than a unit standards approach. On the other hand, FET institutions are clearly being directed towards unit standards in their industry-related offerings. This results in distinctions regarding the requirements for exiting with an FET certificate at the end of the FET band, with a school-based Further Education and Training Certificate (FETC) allowing access to higher education. A further implication, is that the unit standard-whole qualification divide has the potential to perpetuate perceptions that qualifications achieved through FET institutions are inferior to those obtained via schools.

The challenge in achieving an equitable FETC (for exit from FET) across learning sites in FET is located in the perceived value of the qualification that the learner will achieve. This perception is related to the differing requirements for access to academic higher education versus access to the world of work. Matriculation with endorsement is viewed as a mechanism for identifying those learners who will succeed in a university environment. However, only around 14 per cent of learners who enrolled to write the matriculation examinations in 2000 achieved the necessary results to access university. This percentage is reduced by half when considering drop-outs further down the system. In addition, despite these selection criteria, there are high numbers of failures in the first year of university. For other higher education institutions, such as technikons, access to programmes is significantly less restrictive; programmes can be accessed via the formal academic route or via a technical college qualification. Technical colleges themselves also offer higher education programmes, although only in a narrow range of fields (Powell & Hall, 2000).

The inherent difficulty is putting in place learning pathways in FET learning sites that lead to varying lifelong learning opportunities, without prejudicing the value of the qualification that the learner will achieve on exiting FET.

> The danger exists that an attempt to create coherence will result in the compulsory requirements for the FETC to be too prescriptive and thereby create artificial barriers to progression as is the case with the Senior Certificate with matriculation endorsement. Too much flexibility however, inevitably results in social judgements about the "exchange" value of certain qualifications and ultimately prejudices the learners who hold the qualification, negatively (SAQA, 2000b).

In seeking to create an FET sector that can respond to the growing demands of the global economy, there is increasing pressure to view knowledge acquisition in holistic terms (SAQA, 2000d). This necessitates a fundamental paradigm shift regarding where learning takes place. The challenge for the education system in South Africa is whether such a paradigm shift can be translated in the way learning is organised across the

FET system. For colleges, the challenge is whether their definition of the nature of knowledge and skills with which graduates emerge is of a sufficient level, so that colleges can begin to break out of the narrowly-defined and marginalised role they have traditionally played, and the qualifications they offer adequately prepare learners for the challenges of the global economy.

It also requires, however, that at the policy level colleges are not set up to provide inferior programmes. The imperatives of the Skills Development Strategy are aimed at the economic and social demands of the country in order to become globally competitive (DoL, 1997). If FET colleges are to become key public delivery agents of this strategy, a concerted complementary strategy needs to be put in place by the Department of Education to overcome traditional views of the relative value of these colleges in relation to schools, through active advocacy and support, so that the qualifications being offered by colleges achieve an adequate level of exchange value. In this way the ultimate needs of learners across the sector will be met, through enhancing successful job creation once the qualification is achieved.

This also implies an obvious indication that policy implementation will not result in integration, but in a focus on the achievement of equivalence, particularly at the qualification level. Therefore, while schools and colleges will be offering differentiated types of qualifications, the equivalence between these institutions will be achieved through the achievement of high levels of knowledge and skills acquisition via the NQF, which will create an alternative and more advanced form of measurement of the performance of the system as a whole.

Creating the interface between education and work – the learnership challenge

The imperatives of transformation in colleges, from the perspective of economic development, are directly related to the position of colleges at the interface between education and the world of work. It is a clear objective of FET policy that technical colleges provide the key site for equipping learners to engage with the demands of the world of work.

State policy provides two mutually inclusive strategies for achieving this objective in the FET curriculum. The first is through the interrogation of the notion of 'applied competence' as envisaged in the Skills Development Strategy (DoL, 1997). The second is through the operationalisation of this notion through the introduction of 'learnerships' (RSA, 1998e). This outcome informs the distinct role that FET colleges can play in achieving integration.

The notion of applied competence lays the basis for holistic and integrated teaching and assessment. It comprises practical (observable skills), foundational (embedded knowledge and understanding), and reflexive (linking, understanding and adapting performance) competence. The combination of such elements implies 'the ability to put into practice in the relevant context the learning outcomes acquired in obtaining a qualification' (SAQA, 2000d).

The introduction of learnerships potentially lends itself to holistic learning. This is due to a focus in the assessment process on both observable performance and inference over a suitable period of time within the college and workplace setting. It encourages the assessor to make sound judgements about the learner's ability to cope with different environmental pressures and allows for a greater perspective on predicting future performance within those settings. Going beyond the observation of performance and the assessing of rote learning associated with traditional apprenticeships (Omar, 1999), the assessment of applied competence necessitates that learners are able to reflect on their workplace experiences, understand why they adopted a particular approach to problem-solving, and generate alternative possibilities for problem-solving.

Learnerships are legislated by the *Skills Development Act* (RSA, 1998e) to include a complex contractual agreement for a fixed period between the learner, the provider and the employer. The contractual agreement provides a framework for formalising the relationship between these three parties in realising the qualification. Beyond the formality of the agreement, this relationship requires high levels of co-operation to ensure the smooth planning and operation of the learnership. A key characteristic of the learnership, however, is that it may only be submitted for registration if a clear demand has been identified (DoL, 2000). Learnerships, therefore, set up the context for colleges as possible providers to form close working relationships with employers. In doing so, learnerships force colleges to clearly identify the types of qualifications that will best meet the needs of employers. A mechanism is provided to ensure that college programmes become relevant and responsive and that the skills acquired are successfully transferred and applied in the workplace.

Learnerships are located at the core of the Department of Labour's macro-strategy for skills development. The challenges facing the achievement of holistic skills development through learnerships are three-fold. Firstly, as noted above, the learnership must be in response to an identified need. Secondly, and following on from the first, the strength of the learnership concept is that they should offer learners who may not have had exposure to meaningful educational opportunities as a result of apartheid the opportunity to access education and training programmes that will lead to relevant knowledge, skills and work experience for entry into the labour market. Since many learnerships will be offered in areas of the country where there is 'jobless growth', the learnership will need to equip the learner to be able to create and sustain employment. This implies that the learnership must move beyond the narrow confines of traditional apprenticeships and seek to build learners from disparate levels of prior learning, to a situation of competence necessary for meaningful social and economic participation.

This requires high levels of investment of resources to provide sufficient support to learners, both within the college and within the workplace.

Thirdly, there is an inherent need for flexible administration systems in colleges to cope with the demands of balancing and connecting classroom theory and workplace practice. The introduction of learnerships into colleges will require a fundamental shift in the organisational mindset of college lecturers and employers. The learnership may require college personnel to work outside of normal hours and to offer different modules at different times. In this way, the learnership may force colleges to move away from a time-led curriculum and rigid opening hours.

All of these challenges raise critical questions around the feasibility of successful learnerships in the near future. Already learnerships that have been introduced in the hospitality sector have illuminated the complexities involved in developing and implementing learnerships, including difficulties in recruiting learners, time needed for achieving learner outcomes, level of educator training, identifying and negotiating workplace experience, and the administration difficulties highlighted above (DoE, 2000c). When placed in the context of low employment opportunities, the levels of resources required for colleges to successfully facilitate the learnership programme are significant.

As a means of achieving the objectives of FET policy, the learnership provides an ideal theoretical model for colleges to deliver qualifications that contribute to poverty alleviation and job creation. The potential exists, therefore, for the fundamental guiding principles behind policy in the context of transformation to be realised, if these challenges can be addressed. If not, questions should be raised about whether learning in such an ambitious form can achieve the objective of opening access to optimal education and training to the mass of people in the country who have not previously had such access. Alternatively, it may force proponents of the learnership programme to consider possible variations of the concept. For colleges, it will be necessary to become creative in the design and management of such programmes, and to ensure a learning process is in place when implementation occurs.

In addition to establishing the legal framework for learnerships, the *Skills Development Act* also makes provision for the development of Skills Programmes, which would comprise an occupationally-directed learning programme that leads to a credit towards a qualification rather than a full qualification. The purpose of the skills programmes is to allow learners access to short programmes that could be combined towards a qualification, thus allowing more flexibility and mobility. The skills programme is less cumbersome in that it does not require a contract with an employer and demands less time from the college and from a potential employer. However, the Act requires that the skills programme be demand-driven and subject to the requirements of the NQF. The Act does not stipulate that skills programmes require workplace experience, and

therefore does not set stringent requirements for such. This allows flexibility for the college with respect to the level of workplace experience that can be negotiated. It may also allow greater access for learners who are seeking work, as they are able to gain specific skills within shorter periods of time and work at their own pace towards a qualification if they so wish, while seeking gainful employment.
The debate over the relative value of learnerships and the skills programme is premature as learnerships are still in their infancy. However, important considerations relate to the intent of the programme or qualification, the outcomes that are applied in this respect, the quality of teaching, and the approach to assessment that is undertaken. The key guiding principle is that learning in this context moves beyond narrow divides between theory and practice and seeks to achieve an optimal transition to the world of work.

From the policy point of view, while learnerships are seen as a critical mechanism for delivering the Skills Development Strategy, successful implementation will require careful planning and support. Learnerships sit at the heart of achieving coherence between education and work, and require a co-ordinated effort to ensure that colleges are enabled to deliver. As accessible public providers, there is strategic advantage in achieving this coherence, but in doing so the political imperatives must be understood within current realities. This implies that government should not be locked into rigid notions of what the learnership should entail, but should rather be guided by the unique demands of the regional economy in which the colleges operate and create the basis for dynamic and innovative institutional responsiveness.

A recipe for responsiveness: partnerships with employers

The macro-institutional framework for education and training is supported by the promotion of a commitment on the part of both government and the private sector to demand-led skills development. The relationship between the Departments of Education and Labour, especially at the provincial level, will be a key determinant of the extent to which employers buy into the potential role that FET colleges can play in this regard.

The *Skills Development Act* (RSA, 1998e) and the *Skills Development Levies Act* (RSA, 1999b) provide a means to draw employers into the macro-institutional framework and then give them incentives to take responsibility for the training and development of their staff, in line with the broader economic needs of the country. Significant responsibility has been devolved to Sector Education and Training Authorities to establish, promote and be accountable for targets for skills development in their

4 The *Skills Development Act* provides for the collection of a skills levy from employers, initially comprising 0.5 per cent of total payroll in 2000, and 1 per cent of payroll from 2001 onwards. Of this, 80 per cent will be disbursed to the twenty-five SETAs and a certain portion redistributed to employers via the SETAs, while 20 per cent is being channelled into the National Skills Fund to address the skills development of specific marginalised groups.

respective sectors of economic activity. SETAs and employers are required to develop yearly plans to guide the distribution of the skills levy.[4] FET colleges can play a strategic role in assisting these stakeholders in achieving the objectives outlined in their skills plans. From the perspective of colleges as key providers of FET, this provides a significant opportunity. The provincial Departments of Education play a significant role in directing and guiding colleges to take on this opportunity, especially as the relationships between colleges and employers have traditionally been deficient. Beyond parastatals that supported the apartheid apprenticeship strategy, there is generally poor awareness among commerce and industry of what colleges have to offer. Provincial Departments of Education will need to engage in substantial advocacy campaigns to draw employers to the notion of colleges as delivery sites for their skills development.

Fundamental to the notion of responsiveness are the relationships that FET colleges will need to establish with industry stakeholders (in particular employers and SETAs). However, while the Skills Development Strategy provides a useful context for the establishment of such partnerships, it is clear that employers will still have to be convinced of the benefits. The primary challenge is that industry training is generally not a substantive activity in South African companies, with 70 per cent of those engaged in training offering only induction or initial-type training, and 74 per cent of those involved in retraining offering only informal training (Kraak, 1999b). Therefore, the first challenge will be to inculcate in these companies a mind-shift around the nature and benefits of human resource development. The SETAs play a critical role in achieving this.

The National Skills Development Strategy (DoL, 2001) establishes a target of eighty thousand learnerships delivered to people under the age of thirty by 2005, which the SETAs are expected to promote and establish. The SETAs have the means to incentivise employers to deliver learnerships through a range of mechanisms for dispersing the skills levy to employers. SETAs will approve or not approve Workplace Skills Plans submitted to them by employers and will disperse funds on this basis, and on the basis of the Workplace Skills Plans being successfully implemented. Besides being funded for the Workplaces Skills Plans, an added benefit under the notion of 'special initiatives' allows for additional funds specifically geared to incentivising the delivery of learnerships.

The learnership agreement, as legislated by the *Skills Development Act,* establishes the framework for the partnership between the employer, the learner and the provider. This agreement must then be registered with the SETA. White Paper 4 expressly establishes FET colleges as key delivery sites for learnerships. However, this requires that colleges are able to form relationships with SETAs and employers, and for the provincial Departments of Education to play a role in actively brokering these partnerships.

Other avenues for partnership also exist through the National Skills Fund. Through the provision of skills development opportunities aimed at social development, such as the skilling of unemployed and retrenched people, college-employer partnerships in the form of learnerships or skills programmes can access funding grants through the National Skills Fund. Such avenues are facilitated through Provincial Skills Forums and should be in line with provincial and national priorities. Therefore, in the spirit of co-operative governance, the provincial Departments of Education are crucial stakeholders in supporting such initiatives.

The college-employer interface, with respect to learnerships in particular and skills programmes in general, will be a challenge of integrating models for skills development. The demands of human resource development are complicated by the tensions between corporate goals (which are largely governed by a desire for global competitiveness) and national policy goals (which are driven by a desire for democracy and redress).
For colleges and employers, the translation of national policy imperatives into a partnership for human resource development must seek to develop a strategy that embraces this tension. For employers, the incentive provided by the skills levy is an important factor. However, the benefits of such partnerships are based on broader survivalist notions. The decline of traditional large-scale production activity and the need for multi-skilled and adaptive staff require that employers strategise carefully around human resource development. In addition, the decline in job creation (especially in areas of the country that have been dependent on large-scale industries), as well as the looming impact of HIV/AIDS on human capacity, necessitates that stakeholders within communities actively work together to find long-term solutions if local and regional economies are going to survive. As the pressures mount and employers gradually seek to explore the opportunities created by the system, they will be required to meet the state's demand for equity and redress. It is in this context that the leverage for the role of colleges becomes particularly prominent, and college-employer partnerships become a strategic mechanism for economic development.

If colleges are to achieve the types of partnerships described above, the provincial Departments of Education face the challenge of providing capacity development and support to colleges. The enabling conditions necessary for such responsiveness include the need for capacity to understand industry needs, develop appropriate curriculum and programmes, and implement appropriate strategies for teaching and learning. This should comprise a central component of provincial strategies for FET transformation, with respect to the process of mergers and beyond, so that FET Institutions can fulfil this role.

In addition, the provincial Departments of Education are able to build pressure for partnerships into their funding methodologies and provide incentives to colleges through so-called 'earmarked funding' (Kraak, 1999a). Ironically, the need for such partnerships is not explicitly stated in the *Draft Criteria for Declaration of FET Institutions*, but it would be necessary to establish this as a key performance indicator for future college functioning.

Conclusion

FET policy provides the basis for FET colleges to be critical sites for addressing the skills crisis in the country. The ability of these colleges to deliver on this role is profoundly determined by the way in which they are impacted by the policy environment. The original conceptions of FET as an integrated system at all levels have had to shift through a process of functional separation in governance of the transformation process. What has emerged from this process is a fundamental shift from integration and equality to functional differentiation and equivalence. For government, the challenge is to seek how policy divides can be overcome to harness the potential of such colleges to meet the macro-strategy for human resource development.

The steering role of the state must be conducted in such a way that colleges are ultimately empowered to enhance their profile and be key delivery agents for the system. The imperatives of transformation are locked into distinctly construed notions from the different government departments of what this should entail, especially at the curriculum and qualification levels. Institutional and curriculum reform are integrally related in that they are undergoing change in order to respond to the requirements of the NQF as an overarching framework. The success of FET will be determined by how the forces addressing this reform are informed by current realities in the system. Colleges are placed at a complex intersection of policy, and therefore, without coherence in the policy environment to guide them in meeting the objectives of transformation, the sustainability of such institutions will be threatened as they become overwhelmed by market forces. This will result in a significant lost opportunity for meaningful and accessible skills development opportunities.

Chapter 9

The Implementation of the National Qualifications Framework and the Transformation of Education and Training in South Africa: A Critique

Michael Cosser

Introduction

Implementation of the National Qualifications Framework (NQF) effectively began with the establishment of the South African Qualifications Authority (SAQA) office in November 1997, following the promulgation of the *SAQA Act* in 1995. Much behind-the-scenes work had been undertaken by the SAQA Board prior to that date towards drafting the National Standards Bodies (NSB) Regulations and the Education and Training Quality Assurance Bodies (ETQA) Regulations (RSA, 1998c,d). This chapter charts the progress achieved by SAQA in overseeing the implementation of the NQF, provides a critique of NQF implementation to date, and considers implementation of the NQF in the light of the HSRC Round Table thesis proposed by Kraak (2000b:1):

> South African education policy and implementation in the year 2000 has undergone a profound shift away from its original intellectual premises in the early 1990s which stressed integrated education and training (ET), outcomes-based ET, progressive pedagogy, and unified as opposed to stratified systems of both further and higher education. Policy implementation today continues to retain the old sectoral divisions between education and training, and the structural (trinary) distinctions between colleges, technikons and universities. Analysts note a return to more traditional notions of schooling – a "back-to basics" – and a new "managerialism" that emphasises the regular assessment of learner achievement, improving school discipline and the establishment of effective school and district management.

Finally, the chapter proposes certain NQF implementation adjustments for the future.

Progress achieved in the implementation of the NQF

Progress achieved in the implementation of the NQF is documented below according to SAQA's three 'infrastructural deliverables' (SAQA's term for the three areas of implementation according to which its outputs are assessed) – standards setting, quality assurance, and information management.

Standards setting

In the implementation period November 1997 to April 2001, the Directorate of Standards Setting and Development (DSSD), which oversees the implementation of the standards setting system, facilitated the establishment of twelve NSBs and the registration of eighty-nine Standards Generating Bodies (SGBs). Seventy-six SGBs were proposed for registration. A total, therefore, of 165 SGBs were in the standards setting system – either registered or proposed for registration. SAQA received some 8 700 provider-specific qualifications in an outcomes-based format by 30 June 2000 for interim registration on the NQF. It approved 7 300 qualifications for interim registration, and registered forty-one new qualifications and 679 new unit standards. These achievements are attributable chiefly to the work of a professional staff of fifteen – the Director of the DSSD, two Deputy Directors of the Division of Standards Setting (DSS), and twelve NSB Co-ordinators (one for each organising field)[1] – and to the individual and collective efforts of education and training stakeholders drawn from a variety of sectors across all three bands of the NQF – General Education and Training (GET), Further Education and Training (FET), and Higher Education and Training (HET). The registration of qualifications and standards is the result of the deliberations of a board of approximately thirty SAQA members.

Quality assurance

In the same implementation period, the Directorate of Quality Assurance and Development (DQAD) facilitated the registration of the following ETQAs by the Authority:

- ❑ Mining Qualifications Authority;
- ❑ Banking Sector Education and Training Authority[2] (BSETA);
- ❑ Media, Advertising, Printing, Packaging and Publishing Sector Education and Training Authority (MAPPSETA);
- ❑ Tourism and Hospitality Education and Training Authority (THETA);
- ❑ Clothing, Textiles, Footwear and Leather Sector Education and Training Authority (TEXTILES SETA);
- ❑ Construction Education and Training Authority (CETA);
- ❑ Information Systems, Electronics and Telecommunication Technologies Sector Education and Training Authority (ISETT); and
- ❑ Services Sector Education and Training Authority (SSETA).

1 For ease of management, SAQA divides education and training into twelve organising fields, that represent combinations of cognate disciplines. For example, NSB 01 is responsible for Agriculture and Nature Conservation, NSB 02 for Culture and Arts, NSB 03 for Business, Commerce and Management Studies, and so forth.

2 SETAs - bodies established under Department of Labour legislation, tasked with improving the skills base of the workforce and assuring the skills base of those entering the workforce - are responsible for assuring the quality of learning provision in their sectors. One of their roles, therefore, is to function as ETQAs. From a SAQA perspective, they are deemed 'economic sector ETQAs', since they are responsible for quality assurance in each of the twenty-five economic sectors demarcated by the Department of Labour. SETAs apply to SAQA for accreditation as ETQAs.

In addition, two statutory professional bodies (the Security Officers' Board and the South African Nursing Council), one non-statutory professional body (the South African Institute of Chartered Accountants), and one education and training sub-system ETQA (the Council on Higher Education) were accredited.

At the same time, the Directorate of Quality Assurance and Development acted as an interim ETQA for private higher education providers and published, among other documents, criteria and guidelines for ETQAs (SAQA, 1998), providers (SAQA, 1999a), and assessment (SAQA, 2000a), as well as a document on quality management systems for ETQAs and providers (SAQA, 2000d).

Information management

SAQA's major achievement in the area of information management has been the establishment of the National Learners' Records' Database (NLRD), which in addition to recording registered qualifications and standards and the details of NSBs, SGBs, ETQAs and Providers has the capacity to register the learning achievements of up to thirty million learners.

The Strategic Support Unit of SAQA – in part a think-tank attached to the Executive Office, in part a unit providing support to other directorates and divisions within SAQA – has facilitated the publication of a range of pamphlets and booklets on the NQF and the role of SAQA (SAQA, 1999c,d,f and 2000c,e,f,g). The Unit also published a number of issues of the SAQA Bulletin in the course of 2000. In addition, the Unit has facilitated and managed the process of data capture on short courses offered by education and training providers across South Africa, with a view to their informing the generation of unit standards that will lead to qualifications that can be registered on the NQF. Finally, the Unit has spearheaded the process of the drafting of guidelines for NSBs and SGBs on the Further and General Education and Training Certificates.

A critique of NQF implementation

The NQF and delivery

Research carried out by the Human Sciences Research Council in the period November 1999 to February 2000 into the efficacy of the NSBs points up a number of inadequacies in the SAQA machinery that have retarded progress on standards generation (Kraak & Mahomed, 2001). These problems include what the report's authors call 'bureaucratic malaise', lack of direction in SGB formation activity, lack of policy on level descriptors, failure of SAQA to draw the Department of Education into standards generating activity (especially for school subjects in the GET and FET bands), and lack of consensus on the nomenclature, articulation and entrance/exit features of qualifications. By February of 2001 these and other shortcomings had been addressed: SAQA had clear policies on SGB formation (including the issue of SGB overlaps) and level descriptors, had negotiated frameworks for the generation of FET and GET Certificates (including recommendations on nomenclature, articulation and entrance/exit features), and had struck agreements with the Department of Education about standards generation in subject areas (Communication Studies and Language, and Mathematics) key to the fundamental learning components of GET and FET qualifications.

Notwithstanding the difficulties associated with the 'messy, setting-up phase' of NQF implementation – in the words of SAQA's Executive Officer (cited in Kraak & Mahomed, 2001:143) – in one sense the facts speak for themselves: SAQA has achieved a great deal in a relatively short space of time, particularly given the paucity of resources at its disposal. A staff of seventy has been set up to oversee a most ambitious qualifications framework by international standards – a single, integrated framework populated with qualifications and learner achievements across twelve organising fields spanning three bands, including HET. Spatially and temporally – given the open-endedness of Levels 1 and 8 – the framework is the vehicle for lifelong learning.

The difficulties confronting SAQA in regulating the pace of delivery should not be underestimated. For those who have been anxiously anticipating the transformation of education and training, the pace is too slow. For those who fear the effects of too rapid a transformation, or any transformation at all, the pace is too quick. SAQA has to balance these concerns in populating a framework that both registers progress and wins over a general populace fearful to different degrees. Rahmat Omar (2000), a SAQA member,[3] makes the point that you cannot deal with systemic change by tackling all the issues across all the fields: if you are going to succeed in creating a climate for the transformation of education and training, you need to prioritise your actions by focusing on those organising fields where transformation is needed most. The NQF is an ambitious project, and SAQA does not have the resources to please all of the people all of the time.

The inevitable consequence of attempting to cover all the bases in this way is a compromise, and in some instances a fall, in quality. The Authority recognises certain imperfections in recently approved qualifications, for example, but weighs these against the greater cause of inclusivity. Thus the interim registration process has been designed precisely to accommodate the qualifications currently offered by providers nation wide on the premise that it is preferable to bring qualifications into the fold now and to enjoin quality later than to strive for quality now and risk losing the support of those most anxious to see progress.

The NQF as social construct

While quantity for quality may have characterised the registration process, the other (not unrelated) strand that underpins implementation is the promotion by SAQA of

3 Omar is a SAQA board (or Authority) member, 'Authority' being used to denote a board that is actively involved in the standards and qualifications approval process.

the NQF as a social construct. On the face of it, by 'social construct' SAQA means in the first instance a mental construction (of a framework) that is socially determined – shaped by the consensus of those individuals and groups party to its construction. As the SAQA web site puts it, 'The NQF is a social construct whose meaning has been and will continue to be negotiated by the people, for the people' (www.saqa.org.za). Such promotion is a double-edged sword – at once a vanguard action and a defence against possible failure. To understand this paradox, we must examine more closely the notion of the NQF as a social construct.

The description of world view and ideology provided by Roger Fowler (1986:17) in the following quotation provides a useful perspective from which to approach this topic:

> ... human beings do not engage directly with the objective world, but relate to it by means of systems of classification which simplify objective phenomena, and make them manageable, economical subjects for thought and action. In a sense, human beings create the world twice over, first transforming it through technology and then reinterpreting it by projecting classifications onto it. Because classification appears to be natural, members of a community regard their assumptions and types as "common sense". It would be more accurate to call these attitudes "world view" or "theory" or "hypothesis" or "ideology". The last of these terms, "ideology", is often used to accuse a community of holding false or distorted theories of reality. In a sense all theories are distortions, since they are interpretations or representations rather than reflections. If one needs to use the terms "ideology" and "ideological" pejoratively, it seems better to apply them to unexamined, unselfcritical, routinized presentations of the world, rather than to brand world views as false.

According to this theory, the NQF as a framework that seeks to underpin the particular system of education and training that it advocates would be a benign ideology, one that promotes and cultivates a particular approach towards learning for personal and socio-economic development. That the promotion of the NQF is overt – a metacognitive exercise taking full cognisance of its overlay of a further system of classification onto reality beyond the classification referred to in the extract above – may seem to redeem it from being branded a false world view or an ideology in the pejorative sense. However, there is a danger in its proponents unquestioningly rejecting opposing world views through their zealous proselytisation of education and training stakeholders from one ideology (inputs-based education and training) to another (an outcomes-based approach). Happily, the Authority – by virtue of its being composed of a range of stakeholders representing a variety of sectors – has avoided adopting an uncritical approach towards its task. Nevertheless, SAQA staff need to guard against being defensive of an ideology whose conversion imperative is bound to elicit an unfavourable response from certain quarters.

The relationship between the NQF as ideology and the NQF as social construct is clear. The success of the implementation of the NQF depends on the extent to which education and training stakeholders subscribe to its ideology. Thus the Freirean 'we make the NQF road by walking it' – the image of the unfolding of the NQF borrowed from the title of the book by Freire and Horton (1990) – promotes the positive aspect of the NQF as a social construct whose ideology is patent to all. This is the vanguard action spoken of above. The other side of the coin is an understanding that the NQF road is only as navigable as the people willing to walk it – the corollary being that the failure of the NQF can always be ascribed to the notion that its implementation is a stakeholder-driven process.

In assuming that a framework is validated on the basis of the consensual process that led to its construction, SAQA may be in danger of reifying into a system of education and training what was never intended to be more than a guide.

The NQF and the spirit of compromise

In a stakeholder-driven process, the interface of policy and practice is invariably marked by compromise. Another hallmark of the NQF implementation process so far, then, is the extent to which SAQA has had to compromise its position on various issues, and none more so than on the role of the HET sector in the implementation of the NQF. Notwithstanding the extent of HET support for the NQF which SAQA secured during the negotiation phase leading up to the promulgation of the *SAQA Act* in 1995, the sector has demonstrated, chiefly via its representation on the Authority, its reluctance to be deemed a partner equal to all others participating in the implementation process. The list of concessions includes:

- SAQA acceptance of the registration of non-unit standards-based qualifications, following the example of international NQF models, particularly that of the New Zealand Qualifications Authority.[4]
- SAQA promotion of provider-driven SGBs generating qualifications for individual institutions (which calls into question the extent to which such qualifications are 'national' – originally all qualifications were to be national, meaning both nationally applicable and nationally constructed).
- The establishment of a Joint Implementation Plan with the HET sector that will see close university and technikon involvement in ensuring the coherence of the framework from levels 5 to 8. (Originally SAQA, through its NSBs, was to

4 Originally all qualifications were to be based on unit standards. The alteration of this conception was signalled ahead of its confirmation in the NSB Regulations (RSA, 1998c) in the White Paper on Higher Education Transformation: 'The incorporation of academic qualifications within a national framework is not a straightforward matter and, quite properly, it has been the subject of intense debate. SAQA has determined that both unit standards and whole qualifications *[sic]* may be presented for registration on the NQF. This should meet the serious concern among many academic staff that unit standards methodology, and the construction of qualifications from multiple units of learning, are inappropriate foundations for certain academic programmes' (DoE, 1997a:28). The use of the term 'whole qualifications' implies that qualifications based on unit standards are in some sense not whole in terms of their integrity.

ensure coherence of the framework through the registration of qualifications that articulated with one another.)

SAQA's approach appears to have been to accommodate the sector at almost any cost, the price of having the sector opt out of the NQF being too high.

The continued involvement of the HET sector in the NQF process, however, hangs in the balance. Much will depend on the timing and nature of SAQA's response to HET institutions on the submission of their qualifications for interim registration, that will set the tone for the relationship to follow, and on the ability of SAQA not to over-regulate the qualifications generating process (allowing the sector itself to take the lead in standards generation).

NQF implementation and the 'profound shift' thesis

A critique of the thesis in relation to NQF implementation

The assertion in the Round Table thesis that education policy and implementation has undergone a 'profound shift' away from its original premises in the early 1990s may be true of implementation in certain arenas, but it is an overstatement in the case of SAQA, which has consistently promoted the integration of education and training, outcomes-based education and training (OBET), and unified systems of FET and HET.

First, the integration of education (with its traditional orientation towards knowledge acquisition and production) and training (with its traditional orientation towards performance) is embedded in the design of qualifications and standards, that are a composite of the knowledge, skills and values that learners need to attain in demonstrating applied competence in a learning area. While it may be the case that certain standards valorise performance over knowledge, SAQA has been at pains – in stressing the importance of specific outcomes of unit standards not constituting sequences of tasks – to promote a standards generating process that does not result in a narrow vocationalism, for example. There are bound to be exceptions, however, as the need to appease certain stakeholders demanding the immediate registration of their qualifications results in accelerated delivery – an approach that may well have future repercussions for the quality of the framework.

The integration of education and training is promoted also through the discourse used to conceptualise and describe it. In this regard, it is interesting that SAQA is the only role-player operating in the higher education and training sector that consistently speaks of 'education and training' as a single entity – in contradistinction to the international discourse of 'higher education' manifested nationally in the Council on Higher Education and in such publications as the White Paper on the Transformation of Higher Education (DoE, 1997a) referred to above, and the recently released *National Plan for Higher Education* (DoE, 2001).

Second, implementation of the NQF is premised on an outcomes-based approach towards education and training; in fact, the NQF may be said to epitomise such an approach. The approval of qualifications for interim registration hinges precisely on the extent to which providers have made a shift from a predominantly inputs-based approach towards the outcomes-based approach outlined in NSB Regulation 11(1)(c), with its emphasis on the exit-level outcomes and assessment criteria that the qualification embodies. New qualifications are designed on the same premise. There is no sense, then, in which OBET has been compromised by SAQA.

Third, SAQA has consistently promoted the construction of unified systems of FET and HET. The notion of a unified system requires explication, however. Unified in this sense should be understood in the context of the first objective of the NQF, that has to do with the creation of an 'integrated national framework for learning achievements' (RSA, 1995). Such an integrated framework connotes integration on a number of levels: academic and vocational; professional and non-professional; formal, non-formal, and informal learning; historically advantaged and historically disadvantaged. But integration here does not mean a blurring of the divisions that differentiate one type from another (for example, academic from vocational). In this view, we might expect to see universities, technikons and colleges in HET thrown into a fire from the ashes of which might rise a new institutional type – or a model in which technikons approximate universities, possibly along the lines of polytechnics upgrading to universities witnessed in the UK. The intent of the NQF objective is to make provision for the co-existence of university, technikon and college qualifications within a single framework – the unification coming not from the merging of identities, but from the extent to which a unitary framework allows for the *articulation* of university, technikon and college qualifications.

An understanding of 'framework' is important here. A national qualifications framework is, in the first instance, a *framework*. It is, to use the construction metaphor, not the building itself but the frame, the constructional system, that gives shape and strength to the building. The building process involves assembling the materials – the bricks and mortar – into the structure.

Further exemplification of SAQA's approach is evident in its facilitation in the period June to November 2000 of discussions aimed at achieving consensus on the nature of the Further Education and Training Certificate (FETC). The approach has been not to attempt to create a 'one size fits all' certificate but to acknowledge the different requirements of the various sectors (schooling, technical college, industry, NGO, and others) in a spirit of accommodating different types of FETC within one framework – ensuring, through the prescription of minimalist design rules, the articulation of those qualifications.

NQF implementation and the transformation of education and training

The question of the extent to which South African education and training has been transformed through policy implementation over the past decade underpins the Round Table thesis that gave rise to this chapter, and is the focus of one of the questions that posed by the Round Table organisers: 'What are the international trends with regard to transformation in key educational areas such as OBE, integrated ET, unified systems of FET and HET, and qualifications reform?' (Kraak, 2000b:2). This section of the chapter will focus not on international trends but on the extent to which we can reasonably expect transformation to have taken place in South Africa since the onset of NQF implementation.

The attempted replacement of one system with another invariably connotes revolution rather than evolution – in the present case, the 'overthrow' of a largely inputs-based education and training system by an outcomes-based system. In such instances the first five to ten years of implementation usually experience some degree of correction, as the new accommodates to some extent the old, as implementation catches up with policy. This is one perspective from which to view educational and training transformation in South Africa in the decade 1990-1999. Nor does such an apparently reformist view necessarily imply a return to a sectoral approach to education and training; rather, it reflects an understanding of the practical realities of the implementation of certain tenets of policy and the need for concomitant adjustments – as witnessed in the adjustments SAQA has had to make in attempting to keep HET within the NQF fold.

From another perspective, we err in thinking that we can attempt to transform an education and training system overnight (for 'overnight' read five to ten years). Deep transformation – that is, qualitative change in the learning of individuals that results in personal and socio-economic development – will probably take twenty to twenty-five years. If by the end of the first quarter of the twenty-first century we do not see the tangible results of transformation policies, then we have cause to re-evaluate our education and training landscape.

The counter to this position is that credit accumulation and transfer systems (CATS) such as the NQF have not taken hold in any significant way elsewhere in the world. For example, Ensor's (2001:10) review of the international literature on the credit exchange system indicates that there is 'little tangible empirical evidence of the credit exchange discourse working in curriculum reconstruction in practice, or evidence of undergraduate curricula being structured as interdisciplinary offerings on a global scale'. The difficulty with this assessment, however, is twofold. First, it equates CATS with modularisation, thereby failing to distinguish qualifications from the learning programmes that lead to their achievement (a distinction SAQA consistently maintains). Second, it assumes that the implementation of a CATS-type system in South Africa is bound to fail because it has 'in general' (Ensor, 2001:10) not taken hold elsewhere, despite her prior reference to the work of Trowler which suggests that the system has indeed taken hold in ex-polytechnic universities in the United Kingdom. This assumption fails to allow for the vast contextual differences between those developed countries in which such research has been conducted, however, and South Africa, a developing country.

If implementation of the NQF has not lived up to expectations by the first quarter of 2001, does this mean that policy should be changed, or does it mean that implementation mechanisms should be reviewed? SAQA views the imminent ministerial review of the organisation in the latter light – the NQF as the epitome of an outcomes-based education and training system is incontrovertible; what should be addressed is the capacity of SAQA to oversee the implementation of the NQF, and its approach towards that implementation. In this context, the review would focus on the extent to which SAQA has contributed towards creating a climate of transformation as embedded in the five objectives of the NQF, which are to:

- create an integrated national framework for learning achievements;
- facilitate access to, and mobility and progression within, education, training and career paths;
- enhance the quality of education and training;
- accelerate the redress of past unfair discrimination in education, training and employment opportunities; and thereby
- contribute to the full personal development of each learner and the social and economic development of the nation at large (RSA, 1995).

NQF implementation: the road ahead[5]

If the implementation of the NQF is to contribute towards the creation of a climate conducive to the transformation of education and training embedded in the above objectives, SAQA will need to ensure the following:

- strategic decision-making that leads to transformation;
- provision of support to stakeholders;
- retention of support of social partners;
- the affordability of NQF implementation;
- prioritisation of activity;
- support to SAQA staff in NQF implementation; and
- exercise of leadership.

These aspects are discussed in some detail below.

5 This section owes much to the interview with Rahmat Omar (2000) referred to earlier.

Strategic decision-making that leads to transformation

SAQA will need to be strategic in determining how best to ensure that its short-term decisions facilitate the creation of a climate conducive to the transformation of education and training. A case in point is how it handles the Interim Registration process, which sets the tone – for HET in particular – for the unfolding of the process of the registration of new qualifications on the NQF. If SAQA, on the grounds of inclusivity, gives approval to Interim Registration qualifications that it knows to be flawed (because they do not conform to the specifications for qualification design promulgated by the Authority), it runs the risk of legitimising the old and retarding, if not stalling, the process of transforming the old into the new. The way SAQA communicates with stakeholders about the quality of their submissions for Phase II of Interim Registration is critical in this regard.

Provision of support to stakeholders

SAQA now has in place the criteria and guidelines for standards setting and quality assurance. The test will be to draw stakeholders into the NQF process through the provision of adequate guidance in the use of those criteria and guidelines. In the standards setting arena, for example, many SGBs have had to fend for themselves in the generation of standards[6] because SAQA has not had the capacity to provide the requisite on-the-ground support – the result has been, variously, duplication of standards generated in other SGBs, incorrectly formatted standards, or an unnecessarily protracted standards writing process.

Since SAQA does not have the capacity in-house to provide such support, it should pursue a dual strategy of recruiting and, more importantly, *training* consultants to assist with capacity-building and the evaluation of standards, and of establishing partnerships with education and training bodies (NGOs, consortia, and so on) to undertake capacity-building on its behalf and to lend conceptual support to the implementation process. In fact, SAQA has recently begun to employ consultants to undertake the first-pass evaluation of standards before they are evaluated by NSBs.

Retention of support of social partners

SAQA has managed to secure the support of powerful social partners for the NQF – particularly the Department of Education, the Department of Labour, organised business, and organised labour. It will need to ensure that in the next phase of implementation it retains this support by courting the continued buy-in of these partners – through, *inter alia*, satisfying the requirements of

6 In this section, 'standards' includes 'qualifications'. On a temporal level, a qualification is merely a type of standard that is longer than a unit standard. (One credit is equivalent to 10 notional hours of learning, and a standard comprises 120 credits or more.)

- the Department of Education, through facilitating the generation of standards that meet the needs of schooling;
- the Department of Labour, through facilitating the generation of standards that meet the needs of the National Skills Authority, the Sector Education and Training Authorities, and learnerships; and
- organised business and organised labour, through promoting the translation of standards into learning programmes that will contribute to upgrading the skills of the workforce, and through fostering the role of trade unions in skills development and the promotion of equality in the workplace.

The affordability of NQF implementation

As overseer of the implementation of the NQF, SAQA needs to ensure that the development of the NQF is affordable in the short to medium term and sustainable in the longer term. This not only applies to such immediate concerns as ensuring that SGBs have sufficient funds to do their work, but has implications for SAQA's partnerships with such role-players as the Department of Education – an arm of the state and one of the chief beneficiaries of standards generation. The capacity of SAQA to sustain an NQF for South Africa hinges not only on its own immediate capacity to become self-sustaining within a short period of time but also on the support of the state, in the form of financial support through the Ministry of Labour. The British government provided millions of pounds for the generation of standards in the early stages of standards development in the UK; the South African government arguably should have done likewise had it hoped for the nation to capitalise on the skills development that it wants for its people.

The unevenness in the funding of Standards Generating Body initiatives is further cause for concern. As Kraak and Mahomed (2001) point out, the fact that some SGBs have access to additional sources of funding may widen the gap between different SGBs and the ways in which standards are generated and approved. Such widening is already apparent in the different funding bases and options of SGBs in occupationally-directed areas (the professions) versus those in less professionally-oriented areas (culture and the arts, and the human and social sciences). SAQA cannot have a vastly uneven standards generation process if it is committed to both economic and social development.

Prioritisation of activity

With so all-encompassing a mandate as SAQA's, the temptation is to want to cover all the bases by attempting to propagate the NQF in every quarter of the land. In this view, one cannot ensure successful implementation of the NQF unless the greatest number of persons in the greatest number of sectors is exposed to it. An opposing view is that spreading oneself thin in this way is counter-productive, and that one needs to focus on select areas that strategically will pay the greatest dividends.

If the latter approach is adopted, there are various ways in which activity can be prioritised. One is to focus on one or two bands at the expense of the other(s). Thus one SAQA member's proposal has been that SAQA leave the HET sector to go its own way and focus on the FET band. While there is certainly merit in the argument that SAQA should influence the course of deliberations surrounding the FETC, given the place of the matriculation examination in the national psyche, the notion of leaving the HET sector to chart its own transformational course is arguably myopic, particularly given the imperatives that the establishment of the Council on Higher Education imposes on the sector. Another approach, propounded by Rahmat Omar (2000), is to focus on one or more organising fields of the NQF at the expense of others – which might be achieved through an identification of the supposed advocative and socio-economic benefits that would accrue to the country were there to be a massive skills upgrading in a particular area, and the subsequent targeting of that area for standards generation and concomitant skills development. Such prioritisation would need to work in concert with the imperatives of the national Skills Development Strategy, however, since any lack of synchronisation between the Department of Labour and SAQA in terms of focus of activity might serve to undermine the social partnership SAQA is anxious to build with that Department.

SAQA's method of prioritisation to date has been to establish Joint Implementation Plans (JIPs) with various stakeholder groupings. Thus there was a JIP with the HET sector in the last three months of Phase II of the Interim Registration period (April to June 2000) to ensure coherence of submission of qualifications to SAQA for registration and learning programmes to the CHE for accreditation and to the Department of Education for approval for subsidy. There is also a JIP with all role-players in the HET sector – a project driven by the CHE – to ensure coherence of standards generation and registration in the HET band. The establishment of such JIPs should be extended as SAQA identifies strategic areas for prioritisation.

Strategic decision-making is needed also in the area of SGB promotion towards eventual registration. Kraak and Mahomed (2001) illustrate the point with reference to the disjuncture between NSB 07's registration of an SGB for Christian Theology and its concomitant failure to promote the registration of SGBs for Rural and Agrarian Studies and for Urban and Regional Studies – particularly in the face of President Mbeki's naming of rural and urban development as national priorities.[7] This case is symptomatic of a general lack of leadership in standards generating policy. Instead of allowing individual NSBs to craft their own SGB formation plans in relative isolation

7 NSB 07 covers the field of Human and Social Sciences. The sub-fields identified by the NSB within which standards and qualifications are to be generated are: environmental relations; general social science; industrial and organisational governance and human resources development; public policy, politics and democratic citizenship; religious and ethical foundations of society; rural and agrarian studies; traditions, history and legacies; and urban and regional studies. The point, simply put, is that the NSB has not pushed for the registration of SGBs for Rural and Agrarian Studies and for Urban and Regional Studies, which it ought to have done in terms of national priorities - given the need to have national standards and qualifications in these areas.

(notwithstanding deliberations within the Inter-NSB Forum[8]) – and therefore in ignorance not only of the standards generating rationales of other individual NSBs but also of the bigger SGB formation picture – SAQA needs to provide an overarching conception of the role SGBs (can) play in the social and economic development of the country, with clear motivations and roll-out plans for their materialisation. This could be done via its leadership of the Inter-NSB Forum. Such a plan should include a mapping of standards registration onto provider uptake scenarios, so as to avoid a perpetuation of the situation in the UK depicted by Michael Young (personal conversation with the author), in which many of the standards generated (often at great cost) have never been used.

Support to SAQA staff in NQF implementation

Notwithstanding SAQA's recent focus on deploying consultants to assist its staff in the fulfilment of the SAQA mandate, more support needs to be given to staff in the operationalisation of the NQF. This support could take the form of:

- ❑ appointing additional administrative staff (one per NSB) to ensure the smooth functioning of NSBs, thereby allowing NSB Co-ordinators to focus on their core responsibilities as leaders and managers of their organising fields;
- ❑ developing the capacity of NSB Co-ordinators to provide conceptual leadership within their organising fields, and to provide their NSBs and stakeholders with various kinds of assistance in standards generation and evaluation (possibly through assigning one NSB member per organising field to assist the Co-ordinator in the fulfilment of these tasks); and
- ❑ promoting a culture of reflective practice within SAQA that allows professional SAQA staff at every level to step back from their work on a regular basis to review their achievements and mistakes and to chart appropriate courses for the future.

Exercise of leadership

Stephen Covey (1992:101) uses the analogy of the jungle to illustrate the difference between management and leadership. Imagine a group of producers cutting their way through a jungle with machetes, clearing out the undergrowth. The managers are behind them, sharpening their machetes, writing policy and procedure manuals, holding muscle development programmes, bringing in improvement technologies and setting up work schedules for machete wielders – all laudable management activities. The leader is the one who climbs the tallest tree, surveys the entire situation, and shouts, 'Wrong jungle!' The busy, efficient producers and managers respond with, 'Shut up! We're making progress.'

---

8 The Inter-NSB Forum - which comprises two representatives (the Chair and one other member) from each of the twelve NSBs - meets bimonthly to, among other things, consider overlaps in SGB formation.

The SAQA office may have made much progress in overseeing the implementation of the NQF, but that progress is to no avail unless it leads in the direction of real change. True progress is measured not by numbers – number of SGBs registered, number of standards registered – but by the extent to which the vision of an integrated, accessible, qualitative, just, developmental system is appropriated by education and training stakeholders and takes hold in South Africa. In other words, transformation will be measured by the nature and extent of ETQA insistence on *quality* education and training provision.

It is in the context of the quality spiral, then – the feeding back of information on provision of learning into the redesign of standards and the subsequent provision of redesigned learning programmes leading to those standards – that SAQA and its staff need to exercise leadership. Leading the education and training stakeholder community in and out of the two jungles will be the supreme test of SAQA's leadership abilities.

Chapter 10

Developing Skill and Employment in South Africa: Policy Formulation for Labour Market Adjustment

Ian Macun

Introduction

This chapter will examine skills policy, its development and implementation, from a Department of Labour perspective. During the decade of the 1990s there was a rapid development of policy across the further education and training (FET) band, emanating both from the Department of Education and the Department of Labour. Although the relationship between these policy initiatives will be touched on briefly, the main focus will be on policy development and implementation within the domain of Labour.

Approaching FET policy from the perspective of the Department of Labour implies a more clearly defined institutional focus, but also demands an approach to skills policy and its relationship to the economy and the labour market – the demand side, as it is commonly referred to. It is this relationship between skills policy and the labour market that has been dominant not only in the formulation of policy but also around its recent implementation. This is not to suggest that skills policy does not share a number of premises with other areas of education policy, but it engages them in particular ways, in different social contexts and, perhaps, with a greater degree of pragmatism.

The chapter will attempt three tasks:

- ❑ to provide a view of the development of skills policy not purely as chronology, but in relation to the thesis posed for debate by the Round Table;
- ❑ to interrogate the principles of skill policy with a view to achievements over the recent period; and
- ❑ to identify certain constraints and areas of innovation in the policy and its implementation.

It should be borne in mind that skills policy is still in an early stage of implementation. To evaluate it fully in relation to the thesis posed for the Round Table would be premature; thus, the following will remain tentative and a little speculative.

Development of skills policy

The roots of the current skills policy extend back to the Wiehahn Commission Report of 1979. The Wiehahn Commission had far-reaching implications for the restructuring of the labour relations system as a whole and its deliberations included skills shortages and the functioning of the apprenticeship system. The report of the Wiehahn Commission, as well as the Riekert Commission (1979), led to the enactment of the *Manpower Training Act* of 1981, the formation of the National Manpower Commission and the National Training Board (NTB) (SALB, 1979; Standing, Sender & Weks, 1996). After amendments to the *Manpower Training Act* in 1990, twenty-seven Industry Training Boards (ITBs) were established with control over administration and certification of training undertaken in industry. These boards were established on an industry basis and were expected to meet training needs on a day-to-day basis without state intervention (Standing *et al.*, 1996). A number of the ITBs administered levies in their sectors to fund industry-based training initiatives.

An important development occurred in 1994 with the publication by the National Training Board of a national training strategy for the country. In many ways, the national training strategy provided the bridge from the policy framework as it had evolved under the National Party government to the new skills policy of the post-1994, ANC-led government. The strategy contained policy proposals that were consistent with ANC education and training policies more generally. This was made possible by the inclusion of representatives of the Congress of South African Trade Unions (COSATU), first on the NTB and then as members of the task team that formulated the national training strategy. While the post-Wiehahn reforms had served to deracialise industry training, the NTBs proposed a national strategy democratising the governance of industry training.

The first Minister of Labour in the post-1994 government adopted the NTB's national training strategy as a framework for the development of skills policy, and this was followed by the publication of the Skills Development Strategy Green Paper in 1997. The Green paper emerged from a lengthy process of consultation (*Mail & Guardian*, 2001). It built on the NTB's earlier strategy and outlined the key arrangements for the new government's skills strategy. The Green Paper was accepted with minor amendments and paved the way for the promulgation of the *Skills Development Act* in November 1998 and the *Skills Development Levies Act* in April 1999. Broadly speaking, the Skills Development Act sets out the institutional framework for skills development by enacting the establishment of the National Skills Authority (NSA), the Sector Education Training Authorities (SETAs) and institutions within the Department of Labour, including a new planning unit. The *Skills Development Act* also introduced a new learnership system linked to the National Qualifications Framework (NQF). The *Skills Development Levies Act*, on the other hand, deals with the new skills levy and the national skills fund, that is to meet national training objectives, particularly for the unemployed and vulnerable groups in the labour market.

At first glance, the trajectory of skills policy over the past twenty years displays important continuity, especially with regard to institutional arrangements. The NTB bears some resemblance to the current NSA and the ITBs to today's SETAs. A key change has clearly been the transition from employer-driven to stakeholder-driven bodies. The role of the state remains broadly similar, however, as overseer and regulator of what are essentially industry-based or sector-based, arrangements for the administration and delivery of training. The skills levy also has a precursor in the training levies introduced and administered by the former ITBs. The continuity in policy should not obscure the continuous refinement and improvements that have taken place in the policy environment to counter past deficiencies in training. These deficiencies have been well documented,[1] but it is worth noting the main findings of an NTB assessment of the twenty-seven ITBs in 1995. These were that:

- Most ITBs focused on services relating to training accreditation and standard setting: only one-third are directly involved in delivering training.
- A variety of levy and levy/grant systems were used to collect and disburse funds to employers. Collection rates were low in many sectors.
- Many ITBs remained focused on apprenticeship and artisan training, although the focus had been shifting to include other occupational groups.
- ITBs remained focused on technical training for the employed. Only 12 per cent of training was provided to the unemployed.
- ITBs did not operate in all sectors and had limited success in involving small business and micro-enterprises. Even within their own industrial sectors, some ITBs had restricted coverage, incorporating from 50 per cent up to 100 per cent of enterprises in the sector. Some ITBs were dominated by a few large companies – for example, the chemicals, oil, hospitality, electricity, sugar milling and refining, and carbonated soft drink industries. Sectors without ITBs included government and retail, financial, security, and health services.
- The survey revealed considerable spare capacity in the private training centres accredited and granted funds by the ITBs to undertake industry training (NTB, 1995).

Thus, by the late 1980s and first half of the 1990s, the industry training system was characterised by quite severe inefficiencies and limited reach. Coupled to this was the continued racial segmentation in the provision of training through the technical colleges and training centres.

A stress on continuity should, therefore, not detract from the substantial challenges – in the way that education and training had been operating in relation to the economy – that the policy reform process sought to address. There were also important international influences on the development of South African skills policy. The 1980s and 1990s witnessed a number of important reforms in education and training systems internationally. Some of the more important reforms concerned the following:

- a move to *demand-led* training to support the performance of firms;
- *public-private governance partnerships* over training systems;

1 See, *inter alia,* Standing, Sender & Weeks (1996), Kraak, Paterson, Visser & Tustin (2000), and Ziderman & Van Adams (2000).

- a move away from traditional manpower planning to *labour market analysis* in order to inform training authorities and providers of current and emergent skills needs;
- *decentralised control* over the delivery of training to improve responsiveness of training; and
- shifting government's role from the provision of training to *financing and monitoring* training.

These reforms are all mirrored to an extent in the skills policy framework that unfolded in South Africa during the 1990s, not in the sense of policy borrowing but more as a case of modification of international experience to suit South African conditions.

Alongside the continuity, there have been important shifts in the policy framework. Perhaps the most important of these has been the linking of education and training to an outcomes-based approach and to the National Qualifications Framework. The establishment of the South African Qualifications Authority (SAQA) in 1997 ensured that implementation of the NQF was able to begin, supported in different ways by the Departments of Labour and Education. Another important shift has occurred with the introduction of a new learnership system linked to the NQF. The learnerships are fundamental to current skills policy as they are envisaged not only as a vehicle for expanding the old apprenticeship system but also as a way of supporting access to the labour market by new entrants through skill acquisition. The combination of theoretical and practical learning in the learnership has an element of continuity with an NTB recommendation that a system of 'modular performance-based institutional training coupled with controlled on-the-job training and experience' be introduced. This recommendation arose from an NTB investigation into artisan training in 1985 (cited in Standing *et al.*, 1996:455-456).

Governance of education and training has also experienced some shifts, although not as fundamental as was envisaged in certain quarters. *The* NTB's national training strategy recommended the formation of a single Ministry of Education and Training to overcome the historical divisions between policy formation for education and training within government. Neither the old nor the post-1994 governments have acted on this recommendation. Within the ambit of skills policy, however, the role of the Department of Labour has changed in significant ways. Having previously adopted a more distant role in relation to the regulation and provision of education and training, the current legislative framework demands a more active role by government in steering skills development and in ensuring the delivery of training. The latter is particularly important with regard to the operation of the National Skills Fund, established by the *Skills Development Act* and funded through an apportionment of national levy income. While this development does not signify a shift from a market-led to a state-led approach, it does require a workable partnership between government, the NSA, SETAs and training providers.

The shifts in policy over the past decade have been significant, but they have been in keeping with the premises of outcomes-based education and training, unified systems and the integration of education and training.Also important have been the continuities in policy, not merely for the sake of continuity, but in order to build on the strengths of old or existing policy and practice in a pragmatic way.A striking feature of skills policy during the 1990s, as with other areas of labour relations and labour market policy, was its incorporation into a new, co-determinist policy regime, namely that governed by the National Economic Development and Labour Council (NEDLAC). NEDLAC was established by an act of Parliament (*National Economic, Development and Labour Council Act*, 1994) and brings together representatives of organised business, labour, community and development organisations and government. NEDLAC has substantial influence on the formulation of economic and social policy and has ensured that the state has had to relinquish the control that it used to exercise over policy.[2] Both the *Skills Development Act* and the *Skills Development Levies Act* were subject to negotiations at NEDLAC. This process ensured legitimacy, understanding and support from key stakeholder constituencies.The NEDLAC process did, however, add a new focal point for skills policy, that may have detracted from a higher level of co-ordination with areas of education policy that were being developed the Department of Education at the time, particularly policies in the area of further education and training.

Apart from continuities and shifts during the 1990s, skills policy had a steady trajectory from conceptualisation, consultation, modification, and political endorsement to legislative enactment. By the end of the decade, the architecture was in place and implementation was able to proceed.

Policy principles and their implementation

The skills policy that began to be implemented in 1999 has been guided by a number of operational principles that play a crucial role in translating policy into practice, or in giving a certain reality to the premises that underlie policy.These operational principles are institution building, the use of incentives, demand-led skills development, and planning-led skills development.

In April 1999, a new National Skills Authority was constituted and began its task of making recommendations and giving policy advice to the Minister of Labour. Although principally an advisory body, the NSA debates and gives guidance on a wide range of issues relevant to implementation. In doing so, it has been able to interrogate, modify and improve upon a range of regulatory and operational guidelines emanating from the Department of Labour. In this respect, the NSA has demonstrated the value common to many co-determinist type arrangements, but it has also resulted in a lengthier process of decision-making around issues to do with policy implementation.The nature of the relationship between the NSA and the Department is one that has inevitably

2 It is interesting to note that education policy, despite its social significance, has not been brought within the NEDLAC ambit

provoked discussion and debate in the short life of this institution. This will be returned to later.

A more formidable challenge of institution building has been the establishment of the twenty-five new SETAs. This involved the collapse of the existing twenty-seven ITBs and, in a few cases, the formation of entirely new training authorities. The complex interplay of legal, organisational and political issues involved in establishing the SETAs has resulted in institutions that are at different levels of operational efficiency, some of which will require considerable time to perform their functions optimally. Given the strategic importance of the SETAs in facilitating education and training in their sectors, disbursing grants and taking on a quality assurance role, it is likely that the delivery of training will vary across sectors for some time to come.

The use of incentives is critical to skills policy as it is to other areas of education policy, particularly for the higher education sector. For skills development, incentives have been operationalised through the policy covering the disbursement of grants by SETAs to firms from levy income received in the sector. The development of appropriate and acceptable criteria has constituted an area of intermediate policy formation requiring extensive discussion and debate, not only within government but also with the NSA and SETAs. Given the relatively broad or enabling nature of skills legislation, the development of detailed regulation to govern financial and related aspects of the levy has posed a considerable challenge.[3] The underlying issue relates to the appropriate combination of incentives and supports to alter human resource development in enterprises. Micro level interventions are complex at the best of times and this has proved true of the levy/grant system as a way of incentivising the development of an enterprise training culture in South Africa. Although it is too early to assess the grant system, given that it is still in its first year of operation, its success will depend not only on the package of incentives that have been put in place but also on the administrative efficiency of the levy collection and income disbursement by the South African Revenue Service (SARS). The role of the SETAs, particularly in relation to enterprises within their sector, will be another crucial factor determining the success or otherwise of the levy/grant system.

A consistent theme of skills policy during the 1990s has been the importance of education and training being demand-led. The emphasis on demand-led training is most commonly interpreted to refer to the importance of responding to employer needs and hence ensuring training for employment. In theory, this is an important strategic emphasis given the past legacy of training provision, particularly state-supported training provision, being perpetuated on the basis of needs that are difficult to monitor and verify. Given the very low placement rates of beneficiaries of training by the Department of Labour, a reasonable assumption would be that the training provided has not assisted beneficiaries to access employment. On the other hand, available

3 The regulation governing the first year of operation of the levy/grant system is contained in Government Gazette number 20865, published on 7 February 2000.

evidence would suggest that there has been declining investment in private sector industry training despite claims of skills shortages in a number of occupation and skill categories. In relation to this paradoxical situation, the focus of skills development is clearly to stimulate demand and on the delivery of training to meet skills shortages and skills gaps in the labour market. The levy system is intended to contribute to the stimulation of demand and the introduction of planning is intended to ensure improved co-ordination between labour market skills requirements and investment in training. What has become clear, however, is the importance of a defined industrial strategy to serve as a framework within which to stimulate demand in ways that support a broader economic growth strategy.

Although the prospects for economic growth have improved moderately, South Africa remains a low-growth economy with formal sector employment contracting during the latter part of the 1990s. This situation is likely to depress demand for new skills or occupations in aggregate terms. The increased rate of unemployment during the latter part of the 1990s, coupled to the legacy of poor human resource development under apartheid, will undoubtedly stimulate demand for improvements in a range of basic and intermediate skills on which work-based learning can then build, whether in the formal sector or in situations of self-employment. What is apparent is the need to develop a more disaggregated approach to the principle of demand-led training and to develop policy guidelines that are able to guide skills planning and training delivery in ways that are appropriate to economic and labour market developments. In doing so, the levels of skill formation identified by the ILO (Standing et al., 1996:450) can provide a useful grid through which to interrogate specific 'sites of demand' for skills. The ILO outlines the following levels:

- pre-labour market (schooling + adult education + vocational training);
- labour market entry training (induction + apprenticeship + on-the-job + institutional);
- internal labour market training (retraining for performance + retraining for upgrading/mobility);
- adjustment training (retraining for retrenchment + unemployment training); and
- flexibility training (institutional + multi-tasking vs. multi-skilling).

In South Africa, as elsewhere, it is mainly the first two forms of training that have received attention. Pre-labour market training is mainly devoted to formal schooling with weak links to the world of work and little incorporation of vocational education in the curriculum (Kraak & Hall, 1999:21). As indicated above, the levels of labour market entry and internal labour market training are weak and the apprenticeship system has been declining substantially over the past decade. The introduction of the new learnerships is likely to have its greatest impact at this level of skill formation. Despite the high rate of unemployment and substantial job losses, adjustment training has also not received much focus. The Department of Labour launched a scheme for training the unemployed in 1985, but there has been a decline both in the number of persons trained and more dramatically in the numbers placed in employment after training. The extent to which the private sector provides training prior to retrenchment is unknown, although it is unlikely to be significant given the general training record of industry. Non-governmental agencies, such as the Mineworkers Development Agency, do provide training for retrenched workers but the extent of this training is difficult to quantify. It is to be hoped that the substantial amounts of funding that will become available through the National Skills Fund will stimulate the supply of training for labour market adjustment. Given the low rate of labour absorption in the economy, a key challenge will be to ensure the acquisition of workplace skills as part of such training and the delivery of training appropriate to self-employment or to areas of existing or potential demand for skills.

The fifth form of skill formation – flexibility training – is especially important in the context of technological and labour market change. Standing, Sender and Weeks (1996:450) suggest that this is 'likely to show the greatest growth in the next few years, since the increasing pace of technological, workplace and enterprise change, coupled with much more flexible labour markets, mean that a growing proportion of the working age population will find themselves regularly changing job, work status, occupation and sector of employment'.

Ensuring appropriate training delivery for these developments poses challenges to the education sector to adapt and diversify learning programmes to suit the needs of working people in a flexible labour market. It may well be that the demand for training necessary for skill formation at this level will be for education and training of relatively short duration, with a specific focus and with flexible forms of delivery. Such training will also have to articulate with the NQF and will thus require forward planning and investment on the part of education and training providers.

The final operational principle is that of planning for skills development. The *Skills Development Act* introduces planning in four ways:

- *National Skills Development Strategy*: The *Skills Development Act* refers to a National Skills Development Strategy (NSDS). It is one of the functions of the National Skills Authority to advise the Minister of Labour on a national strategy. The role of the NSDS is to provide a broad framework within which skills development is to take place. It is intended that this strategy will identify a series of objectives to guide strategic planning for skills development and to guide the implementation of skills development. The strategy will also contain a number of targets that will serve as mechanisms for managing the implementation of skills development by the SETAs.

- *Sector Skills Plans (SSPs)*: These are the responsibility of the SETAs who draw up their plans, submit them to the Department of Labour and receive grant payments partly on the basis of their plans. During September 2000, the first twenty-five SSPs were drafted by the SETAs and submitted to the Skills Development Planning Unit.

- *Workplace Skills Plans (WSPs)*: The Act makes a passing reference to SETAs having to approve workplace skills plans. This aspect has been further elaborated in a recent regulation dealing with the way in which grants are to be disbursed back to individual enterprises.

- *Skills Development Planning Unit*: The Act requires the establishment of a Skills Development Planning Unit (SPDU) within the Department of Labour, which has to, inter alia, assist in the development of an NSDS and liaise with SETAs regarding their Sector Skills Plans. The SDPU was established in June 1999 and has since been playing an active role in supporting the above three dimensions of strategic planning for skills development.

The purpose of planning for further education and training is to establish objectives and targets and to translate them into a schedule of operational activities for a set period of time. This should facilitate effective budgeting and the distribution of resources and, in this sense, provides a strategic management tool. A second purpose of planning, as with planning in other FET systems and for education in general, is to anticipate future activities (Gasskov, 2000). To achieve this requires the use of labour market information, and the current skills development strategy is premised on the flow of information from enterprises to SETAs, and from SETAs to the SDPU. In this way, there is both bottom-up dimension to planning and through the formulation of a national strategy, a top-down approach. Given the relatively poorly-developed state of labour market information, however, deviations from planned operations are very likely to occur and adjustments to plans at all levels are to be anticipated (Gasskov, 2000).

Critical issues, constraints and innovations

Policy for skills development has undergone a series of refinements and some significant shifts over the past two decades, to the point where a new strategy for skills development is now in the early phases of implementation. To date, implementation has brought into sharp focus the ambitious nature of the reform process that is under way. It is a process that requires new institutions to be developed, new funding systems to become effective, an outcomes-based learning and qualifications infrastructure to be developed, the use of skills planning at all levels of the system, and much more. Undertaking such a process stretches capacity in all areas: within government, in the new SETAs and among employers who are required to adapt to a number of new legislative requirements. The implications of the *Employment Equity Act* (1998a) and its relationship to skills development, has emerged as a particularly important theme for the Department of Labour to address.

Within this scenario, there are a number of critical issues that compete for attention in policy debates. One clear issue relates to SAQA and the implementation of the NQF. There have been criticisms of SAQA's capacity and the speed with which it has been able to register qualifications in an outcomes-based format. This issue is dealt with more fully in other chapters in this collection, but given the importance of the NQF for the transformation of education and training, it is to be hoped that the focus of debates will be on ways of improving the implementation of the NQF. Another issue deserving attention is how best to build the capacity of training providers to respond to the new policy environment, both public and private providers delivering education and training at different levels. How to develop closer linkages between trade and industry policies and further education and training will be critical to ensuring the success of a demand-led skills strategy. Finally, the ability of government and SETAs to ensure sufficient participation in the levy/grant system on the one hand, and their ability to effectively utilise the monies made available through the new skill policy on the other hand, will be fundamental to the long-term success of the strategy. Within this diverse range of issues that could focus policy debates, one that will be highlighted relates to the governance of the system.

Governance of education and training can be viewed in at least two different ways. Firstly, governance involves the level of state intervention in the functioning of education and training. Related to this is the nature of the relationship between government and intermediary institutions that control the implementation of skills development. Secondly, governance could be said to relate to the operation of government itself – that is, the degree of co-ordination of education and training between government departments with responsibility for education and training. These two dimensions are worth considering briefly in relation to implementation of policy.

Traditionally, debates about government intervention revolve around two different perspectives. On the one hand, there is the view that employers are unlikely to invest in training unless constraints and/or incentives are imposed upon them to do so. In this case, the assumption is that the state needs to design interventions to enhance the level of training. On the other hand, the neo-classical view would be that employers are in a position to define training needs and to ensure delivery against those needs, as they are able to see to the interests of their staff. In this case, the market can solve the problem of training by leaving the solution to employers, individuals and organised workers (Ashton & Green, 1996:179). The history of vocational education and training in South Africa has tended towards the second view and the result has clearly been one of market failure – hence the policy reforms of the past decade. Skills development policy has, however, not swung back to the first view but encapsulates a hybrid of the state-led versus market-driven polarity. With the creation of intermediary institutions – the NSA and SETAs, whose internal governance is led by stakeholder representatives – different interests are combined to decide on how best to govern and implement skills development. This arrangement allows for employers, employees and other representative groupings to exercise substantial control over the way in which resources for training are allocated. The role of government, therefore, remains important but also potentially contested.

In the implementation of skills policy this relationship between government, the NSA and SETAs is inevitably complex, but the Department of Labour has correctly chosen a key role in governance by retaining a number of functions within the Department of Labour rather than constituting a wholly independent, tripartite body to steer the implementation of skills policy. This does not deny stakeholders a real role in governance, but it does allow for the exercise of substantial influence by government and means that, in practice, there is substantial pressure placed on government to perform a number of operational functions that test its capacity and require it to play a key role in co-ordinating implementation.

The structure of governance for skills development is only possible within the labour arena in South Africa, given the presence of organised interest groups within this sphere and given the emergence of an ethos and practice of co-determinism during the 1990s. In this context, there is a clear imperative towards co-ordination between the Departments of Labour and Education to ensure complementarity between the education system and industry. The notion of an integrated system, perhaps represented by a single government department with responsibility for further education and training, no longer appears to be a realistic option. The policy frameworks that have developed during the 1990s in the area of further education and training address very different imperatives in ways that mirror the functioning of different government departments and it is unlikely that a third wave of policy reform would be feasible at this stage. The recent move towards a government-wide Human Resource Development Strategy, led by the Departments of Education and Labour, could serve as a new mechanism for ensuring co-ordination in the area of education, training and the labour market and an alternative way of overcoming sectoral divisions.

Conclusion

The progress of skills policy over the past decade would suggest that there has been a steady progression towards a framework that remains broadly consistent with the idea of an integrated education and training system. It has been formulated and implemented in ways that are consistent with the characteristics of the broader labour relations regulatory framework, but this is also consistent with practice in other countries. More importantly, the governance model adopted for skills policy in South Africa is one that is most likely to lead to improvements in skills development in the economy and in society as it has been able to establish a structured relationship between the state and the market.

Finally, it is worth noting the cautionary tone adopted by the authors of a recent joint study by the International Labour Organisation and the World Bank (Gill, Fluitman &

Dar, 2000). In their introduction, they state:

> Governments often expect their vocational education and training (VET) systems to perform feats that they would not expect from other systems such as general education. Governments have perceived an increased demand for training if the labour supply shows rapid growth, if employment grows quickly, or if unemployment increases significantly. They have called upon VET systems to help unemployed young people and older workers get jobs, reduce the burden on higher education, to attract foreign investment, to ensure rapid growth of earnings and employment, to reduce the inequality of earnings between the rich and the poor, and so on. The list is disconcertingly long. These high expectations have resulted in heavy government involvement in VET, but the record has been disappointing.

During the coming phase of implementing skills development in South Africa, it would appear that not only are reasonable expectations required, but also a creative and dynamic partnership between government and the institutions that have been designed to implement the policy in the interests of society and the economy.

Bibliography

African National Congress (ANC). 1990a. Discussion Document on Economic Policy. Pamphlet. Johannesburg: ANC.

African National Congress. 1990b. Recommendations on Post-apartheid Economic Policy. *Transformation*, 12:2-15.

African National Congress. 1992. ANC Policy Guidelines for a Democratic South Africa. Adopted at the National Policy Conference. Johannesburg: ANC.

African National Congress. 1994a. *An Implementation Plan for Education and Training. Johannesburg:* ANC.

African National Congress. 1994b. *A Policy Framework for Education and Training. Johannesburg:* ANC.

African National Congress. 1994c. *The Reconstruction and Development Programme. Johannesburg:* Umanyano Publications.

Ashton, D. 1999. The Skill Formation Process: A Paradigm Shift? *Journal of Education and Work*, 12(3):347-351.

Ashton, D. and F. Green. 1996. *Education, Training and the Global Economy*. Cheltenham: Edward Elgar.

Association for the Development of Education in Africa (ADEA). 1996. *Formulating Education Policy: Lessons and Experiences from Sub-Saharan Africa. Six Case Studies and Reflections from the ADEA Biennial Meetings, October 1995*. Tours, France: ADEA.

Association for the Development of Education in Africa. 2000. What Works and What's New in Education: Africa Speaks! Proceedings of the ADEA Biennial Meeting, Johannesburg, 5-9 December 1999.

Badat, Saleem. 1998. Education Politics in the Transition Period. In Peter Kallaway, Glenda Kruss, Aslam Fataar and Gari Donn (eds.), *Education After Apartheid: South African Education in Transition.* Cape Town: UCT Press.

Badat, S., F. Barron, G. Fisher, P. Pillay, and H. Wolpe. 1994. Differentiation and Disadvantage: The Historically Black Universities in South Africa. Report to the Desmond Tutu Educational Trust. Bellville: Education Policy Unit, University of the Western Cape.

Ball, S.J. 1999. *Educational Reform and the Struggle for the Soul of the Teacher.* Education Policy Studies Series, 17:1-38.

Beck, U. 2000. The Cosmopolitan Perspective: Sociology of the Second Age of Modernity. *British Journal of Sociology*, 51(1):79-105.

Bernstein, B. 1996. *Pedagogy, Symbolic Control and Identity*. London: Taylor & Francis.

Bird, A. and G. Elliot. 1993a. An Integrated Approach to Post-compulsory Education. Paper presented to a policy workshop of the Centre for Education Policy Development and the ANC Education Department.

Bird, A. and G. Elliot. 1993b. A Framework for Lifelong Learning: A Unified Multi-path Approach to Education and Training. A draft ANC/COSATU discussion document prepared for the first ANC National Training Policy Workshop.

Bloomer, M. 1997. *Curriculum Making in Post 16 Education: The Social Conditions of Studentship*. London: Routledge.

Braverman, H. 1974. *Labour and Monopoly Capital. New York:* Monthly Review Press.

Brown, P. 1999. Globalisation and the Political Economy of High Skills. *Journal of Education and Work*, 12(3):233-253.

Buenfil-Burgos, Rosa Nidia. 2000. Globalisation, Education and Discourse Political Analysis: Ambiguity and Accountability in Research. *International Journal of Qualitative Studies in Education*, 13(1):1-24.

Castells, M. 1996. *The Information Age: Economy, Society and Culture. Volume I.* Oxford: Blackwell.

Castells, M. 1997. *The Information Age: Economy, Society and Culture. Volume II.* Oxford: Blackwell.

Castells, M. 1998. *The Information Age: Economy, Society and Culture. Volume III.* Oxford: Blackwell.

Chall, J.S. 2000. *The Academic Achievement Challenge*. New York: Guildford.

Chisholm, Linda. 1992. Policy and Critique in South African Educational Research. *Transformation*, 18:149-160.

Chisholm, Linda and Bruce Fuller. 1996. Remember People's Education? Shifting Alliances, State-Building and South Africa's Narrowing Policy Agenda. *Journal of Education Policy*, 11(6):693-716.

Christie, Pam and Jonathan Jansen (eds.). 1999. *Changing the Curriculum: Studies in Outcomes-based Education in South Africa.* Cape Town: Juta.

Clements, M.A. Undated. The National Curriculum in Australia. http://www.ecel.uwa.edu.au/gse/erp/vol23no1/clements.html

Cloete, N. and I Bunting. 1999. Higher Education in South Africa in 1999: Towards a Single Co-ordinated System: A Reflective Piece for the TELP Leadership Seminar. Mimeo. Pretoria: CHET.

Cloete, N. and I. Bunting. 2000. *Higher Education Transformation: Assessing Performance in South Africa.* Pretoria: CHET.

Collins, R. 1998. *The Sociology of Philosophies: A Global Theory of Intellectual Change.* Cambridge, MA: Harvard University Press.

Committee of Technikon Principals (CTP). 1995. *A Framework for the Introduction of Degrees at Technikons.* Pretoria: CTP.

Committee of Technikon Principals. 2000. *Response to the Report of the Council on Higher Education Task Team: 'Towards a New Higher Education Landscape'.* Pretoria: CTP.

Congress of South African Trade Unions (COSATU). 1993a. COSATU, the Way Forward: Building the Programme for Economic Reconstruction and Development. Discussion document of the COSATU Executive Committee, March. Johannesburg: COSATU.

Congress of South African Trade Unions. 1993b. Discussion Paper on the Way Forward. Discussion document of the COSATU Executive Committee, January. Johannesburg: COSATU.

Council on Higher Education (CHE). 2000a. Size and Shape Task Team Discussion Document. April 7. Pretoria: CHE.

Council on Higher Education. 2000b. *Towards a New Higher Education Institutional Landscape: Meeting the Equity, Quality and Social Development Imperatives of the Twenty-First Century*. Report of the Size and Shape Task Team. July. Pretoria: CHE.

Covey, Stephen R. 1992. *The Seven Habits of Highly Effective People*. London: Simon & Shuster.

Davis, Z. 1996. The Problem-centred Approach and the Production of the Vanishing Pedagogue. Paper presented to the Kenton-at-Wilgespruit Conference. October.

De Clerq, Francine. 1998. Effective Policies and the Reform Process: An Evaluation of the New Development and Education Macro Policies. In Peter Kallaway, Glenda Kruss, Aslam Fataar and Gari Donn (eds.), *Education After Apartheid: South African Education in Transition*. Cape Town: UCT Press.

Department of Education (DoE). 1995a. Education and Training in a Democratic South Africa: First Steps to Development a New System. White Paper on Education and Training. Notice 196 of 1995, 15 March 1996. *Government Gazette,* 357(16312).

Department of Education. 1995b. *Report of the Committee to Reivew the Organisation, Governance and Funding of Schools* (Hunter Report). Pretoria: DoE.

Department of Education. 1996a. *Curriculum Framework for General and Further Education*. Pretoria: DoE.

Department of Education. 1996b. *Green Paper on Higher Education Transformation.* Pretoria: DoE.

Department of Education. 1996c. The Organisation, Governance and Funding of Schools: Education White Paper 2. Notice 130 of 1996, February. *Government Gazette*, 368(16987).

Department of Education. 1997a. *Education White Paper 3. A Programme for the Transformation of Higher Education*. Pretoria: DoE.

Department of Education. 1997b. *Report of the National Committee for Further Education: A Framework for the Transformation of Further Education and Training in South Africa*. Pretoria: DoE.

Department of Education. 1998a. *Education White Paper 4: A Programme for the Transformation of Further Education and Training: Preparing for the Twenty-First Century through Education, Training and Work*. Pretoria: DoE.

Department of Education. 1998b. *Green Paper on Further Education and Training: Preparing for the Twenty-first Century through Education, Training and Work.* Pretoria: DoE.

Department of Education. 1998c. *National and Institutional Planning Framework for the Higher Education System*. Pretoria: DoE.

Department of Education. 1999a. *Call to Action: Mobilising Citizens to Build a South African Education and Training System for the 21st Century*. Statement by Professor Kader Asmal, Minister of Education, 27 July 1999. Pretoria: DoE.

Department of Education. 1999b. *Developments in Education since the 1994 Elections: Our Current Challenges and Plans for the Future*. Report on the National Policy Review Conference on Education and Training, 9-12 October, Johannesburg.

Department of Education. 1999c. *Implementation Plan for Tirisano – January 2000 to December 2004*. Pretoria: DoE.

Department of Education. 1999d. *National Strategy for Further Education and Training 1999-2001: Preparing for the Twenty-first Century through Education, Training and Work*. Pretoria: DoE.

Department of Education. 2000a. *Annual Report 1999*. Pretoria: DoE.

Department of Education. 2000b. *Building a New Institutional Landscape for the FET System: Draft Criteria for the Declaration of FET Institutions*. Pretoria: DoE.

Department of Education. 2000c. The Learnership as a Mode of Delivery: Experiences of the Hospitality, Travel, and Tourism Sector. Appendix 7 of Open Learning in South African General and Further Education and Training. Unpublished Policy Report.

Department of Education. 2000d. Minutes of the Council of Education Ministers Meeting, 19 June 2000, Pretoria.

Department of Education. 2000e. National Curriculum Framework for Further Education and Training: Draft Document. Pretoria: DoE.

Department of Education. 2000f. *A South African Curriculum for the Twenty-first Century. Report of the Review Committee on Curriculum 2005* (Chisholm Report). Pretoria: DoE.

Department of Education. 2001. *National Plan for Higher Education*. Pretoria: DoE.

Departments of Education and Labour. 2001. *Human Resource Development Strategy for South Africa. A Nation at Work for a Better Life for All*. Pretoria: Government Printer.

Department of Finance (DoF). 1996. *Growth, Employment and Redistribution: A Macroeconomic Strategy*. Pretoria: DoF.

Department of Labour (DoL). 1997. *Green Paper: Skills Development Strategy for Economic and Employment Growth in South Africa*. Pretoria: DoL.

Department of Labour. 2000. *Standards and Qualifications for Occupation-directed Education Training and Development Practitioners*. Pretoria: DoL.

Department of Labour. 2001. *The National Skills Development Strategy: Skills for Productive Citizenship for All*. Pretoria: DoL.

Department of National Education (DNE). 1991. Education Renewal Strategy: Discussion Document. Pretoria: UNISA.

Department of National Education. 1992. *Education Renewal Strategy: Management Solutions for Education in South Africa*. Pretoria: DNE.

Department of National Education. 1995. A Qualification Structure for Universities in South Africa. NATED 02-116, March 1995 revision. Pretoria: DNE.

Eberstadt, M. 1999. The Schools they Deserve: Howard Gardner and the Remaking of Elite Education. *Policy Review*, 97. http://policyreview.com/oct99/eberstadt.html

Education Review Office. 2000. *In Time for the Future: A Comparative Study of Mathematics and Science Education*. Wellington, New Zealand: Education Review Office.

Engines for Education. 2000. http://www/ils.nwu/edu/~e_for_e/NODE-219-pg.html

Ensor, Paula. 1995. Constructing 'Good Practice': Issues of Apprenticeship and Alienation in an Initial Mathematics Teacher Education Programme. In G. Kruss and H. Jacklin (eds.), *Realising Change: Education Policy Research*. Kenwyn: Juta.

Ensor, Paula. 2001. Curriculum Restructuring in Higher Education in South Africa in the 1990s. Unpublished paper. University of Cape Town.

Erwin, A. 1990. An Economic Policy Framework. Paper presented at the Workshop on Future Economic Policy for South Africa, Harare, May.

Erwin, A. 1992. Economic Reconstruction. *African Communist*, 129:13-23.

Figaji, B. 1999. Higher Education in South Africa: Differentiation or Convergence? Inaugural Professorial Lecture, Peninsula Technikon, Bellville, Western Cape.

Finegold, D. 1991. Education, Training and Economic Performance in Comparative Perspective. *Oxford Studies in Comparative Education*, 1:57-68.

Finegold, D. and D. Soskice. 1988. The Failure of Training in Britain: Analysis and Prescription. *Oxford Review of Economic Policy*, 4(3):21-51.

Finegold, D. et al. 1990. *A British Baccalaureat: Ending the Division between Education and Training. Education and Training Paper No. 1*. London: Inst. for Public Policy Research.

Fowler, Roger. 1986. *Linguistic Criticism*. Oxford: OUP.

Freire, Paulo and Myles Horton. 1990. *We Make the Road by Walking: Conversations on Education and Social Change*. Edited by John Peters. Philadelphia: Temple University Press.

Gardner, H. 2000. Paroxysms of Choice. *New York Review of Books*, XLVII(16):44-49.

Gasskov, V. 2000. *Managing Vocational Training Systems. Geneva:* ILO.

Gee, J.P. 1999. Progressivism and the 'Code': A Paper. http://www.appstate.edu/~moormang/wwwboard2/messages/123.html

Gelb, S. 1991. South African's Economic Crisis: An Overview. In S. Gelb (ed.), South *Africa's Economic Crisis*. Cape Town: David Philip.

Gelb, S. 1992. The Political Economy of the Black Middle Class in a Democratic South Africa. Paper commissioned by NEPI.

Gibbons, M., C. Limoges, H. Nowotny, S. Schwartzman, P. Scott and M. Trow. 1994. *The New Production of Knowledge: The Dynamics of Science and Research in Contemporary Societies*. London: Sage.

Gill, I., F. Fluitman and A. Dar (eds.). 2000. *Vocational Education and Training Reform – Matching Skills to Markets and Budgets*. New York: ILO, World Bank and OUP.

Goedegebuure, L. 1992. *Mergers in Higher Education: A Comparative Perspective*. Uitgeverij Lemma: CHEPS.

Gore, J.M. 1997. On the Limits to Empowerment through Critical and Feminist Pedagogies. In D. Carlson and M. Apple (eds.), *Critical Educational Theory in Unsettling Times*. Minneapolis: Minneapolis University Press.

Gramsci, A. 1986. *Selections from the Prison Notebooks*. London: Lawrence & Wishart.

Green, A. and A. Sakamoto. 2000. *The Place of Skills in National Competitive Strategies in Germany, Japan, Singapore and the UK*. London: Institute of Education.

Green, A., A. Wolf and T Leney. 1998. *Convergence and Divergence in European Education and Training Systems*. London: Bedford Way Papers and Institute of Education.

Griffith, R. 2000. *National Curriculum: National Disaster? Education and Citizenship*. London: Falmer.

Griffiths, T. and D. Guile. 1999. Learning and Pedagogy in Work-based Contexts. In P. Mortimore (ed.), *Understanding Pedagogy and its Impact on Learning*. London: Sage.

Groener, Z. 1998. Political Roots of the Debate about the Integration of Education and Training. In W. Morrow and K. King (eds.), *Vision and Reality: Changing Education and Training in South Africa*. Cape Town: UCT Press.

Guile, D. and M. Young. (forthcoming, 2001). Transfer and Transition in Vocational Education: Some Theoretical Considerations.

Handy, C. 1994. *The Empty Raincoat*. London: Hutchinson.

Hargreaves, Andy and S. W. Moore. Educational Outcomes: Modern and Post Modern Interpretations. *British Journal of Sociology of Education*, 21(1):27-43.

Hargreaves, Andy *et al.* 1998. International Handbook of Educational Change. Great Britain: Kluwer Academic.

Hartshorne, Ken. 1999. *The Making of Education Policy in South Africa*. Cape Town: OUP Southern Africa.

Hess, Frederick. 1997. Initiation without Implementation: Policy Churn and the Plight of Urban School Reform. Paper prepared for the Conference on Rethinking School Governance, at the Kennedy School of Government, Harvard University, Cambridge, Massachusetts, USA, 12-13 June.

Hirsch, E.D. 2000. The Roots of the Education Wars. http://www.tc.umn.edu/~athe0007/HirschArticle.html

Human Sciences Research Council (HSRC). 1981a. *Provision of Education in the Republic of South Africa: Report of the Main Committee of the HSRC Investigation into Education*. Pretoria: HSRC.

Human Sciences Research Council. 1981b. *Provision of Education in the Republic of South Africa: Report of the Work Committee on Technical and Vocational Education*. Pretoria: HSRC.

International Labour Organisation (ILO). 2000. Conclusions on Human Resources, Training and Development. Paper presented to the ILO 2000 Conference, Geneva.

James, Wilmot (ed.). 2000. Values, Education and Democracy: Report of the Working Group on Values in Education. Prepared for the Minister of Education, 8 May.

Jansen, Jonathan D. 1995. Understanding Social Transition through the Lens of Curriculum Policy. *Journal of Curriculum Studies*, 2(3):245-261.

Jansen, Jonathan D. 1999a. Curriculum Reform Since Apartheid: Intersections of Policy and Practice in the South African Transition. *Journal of Curriculum Studies*, 31(1):5-6.

Jansen, Jonathan D. 1999b. Lessons Learned (and Not Learned) from the OBE Experience. In N. Bak (ed.), Making OBE Work?, Conference of the Western Cape Education Department, Kromme, Rhee Cape Administration Academy, 13-15 December.

Jansen, Jonathan D. 1999c. Setting the Scene: Historiographies of Curriculum Policy in South Africa. In J.D. Jansen and P. Christie (eds.), *Changing Curriculum: Studies on Outcomes-based Education in South Africa*. Cape Town: Juta.

Jansen, Jonathan D. 1999d. The State and Curriculum in the Transition to Socialism: The Zimbabwean Experience. In N. McGinn and E. Epstein (eds.), Comparative *Perspectives on the Role of Education in Democratisation*. Frankfurt am Main: Peter Lang.

Jansen, Jonathan D. 2000a. *Framing Education Policy After Apartheid: On the Politics of Non-reform in South African Education, 1990-2000*. Johannesburg: Centre for Development Enterprises.

Jansen, Jonathan D. 2000b. Taking Gibbons on a Walk through a South African University. In Andre Kraak (ed.), *Changing Modes: New Knowledge Production and Its Implications for Higher Education in South Africa*. Pretoria: HSRC.

Jessup, G. 1991. *Outcomes: The Emerging Model of Vocational Education and Training*. London: Falmer.

Kahn, Michael J. 1996. Five Years Gone: A Case Study of Education Policy Implementation in the Transition to Democracy in South Africa. *International Journal of Educational Development*, 16(3):281-289.

Kallaway, Peter, Glenda Kruss, Aslam Fataar and Gari Donn. 1998. *Education After Apartheid*. Cape Town: UCT Press.

Kaplan, D. 1990. Comment on the ANC Economic Policy Recommendations. *Transformation*, 12:21-24.

Kaplan, D. 1991. The South African Capital Goods Sector and the Economic Crisis. In S. Gelb (ed.), *South Africa's Economic Crisis*. Cape Town: David Philip.

Kaplinsky, R. 1990. A Policy Agenda for Post-apartheid South Africa. *Transformation*, 16:49-55.

Keep, E. 1999. UK's VET Policy and the 'Third Way': Following a High Skills Trajectory or Running up a Dead-end Street. *Journal of Education and Work*, 12(3).

Khuzwayo, M. 1999. The NETF and the History Syllabus Revision Process. Unpublished Masters dissertation, University of Durban-Westville.

King, K. 1998. Policy Coherence in Education, Training and Enterprise Development in South Africa: The Implementation Challenges of New Policies. In W. Morrow and K. King (eds.), *Vision and Reality: Changing Education and Training in South Africa*. Cape Town. UCT Press.

Kraak, Andre. 1997. Formulating Alternatives to Neo-liberal Conceptions of Industrial Training: A 'Macro Institutional' Assessment of Skills Development Strategies. *Southern African Review of Education with Education with Production, 3*.

Kraak, Andre. 1998. *Competing Education and Training policies: A 'Systematic' versus 'Unit Standards' Approach*. Occasional Papers Series 1998/1. Pretoria: HSRC.

Kraak, Andre. 1999a. Planning Imperative: New Policy Framework for FET. In Andre Kraak and G. Hall, *Tranforming Further Education and Training in South Africa: A Case Study of Technical Colleges in KwaZulu-Natal*. Pretoria: HSRC.

Kraak, Andre. 1999b. Problems facing Further Education and Training. In Andre Kraak and G. Hall, *Tranforming Further Education and Training in South Africa: A Case Study of Technical Colleges in KwaZulu-Natal*. Pretoria: HSRC.

Kraak, Andre (ed.). 2000a. *Changing Modes: New Knowledge Production and its Implicaitons for Higher Education in South Africa*. Pretoria: HSRC.

Kraak, Andre. 2000b. HSRC Policy Proposal. An Education Policy Retrospective, 1990-2000: Analysing the Process of Policy Implementation and Reform. Unpublished paper. Pretoria: HSRC.

Kraak, Andre. 2001. Debating Castells and Carnoy on the Network Society: Towards a New International Politics and Development Regime. In N. Cloete and J. Muller, *The Challenges of the Global: South African Debates with Castells*. Cape Town: Pearsons and Maskew Miller Longman.

Kraak, Andre and Hall, G. 1999. *Transforming Further Education and Training in South Africa – A Case Study of Technical Colleges in KwaZulu-Natal*. Pretoria: HSRC.

Kraak, Andre and Nisaar Mahomed. 2001. Qualifications Reform in Higher Education. An Evaluation of the Work of National Standards Bodies. In Mignonne Breier (ed.), *Curriculum Restructuring in Higher Education in Post-apartheid South Africa*. Cape Town, Education Policy Unit, University of the Western Cape.

Kraak, Andre, A. Paterson, A. Visser and D. Tustin. 2000. *Baseline Survey of Industrial Training in South Africa*. Study commissioned by the Labour Market Skills Development Programme (European Union and Department of Labour). Pretoria: HSRC and Bureau of Market Research.

Lasonen, J. and M. Young. 1998. *Strategies for Achieving Parity of Esteem in European Secondary Education*. Finland: University of Jyvaskyla.

Lauder, H. 1999. Competitiveness and the Problem of Low Skill Equilibria: A Comparative Analysis. *Journal of Education and Work*, 12(3).

Lave, J. and E. Wenger. 1991. *Situated Learning: Legitimate Peripheral Participation*. Cambridge: CUP.

Levin, R. 1991. People's Education and the Politics of Negotiations in South Africa. *Perspectives in Education*, 12(2).

MacDonald, H. 1998. Why Johnny's Teacher Can't Teach. *City Journal*, 8(2). http://www.city-journal.org.html/8_2_al.html

Mail and Guardian. 2001. Supplement: Skilling SA. February 2-8.

Malherbe, E.G. 1937. *Educational Adaptations in a Changing Society*. Cape Town and Johannesburg: Juta.

Manganyi, N.C. 2001. Public Policy and the Transformation of Education in South Africa. In Y. Sayed and J.D. Jansen (eds.), *Implementing Education Policy after Apartheid*. Cape Town: UCT Press.

Mannheim, K. 1936/1991. *Ideology and Utopia: An Introduction to the Sociology of Knowledge*. London: Routledge.

Maqutu, T.Z., Jairam Khumalo and Jonathan D. Jansen. 1999. *A Very Noisy OBE. A Report on the Implementation of OBE Inside Grade 1 Classrooms*. Durban: Centre for Education Research, Evaluation and Policy, University of Durban-Westville.

Mathews, John. 1988. *Tools for Change: New Technology and the Democratisation of Work*. Sydney: Pluto.

Mbeki, T. 1999. The State of the Nation Address of the President of South Africa, Thabo Mbeki, to the National Assembly, Cape Town, 25 June 1999.

Mbeki, T. 2000. The State of the Nation Address of the President of South Africa, Thabo Mbeki, to the National Assembly, Cape Town, 4 February 2000.

McLaughlin, M. 1998. Listening and Learning from the Field: Tales of Policy Implementation and Situated Practice. In Andy Hargreaves *et al., International Handbook of Educational Change*. Great Britain: Kluwer.

Mkwanazi, Z. *et al.* 1995. The Ongoing Process of Change: Policy and Conflict in South African Education and Training. *Quarterly Review of Education and Training in South Africa,* 2(3).

Moore, R. and J. Muller. 1999. The Discourse of 'Voive' and the Problem of Knowledge and Identity in the Sociology of Knowledge. *British Journal of the Sociology of Education,* 20(2):189-206.

Moore, R. and M. Young. 2001. Knowledge and the Curriculum in the Sociology of Education: Towards a Reconceptualisation. *British Journal of the Sociology of Education,* 20(2).

Mosala, I. 2000. Presentation to the Seminar on the Size and Shape of Higher Education, University of the Witwatersrand, 13 September.

Muller, J. 2000a. *Reclaiming Knowledge: Social Theory, Curriculum and Education Policy*. London: Routledge Falmer.

Muller, J. 2000b. The Sound and Fury of International School Reform: A Critical Review. Mimeo.

Murray, Robin. 1988. Life After Henry (Ford). *Marxism Today,* 3.

National Commission on Higher Education (NCHE). 1996a. Discussion Document: A Framework for Transformation. Pretoria: NCHE.

National Commission on Higher Education. 1996b. A Framework for Transformation. Pretoria: NCHE.

National Commission on Higher Education. 1996c. Notes on the NCHE Consultative Meeting with University and Technikon Principals (CUP and CTP), June 1, HSRC Building, Pretoria.

National Education Policy Initiative (NEPI). 1992. *Human Resources Development: Final Report of the HRD Research Group*. Cape Town: OUP.

National Education Policy Initiative. 1993. *The Framework Report*. Cape Town: OUP.

National Training Board (NTB). 1994. A National Training Strategy Initiative. Discussion Document. Pretoria: NTB.

National Training Board. 1995. *Funding of Training in South Africa. The Final Report*. Pretoria: NTB.

National Training Board and Human Sciences Research Council (NTB/HSRC). 1991. *Investigation into a National Training Strategy for the Republic of South Africa.* Pretoria: NTB/HSRC.

Nzimande, Blade. 2001. Interview on the Role of Parliament in Making and Contesting Education Policy. In Y. Sayed and Jonathan D. Jansen (eds.), *Implementing Education Policy After Apartheid.* Cape Town: UCT Press.

Omar, Rahmat. 1999. A New Approach to the Development of Skills: The Skills Development Act of 1998. *SAIDE Open Learning Through Distance Education,* 5(1).

Omar, Rahmat. 2000. Personal interview with the writer, Johannesburg, University of the Witwatersrand, October 17.

Orr, L. 1997. Globalisation and the Universities: Towards the 'Market University'? *Social Dynamics,* 23(1):42-64.

Payne, G. 2000. Review Symposium: The Curriculum of the Future. *British Journal of the Sociology of Education,* 21(3).

Piore, M. and C. Sabel. 1986. *The Second Industrial Divide.* New York: Basic Books.

Powell, L. and Hall, G. 2000. *Quantitative Overview of South African Technical Colleges.* Johannesburg: National Business Initiative.

Ravitch, D. 2000. *Left Back: A Century of Failed School Reforms.* New Jersey: Simon and Schuster.

Recent Trends in Norwegian Educational Reforms. Undated. http://www.lil.no/biblioteket/forskning/arb82/82-02.html

Reddy, Jairam. 2000. Response to the Discussion Document on the Size and Shape Task Team of the Council on Higher Education. *Perspectives in Education,* forthcoming.

Reich, R. 1991. *The Work of Nations.* London: Simon and Schuster.

Rensburg, Ihron L. 1996. Collective Identity and Public Policy: From Resistance to Reconstruction in South Africa, 1986-1995. Unpublished Doctoral dissertation, Stanford University, California.

Rensburg, Ihron L. 1998. Qualifications, Curriculum, Assessment and Quality Improvement: Laying the Foundations for Lifelong Learning. Report on the National Policy Review Conference on Education and Training, 9-12 October, Johannesburg.

Republic of South Africa (RSA). 1981. *Manpower Training Act.* Act No. 56 of 1981.

Republic of South Africa. 1993a. *Interim Constitution of South Africa.*

Republic of South Africa. 1993b. *Technikons Act.* Act No. 23 of 1993.

Republic of South Africa. 1994. *National Economic Development and Labour Council Act.* Act No. 35 of 1994.

Republic of South Africa. 1995. *South African Qualifications Authority Act.* Act No. 58 of 1995.

Republic of South Africa. 1996a. *The Constitution of South Africa.* Act No. 108 of 1996.

Republic of South Africa. 1996b. *South African Schools Act.*

Republic of South Africa. 1997. *Higher Education Act.*

Republic of South Africa. 1998a. *Employment Equity Act.* Act No. 55 of 1998.

Republic of South Africa. 1998b. *Further Education and Training Act.* Act No. 98 of 1998.

Republic of South Africa. 1998c. Regulations under the South African Qualifications Authority Act, 1995 (Act No. 58 of 1995). *Government Gazette*, No. 18787 (28 March).

Republic of South Africa. 1998d. Regulations under the South African Qualifications Authority Act, 1995 (Act No. 58 of 1995). *Government Gazette*, No. 19321 (8 September).

Republic of South Africa. 1998e. *Skills Development Act.* Act No. 97 of 1998.

Republic of South Africa. 1999a. *Public Finance Management Act.*

Republic of South Africa. 1999b. *Skills Development Levies Act.* Act No. 9 of 1999.

Riekert Commission. 1979. *Report of the Commission of Inquiry into Legislation Affecting the Utilisation of Manpower*. R.P.32/1979.

Royal Society of the Arts (RSA). *Redefining School.* London: RSA.

Sabatier, Paul A. (ed.). 1999. *Theories of the Policy Process.* Boulder, Colorado: Westview.

Samoff, Joel. 1996. *Frameworks! South African Education and Training Policy Documents, 1994-1996*. Durban: Macro-Education Policy Unit, University of Durban-Westville.

Saxe, D.W. 1996. A Review of E.D. Hirsch Jr's 'The Schools We Need and Why We Don't Have Them'. *Network News and Views,* 11. New York: Doubleday.

Scott, P. 1995. *The Meanings of Mass Higher Education.* Buckingham: Open University Press.

Sedunary, E. 1996. Neither New nor Alien to Progressive Thinking: Interpreting the Convergence of Radical Education and the New Vocationalism in Australia. *Journal of Curriculum Studies*, 28(4):369-396.

Simic, C. 2000. Working for the Dictionary. *New York Review of Books,* October 19:9.

Slaughter, S. and L. Leslie. 1997. *Academic Capitalism: Politics, Policies and the Entrepreneurial University.* Baltimore and London: Johns Hopkins University Press.

Smithers, A. 1995. *The New Zealand Qualifications Framework*. Auckland: Business Forum.

Smyth, J. and A. Dow. 1998. What is Wrong with Outcomes? Spotter Planes, Action Plans and Steerage of the Educational Workplace. *British Journal of Sociology of Education,* 19(3):291-303.

South African Labour Bulletin (SALB). 1979. Focus on Wiehahn, 5(2).

South African Qualifications Authority (SAQA). 1998. *Criteria and Guidelines for ETQAs.* Pretoria: SAQA.

South African Qualifications Authority. 1999a. *Criteria and Guidelines for Providers.* Pretoria: SAQA.

South African Qualifications Authority. 1999b. *The NQF and the National Learners' Records' Database (NLRD)*. Pretoria: SAQA.

South African Qualifications Authority. 1999c. *The NQF and SETAs*. Pretoria: SAQA.

South African Qualifications Authority. 1999d. *The South African Qualifications Authority.* Pretoria: SAQA.

South African Qualifications Authority. 2000a. *Criteria and Guidelines for the Assessment of NQF-registered Unit Standards and Qualifications*. Pretoria: SAQA.

South African Qualifications Authority. 2000b. The Further Education and Training Certificate. Discussion Document for Public Comment. Pretoria: SAQA.

South African Qualifications Authority. 2000c. *The NQF: An Overview*. Pretoria: SAQA.

South African Qualifications Authority. 2000d. *The National Qualifications Framework and Curriculum Development*. Pretoria: SAQA.

South African Qualifications Authority. 2000e. *The NQF and Quality Assurance*. Pretoria: SAQA.

South African Qualifications Authority. 2000f. *The NQF and Standards Setting*. Pretoria: SAQA.

South African Qualifications Authority. 2000g. *Quality Management Systems for ETQAs*. Pretoria: SAQA.

South African Universities Vice Chancellors Association (SAUVCA). 2000. SAUVCA's Response to the CHE's Report. Mimeo issued by SAUVCA and authored by Piyushi Kotecha, September.

Spencer Deans. 2000. Addressing the Problem of Failing Schools. Mimeo.

Spira, J.L. 1998. Integrating Principles of Progressive Education into Technology-based Learning. Commentary. http://horizon.unc.edu/TS/commentary/1998-10.asp.

Standing, G., J. Sender and J. Weeks. 1996. *Restructuring the Labour Market: The South African Challenge*. Geneva: ILO.

Stone, J.E. 1996. Developmentalism: An Obscure but Pervasive Restriction on Educational Improvement. *Education Policy Analysis Archives*, 4(8). http://www.olam.ed.asu.edu/epaa/v4n8.html

Subotzky, George. 2000. Complementing the Marketisation of Higher Education: New Modes of Knowledge Production in Community-Higher Education Partnerships. In Andre Kraak (ed.), *Changing Modes: New Knowledge Production and its Implications for Higher Education in South Africa*. Pretoria: HSRC.

Taylor, N. and P. Vinjevold. 1999. *Getting Learning Right*. Johannesburg: JET.

Taylor, S., F. Rizvi, B. Lingard and M. Henry. 1997. *Education Policy and the Politics of Change*. London: Routledge.

Tikly, Leon. 1997. Changing South African Schools? An Analysis and Critique of Post-election Government Policy. *Journal of Education Policy*, 12(3):177-188.

Traub, J. 2000. The Curriculum Crusades. Salon. http://salonmag.com/news/feature/2000/05/31/curriculum/print.html

Tyack, D.B. 1974. *The One Best System*. Cambridge: Harvard University Press.

Van Wyk de Vries Commission. 1974. *Main Report of the Inquiry into Universities*. Pretoria: Government Printer.

Walkerdine, V. 1988. *The Mastery of Reason*. London: Routledge.

Webster, Eddie and G. Adler. 1999. Towards a Class Compromise in South Africa's 'Double Transition': Bargained Liberalisation and the Consolidation of Democracy. Unpublished mimeo, Sociology Department, University of the Witwatersrand, Johannesburg.

Wenger, E. 1998. *Communities of Practice*. Cambridge: Cambridge University Press.

Wiehahn Commission. 1979. Report of the Commission of Inquiry into Labour Legislation. R.P.47/1979.

Wolpe, Harold. 1994. Introduction: Context Principals and Issues in Policy Formation for Post Secondary Education. In *Draft Policy Proposals for the Reconstruction and Transformation of Post Secondary Education in South Africa,* Policy Documents Number One. Cape Town: Education Policy Unit, University of the Western Cape.

Young, Michael (ed.). 1971. *Knowledge and Control: New Directions for the Sociology of Education*. London: Collier Macmillan.

Young, Michael. 1992. Qualifications for a High Skill Future: Lessons from the United Kingdom. Paper presented at the NEPI Conference on Human Resources Policy for a New South Africa, Durban, May.

Young, Michael. 1998. *The Curriculum of the Future: From the New Sociology of Education to a Critical Theory of Learning*. London: Falmer.

Young, Michael. 2000. Bringing Knowledge Back In. Towards Curriculum for Lifelong Learning. In A. Hodgson (ed.), *Policies and Practices for Lifelong Learning*. London: Kogan Page.

Young, Michael. 2001. Contrasting National Approaches to the Role of Qualifications in the Promotion of Lifelong Learning. Paper presented to the Society for Research in Higher Education Conference on Globalisation and Higher Education – Views from South Africa, Cape Town, March 27-29.

Ziderman, A. and A. Van Adams. 2000. South Africa. In I. Gill, F. Fluitman and A. Dar (eds.), *Vocational Education and Training Reform.* New York: ILO, World Bank and OUP.